THEY MET IN PARIS

'PASSION'

They Met In Paris

'Passion'

An Anthology on Passion by Ten Passionate Women Writers Who Met in Paris

Conceived by Carole Lethbridge

Miriam Wride, Louise Wawatai, Judith Bunn,
Carole Lethbridge, Valerie McCrae, Anne Whaite, Diana Wilde,
Roslyn Phillips, Susan Mansfield, Sierra Phillips

Published by T.M.I.P. Publishing©
Blue Mountains NSW Australia

This publication is copyright. Apart from any use as permitted under the Copyright Act 1968, no part may be reproduced by any process without prior written permission from the publisher.

Requests and inquiries concerning reproduction should be addressed to The Publisher

PO Box 307, Wentworth Falls NSW Australia 2782

tmip.publishing@gmail.com

First published 2014
Reprinted 2015

National Library of Australia Cataloguing-in-Publication data

Title: They Met In Paris: Passion

Authors: Bunn, Judith. Lethbridge, Carole. Mansfield, Susan. McCrae, Valerie. Phillips, Roslyn. Phillips, Sierra. Wawatai, Louise. Whaite, Anne. Wilde, Diana. Wride, Miriam.

ISBN: 9780992514709 (paperback)

Subjects: Short stories.
Emotions – Memoir.

Dewey Number: A823.085

Passion concept: Carole Lethbridge©
Cover and layout design: Carole Lethbridge©
Cover photography Paris 2012: Kelly O'Neill©

Acknowledgements

Thank you to Paris for inspiring all of us to continue with our writing, and a special thank you to Kelly O'Neill who was also with us in Paris and took the wonderful photograph that has been used for the cover.

Thank you also to the writers in this book who have shared many personal details of their journey through life.

Disclaimer

Many of the names and some situations in these ten stories have been changed for privacy reasons.

ABOUT THE WRITERS

The ten writers involved in writing this anthology on Passion met in Paris in October 2012. They had arrived from Melbourne, Sydney, Darwin, the NSW Blue Mountains and the NSW Central Coast to attend a memoir writing course organised by the Australian Writers' Centre, facilitated by Patti Miller.

The ten women writers are from a diverse range of backgrounds but they all have in common a love of writing and literature.

The group stayed connected and in November 2013 it was suggested by one of the group that they consider collaborating on this anthology of stories about Passion.

Passion is a positive or negative, strong, barely controllable emotional and intense desire or enthusiasm for something.

Each writer chose a subject, and the task of writing their stories commenced towards the end of 2013. The stories are mostly factual, written from the writer's personal experiences and knowledge.

Day one of the memoir writing course

It's autumn, mid-October 2012, a cool and sunny morning, and I'm standing at the window of the apartment in Paris, waiting for the memoir writers to arrive. I look at my watch. They will be here soon.

I have met the writing group already. We had flight recovery drinks at Café Sarah Bernhardt in the Place du Châtelet on the first evening, and on the second day a champagne brunch with exquisite cheeses and on the third, a welcome lunch in the mirrored Belle-Époque splendour of Vagenende in the Boulevard St Germain, but the whole time I've been restlessly waiting for the writing to begin. What words, what insights, what memories and longings, what stories will unfold?

The apartment where I wait is in the rue Quincampoix on one side of a small square. The street has been here for many centuries – I've seen it on a sixteenth-century map of Paris, the markets of Les Halles in one direction and the Marais in the other. The chestnut trees in the square are starting to lose their leaves, forming a golden carpet on the paving stones. Behind the trees the coloured pipes of the Pompidou Centre, but no buskers or tourists have gathered outside yet. Later on there will be mime artists, a brass band, jugglers, even a didgeridoo player, all performing for the ever-changing flood of visitors, but now it is quiet.

I have been out already this morning, down the cobbled street and around the corner into the *boulangerie* in the rue St Martin to buy a *tarte aux framboises* for morning tea. It's one of my favourite tasks, standing in the *boulangerie* deciding whether to have the macarons, or the *chouquettes*, or the *tarte aux figues* to share with the writing group after we have done an hour or so of writing. Walking back, carefully holding the dainty pastries, the cool air on my face, the smell of coffee wafting from every café I pass, I feel my heart expand with delight.

I know the writers are finding their way across Paris from their apartments to the rue Quincampoix. Some are coming from near the Eiffel Tower, others from the Left Bank and the famous literary *quartier* of Montparnasse, others are not far away in the Marais. Today I think they will come straight to writing class because they don't really know each other yet, but soon they will meet in the café across the square and have a coffee each morning before they start. Soon they will not be a group of strangers, but a group of writers sharing their journeys, daring to reveal their hearts and minds. They are all women, all different ages, all willing to take the risk of memoir writing, the dangerous work of exploring the self.

Now everything else is ready; the chairs and the whiteboard and the notes are arranged. Pens and books and the computer and printer wait. I look at my watch again and at that moment there's a knock at the door. I open it and there they all are, a crowd of writers on the stairs and landing.

'*Bonjour*,' I say.

They laugh and come milling into the writing room. Before we begin, I wonder again what words, what insights, what memories and longings, sorrows and joys, what stories will unfold this year?

Patti Miller

THE TEN STORIES

Passion for Travel	Miriam Wride	3
Passion for Paris	Louise Wawatai	33
Passion for Reading	Judith Bunn	55
Passion for Food	Carole Lethbridge	83
Passion for Romance	Valerie McCrae	113
Passion for Life	Anne Whaite	137
Passion for Women	Diana Wilde	155
Passion for Family	Roslyn Phillips	189
Passion to Protect	Susan Mansfield	217
Passion for Vintage	Sierra Phillips	247
Epilogue	Carole Lethbridge	271

Passion

for

TRAVEL

Miriam Wride

Miriam Wride

Miriam was born in Sydney but lived in Melbourne until she was nine years old. She attended primary school in Heidelberg before her father retired from the army and the family moved back to Sydney to be near her mother's family. Miriam went to high school and university in Sydney. Her first full time position after leaving high school was with the National Bank.

Her dream from the very first day at school was to become a teacher and later her university studies convinced her that this was possible. Miriam's love of learning and geography led her into a degree: Bachelor of Commerce – Economic History, Economics and Geography. Geography became the subject that stayed and made her observant of the natural world and fascinated by human interactions.

She took a teaching post in the country where she met up with a childhood friend whom she married and had two children with. He introduced her to travel but with a twist that left her with a need to travel regularly. Travel left Miriam with permanently itchy feet.

How did they meet in Paris?

We had enrolled in a memoir writing course in Paris to improve our writing skills. We all shared a common bond, writing and Paris or at least the idea and romance of Paris. We met daily in an apartment in the 4th *arrondissement* (district). We came together from our separate apartments on a daily basis; some walked and others came by the metro. It was as if we were headed to our regular work. There were three glorious weeks of writing, visiting cafés, restaurants and the sights. We learnt titbits about each other as we read our assignments, snippets of our lives: it was memoir writing. There was a lot of laughter and tears and no matter how our writing ended, we had shared a moment in our own history.

The world is a book and those who do not travel read only one page. – (St Augustine)

Somewhere along the journey of my self-discovery I realised I was absolutely passionate about travel and, in later years, more passionate about exploring Paris and France.

Travel is exhilarating because everything I experience is an assault on my senses: the language, the people, the châteaux, palaces, history and geography. When I'm at home it's all so ordinary. I yearn to travel to Paris so often that it becomes ordinary, although I cannot at this moment imagine how Paris could ever be ordinary. We all make connections with our world and we try to take note of particular flavours and smells (not Vegemite, more like chocolate and perfume) and colours. I love the food, the language, culture and architecture of a world different to home.

In the past when I travelled home from France, I found I still had unfinished business. I felt I hadn't seen enough, I hadn't met enough people, I hadn't sampled enough food and sat in enough restaurants, I hadn't walked enough streets, spent time in enough gardens or explored all the castles and churches I was passionate about.

I sometimes wonder if the passion for travel started with my grandmother who travelled extensively. We lived in Melbourne when I was young and my grandmother lived in Sydney. The ocean liners she travelled on, the *Arcadia*, the *Oriana* and others, often docked at Port Melbourne on their way back to Sydney. My nanna had always brought back a wonderful selection of souvenirs for my cousins and me; I loved the dolls and the jewellery the most. As my cousins lived in Sydney, at times I had first choice of the treasures she'd brought back with her. On one occasion, I chose a doll I named Susan. Susan had beautiful shiny fair hair which was fashioned in a Sandra Dee style, rolled into a continuous curl at shoulder level. She was tall and when I took her hand I could make her legs walk. Her head turned from side to side as her blue eyes opened and closed. She was dressed in a pale blue outfit and white shoes. I still have her.

As a little girl I travelled every Christmas with my family up the Hume Highway to Sydney and back again. I always remembered the journey up but never the return journey. Perhaps it was the anticipation of seeing all the cousins or, more likely, wondering what Christmas gifts I would receive. I would lie on the back seat (no seat belts then) of the two-tone yellow Vanguard and watch the branches of the trees flicking by as we headed north. I remember the grassy fields and the paddocks with cows, and I especially remember the clickety-clack of the old wooden bridge over the Murrumbidgee River at Gundagai. Gundagai was a major milestone in the journey – more than halfway. The car had a bench seat in the front that folded down into a camp bed. The journey took two days and we pulled off the road at Holbrook to have a sleep. There was no double-lane super highway in the 1950s.

In 1960 we moved to Sydney where most of our extended family lived. This meant I was able to witness many of my grandmother's overseas departures from Sydney's Circular Quay and the finger wharves at Woolloomooloo. I loved her large travel trunk that opened like a double-door refrigerator. On the left-hand side there were a myriad of drawers for her special things, her underwear, her shoes and her jewellery. On the right there were hangers for her ball gowns and her fur coat. The trunk had a particular smell of perfume and naphthalene, a smell that always reminded me of not only my nanna, but also of old houses and old ladies.

It was an age of long voyages, fine dining and entertainment. As children, we ran and explored the ship's corridors and up and down the grand staircases until the ship's siren signalled for us to disembark. People on the wharf threw streamers to the ship as a farewell. The streamers were a tradition in those days to try to keep the departing passengers and the left-behind family and friends attached to one another.

Perhaps my immense passion for travel really did start then.

I didn't go anywhere overseas until after my own children were born. It was my desire as a parent to share and show them the world. Initially it was short trips to Tasmania, the Great Barrier Reef and the Great Ocean Road. As a family, we thoroughly enjoyed these holidays, saw many beautiful places and had some wonderful experiences.

When I finally went to Europe in 2003, I followed in the footsteps of my youngest daughter. Her favourite places became mine. In France, my passion for travel was realised.

I had arrived to meet JT (my daughter) at Charles De Gaulle airport. The flight was early due to a strong tail wind. This meant I landed at 5.30 am and had to alight in the dark. The doors to the terminal were closed and even the lights were off. No one was home! I eventually found the baggage carousel and made my way out of the airport. There were no immigration officials to stamp my passport or anyone to notice my arrival. I then had to wait for my daughter to come to the airport and take me to our accommodation. JT had spent twelve months on exchange at a French school. She was familiar with the French railway and Paris so I waited, not knowing that JT couldn't leave until around 6 am and then it would take her another one and a half hours to arrive. It was such a lousy introduction to France that it's now hard to imagine how I ever fell in love with the place.

JT had booked a backpacker hotel in the 13th arrondissement. To my horror I had to hand over my passport to the manager. (Thank goodness they no longer do this.) I had a new suitcase; it was round and had four wheels, which was most unsuitable for the staircase. (With constant use and cobblestone streets, I eventually lost all the wheels.) The stairs were circular and narrow. My suitcase and me alongside didn't quite fit going up the stairs. It was a struggle to push it in front of me all the way to the third floor. I was grateful that my daughter had thought that perhaps I wouldn't like to share with strangers; fortunately we had our own room. I soon learnt to have the first shower, because although it worked, the drain was blocked, so the floor quickly became flooded. This was not another good start to Paris and France – although it became a theme of most bathrooms, showers and toilets that frequently didn't work.

JT and I only had a few days in Paris. We saw the Eiffel Tower, Notre Dame and Sacré Cœur in a whirlwind. It was a bright sunny summer morning when we decided to leave Paris to go by taxi to La Defence to pick up a hire car. Even though it was daylight, it was scary being driven around the Arc de Triomphe, with its many variable lanes with no line markings, by the taxi driver. Apparently, although I had not been able to verify this, if you have a smash on this roundabout you are not covered by insurance! You have to negotiate with the other driver for any compensation for damages. We hired the car, a black VW Golf, and set off to see JT's favourite places in France shown to her by her host parents.

I don't think I have ever been to France when there hasn't been a major renovation in progress with scaffolding and hanging dust nets. When we arrived in Reims their cathedral was decked in scaffolding along one side, the front and to the dizzy heights of the spires. Despite this, I still managed to see some of the fabulous carvings, statues and mouldings on the outside. Church carvings and windows were the storybooks of the Middle Ages, told in stone and stained glass. On the outside of Reims Cathedral was a series of stained glass pictures showing what I thought was a man climbing in and out of a bathtub. I have since learnt that it was Clovis converting to Christianity while getting in and out of a baptism font. He was shaped like a barrel and of course was naked. Elsewhere in the grounds of the Cathedral many of the statues had been damaged over time and during various wars, and the cost of repairing each life-size statue now was around 100,000€.

Reims Cathedral was where most kings and queens of France were crowned. Like other French cities, Reims has a mostly medieval town centre, with loads of alfresco cafés, restaurants and blackboards advertising the *plat du jour*. Our lunch that hot summer's day was lobster that had only minutes before been swimming around in a water tank.

The present Cathedral in Reims replaced an older church destroyed by fire in 1215, which had been built on the site of the basilica where Clovis was baptised in 496. The older church, a basilica, had originally been built on top of Roman baths. There are stories which suggest that after the St Denis Basilica in Paris was built, many of the bishops in the rest of France set fires to get rid of their small, dark Romanesque churches so they could be rebuilt in this new grand Gothic style.

The Reims Cathedral also has an effigy of Saint Denis, who appears on many other French churches, holding his head after having been decapitated. He was martyred after he apparently walked twenty kilometres from Montmartre to St Denis holding his head. While Reims Cathedral is the place of coronations for most of the kings of France, St Denis Basilica in Paris is where many kings and queens of France are buried.

Walking a little further from Cathedral Reims, there is the Basilique Saint-Remi with its many roman sarcophagi situated outside and opposite Taittinger, one of the great champagne houses of France. Our Taittinger tour was conducted in French and my daughter translated for me as we wandered down into the very chilly limestone caves dug out by the Romans for lime wash. Here were stored one million magnums of champagne in the ten kilometres of tunnels to mature before they travelled the world to be drunk or smashed on the sides of newly launched ships. At the end of the tour, as we sipped our chilled champagne, our enjoyment was interrupted when a woman very loudly and raucously asked our guide, 'How on earth, darling, did the Romans get all that limestone down here?'

Mon Dieu! I had to turn away.

My next experience with the French lunch culture, in Épernay near Reims, home of Moet, left me very annoyed. As an Aussie on tour I was shocked that all the shops were shut between 12 and 2 pm, and I wanted to shop. After all, I was a tourist with limited time and I was forced to stop and have lunch. It was warm and sunny so we sat under huge umbrellas in the centre of town to eat our freshly made baguettes. The bread was warm and crunchy on the outside and soft on the inside, filled with ripe heritage tomatoes, mature cheese and freshly cut thick ham with Dijon mustard. As an aside, I eventually got over my annoyance and enjoyed my many French lunches.

JT's host family in France lived in a small town outside Paris to the southeast, on the Aube River. The town was just what I imagined a French country village would look like. The car park was in the centre of town next to the *Mairie* (town hall) and many of the houses there had double gates, the size for a large carriage to fit through, leading into an inner courtyard. This maintained privacy for the families and in many cases there were also lawns and gardens. JT's host family lived in a house in the centre of town without a garden.

JT's host mother's business was on the ground floor and then upstairs via a circular iron staircase was the living room, dining room and kitchen. There was also one bedroom and bathroom on this level. There were two more bedrooms up another level, one of which had originally been part of the adjoining house. The family had bought an extra room from the owner next door and had knocked a doorway into the other house from their hallway for the additional bedroom! The back of the house was on the Aube River. JT's host father had decided that lack of parking for the family was a problem, so he built a bridge across the river at the back of the house to gain access for their vehicles to their basement garage. Naturally he ignored planning and construction permission. The bridge was needed, so he built it. Only in France!

The host family spoke no English and JT's Year 10 French didn't cut the mustard. Their mission over the twelve months she was there was obviously to communicate, so they agreed to teach each other their respective languages. On my arrival I found labels everywhere in the apartment: evidence of the English lessons. My daughter tested the family's English vocabulary and grammar every Friday night. I found it very funny that she had gone to such lengths during her stay with them to teach them English, when she was really there to learn French.

In 2008 my husband and I decided to visit Ypres because it was the anniversary of WWI. We arrived at Passendale (Belgium) from Lille (France), amidst a crowd of children from Canada on a school excursion, war veterans from almost everywhere, Belgians and other tourists.

I was surprised by the size of the cemetery. It was a Commonwealth-only cemetery and there were thousands of little white crosses all neatly organised in lines of perfect symmetry. The crosses commemorated the soldiers with names and countries of origin; soldiers without names but known countries of origin and then soldiers without names and unknown countries of origin. These ones were just inscribed *a soldier*. I became teary because it was so sad that no one knew who these soldiers were. It was one of those visits where, with the benefit of hindsight, we should have stayed longer.

We then headed to Polygon Wood, home of the Australian

5th Battalion. It was nearly 11 am and still drizzling. When a lone bagpiper walked into the cemetery I found myself tearing up again as he played. I whispered to a lady standing close to me, 'I feel the weight of history on my shoulders.'

She looked at me perplexed and replied, '*Pardon?*'

'I'm sorry!' Then she smiled at me – she obviously understood me.

She said in English, 'As Belgians, we are very grateful to you Australians for fighting and saving us in WWI. We come on the last Sunday of the month to this cemetery. Thank you!'

By then I was really crying and the rain was getting heavier.

The landscape was very flat and you could still see the occasional concrete bunker that housed artillery from WWI in the middle of the wheat fields. Occasionally there was a mound of earth and we later learnt that these mounds were often fought over for months at a time during the war. We also discovered during heavy rains the sides of the road filled with water and men and horses drowned in these fields, as well as being shot and blown up. In many cases their bodies were never found.

We headed to the nearby town of Ypres for lunch and to dry off. The restaurant we found was very crowded, and the waiter was trying to shoo off people who were only there for a coffee. Because of the rain everyone was trying to find shelter. We were welcomed because we wanted lunch. The *plat du jour* was fresh bread, assorted pickles, paté, salami and then beef stew and pancakes – all for 17€.

We then visited the Menin Gate in Ypres where the names of the missing soldiers with no known graves are carved into the stone arch. There were so many names it was hard to comprehend the incredible losses suffered by so many.

We also visited the local war museum, the In Flanders Field Museum in Ypres, which was located in the old restored *Hôtel de Ville* (local town hall). The stone carvings on the outside were immaculate in their intricacy and beauty and the building had a fairytale air about it. The museum itself was definitely worth visiting. There were dioramas and audiotapes of soldiers reading their letters and recounting their

Passion for TRAVEL

experiences on the battlefields. In the background was a sound and light show with the noise of exploding artillery. The uniforms, letters and machinery on display were amazing.

We left the museum to return to our car. There was no car. Despite the previous warning from a local who had wagged his finger at us, my husband had insisted on parking in an obvious tow-away zone. Parking had been difficult to find and he had thought that everything would be fine. Anyway, it appeared the car had been towed away. Now we had another unplanned adventure.

First, we went to the police station where they said they could have taken us to the car but it was a public holiday. So with the address for the locality of our car in hand, we headed off to find a taxi. There were none around. I stood on the corner hoping to wave down any passing cab, trying to overcome my anger at this turn of events. My husband had gone to chat with the local barman across the road. As I stood on the windy street corner, a car pulled up beside me. A man wound down his car window and asked a question in French, of which I understood nothing. However, I got the idea that they wanted directions. The man understood my *Je ne comprend pas*, but his wife thought that if she yelled at me then I would understand. I laughed out loud; it was like our attitude in Australia to foreigners.

The barman that my husband had been talking to managed to organise a taxi to take us to our impounded car. We had to pay a fine of 120€ to retrieve the car, as well as 40€ for the taxi. As we left, I asked why they took our car. The reply was because it (the car) was French. What better reason could they have?

We travelled to the battlefields again in 2012, this time to Normandy. On this trip we explored the many WWII Normandy beaches where the invasion took place. We stayed in Honfleur, a seaside town at the mouth of the Seine opposite Le Havre and drove to Villers-Bretonneaux, Amiens, Caen and Bayeux to start. We stopped at nearly every beach along the Normandy coast involved in Operation

Overlord from Juno to Omaha. It was a challenge to pick out all the international flags fluttering, and reflect on the stories of the calamities that befell the armies on these beaches.

At Villers-Bretonneux and nearby Amiens we saw the battlefields of the Somme. We visited the Australian cemetery at Villers-Bretonneux and climbed its tall commemorative tower to survey the landscape. It was open to the weather and was cold, wet and windy. It was not snowing, but I felt as though it should be. I was dressed in my blizzard-proof blue jacket, beanie, a woolly scarf and fur-lined gloves yet I was still cold. My father would have said this was a *lazy* wind – it went right through you, not around you. The battlefields were as flat as a tack. It was hard to imagine the fighting that would have taken place over this landscape.

We lunched in a restaurant in the nearby town which was full of French families. We studied the French menu with great concentration. We understood the word steak but everything else was a mystery. We asked our waitress, a very young French girl to explain a couple of the dishes, but she spoke no English. She took off and accosted some of the patrons in the restaurant until she found one gentleman willing and able to come to our table and explain the menu. They were both kind but we were very embarrassed. It surprised us that our waitress spoke no English given that English is compulsory in schools these days and Villers-Bretonneux had Australian flags everywhere.

We next went to Amiens to see the cathedral that was inspiring for its size, history and for the many mistakes in its design. I wandered inside and my husband had an ABC (another bloody cathedral) moment and remained in the car. It was obvious that the cathedral had been added to many times and the additions were of different architectural periods – Baroque, Romanesque and Gothic. In fact, when it was originally built it was too big for the stress and strains that the huge vaulted ceilings put on its walls. It was built this size at the time because the bishop wanted a cathedral bigger than any other to house a relic relating to John the Baptist.

Inside, the internal wooden beams holding the roof were the size of gargantuan ancient tree trunks. There were more beams holding up these beams. As the roof was obviously too high, it had threatened to push the walls outwards, which would have brought the whole structure down. As I walked around I was amazed by the magnificent stained-glass windows, the huge carved altar and ornate silver candelabras and relic boxes. There were iron rods along the floors which I later discovered were necessary to tie the building together. They also corrected the bowing and stresses by placing enormous stone buttresses against the outside to keep the walls from falling outwards. There was so much corrective work done over the centuries, I would be amazed if there had been no major fatalities.

The coastline of Normandy is also dotted with many beautiful towns such as Deauville and Trouville. They are twin towns with exquisitely ornate houses that were built for the very rich Parisians who holidayed there. The lace ironwork running along the rooftops and the carved timber lace edges on the roof gutters were worthy of many photographs. I made my husband stop the car frequently so I could run back and snap photos. Deauville is sometimes referred to as the Parisian Riviera and real estate is priced accordingly. An estuary and railway line separate the two towns. In the last three centuries trendy Parisians regularly visited the famous racecourse in Deauville. Coco Chanel established her first shop and Parisians visit the annual film festival there.

In Trouville we were drawn to the fish market near the pier where the variety of fish and crustaceans was incredibly extensive. A French fisherman directed us to a seat. He spoke no English but we were very good at pointing and nodding and we managed to order oysters, fish, prawns, langoustines and champagne. Our oysters were freshly shucked; the langoustines were cut in half long ways. We were in heaven that day, watching the sea roll in, seated on aluminium chairs at a high table behind the plastic curtains.

Our passion for *fruits de mer* was revived every time we were able to source fresh seafood in speciality restaurants around the coast of France. Some of these restaurants included *bouillabaisse* in Marseille, seafood platters in Arcachon, La Rochelle, Saint-Malo and Île de Ré. There were many excellent seafood restaurants, many with separate preparation areas, usually on the outside corner of the establishments. They were set up like this mostly for patrons to choose their seafood to take home.

Île de Ré on the west coast of France near Saint-Nazaire was the first French island we visited. It's still almost totally dedicated to the collection of salt. In earlier times the salt collectors used donkeys that carried baskets of salt straddled over their backs. The donkeys had their legs covered with pieces of cut-off old pyjamas to stop the weeds from cutting them (all the postcards show the donkeys with their striped pyjamas). We stayed at a boutique hotel in the Port Saint-Martin. It had been both a British and French fortified harbour. The staff were very attentive and kindly lent us a laptop during our stay. We had one night in an extremely pleasant room, but the following night we had the whole hotel to ourselves and the staff upgraded us to an even more luxurious room. The room was gigantic and decorated with Turkish carpets and heavily carved furniture. We could even see the harbour through a tiny window. The bathing area had separate rooms for the shower, bath, toilet and basin. We later found out that in peak season it would have cost us 750€ per night. The room was named after a poet from the island, Pierre, who wrote constantly about Turkish women. Apparently Johnny Depp regularly stayed on this island.

It was winter during our stay there and while it was sunny during the day and the skies were blue, the nights were very cold and windy. The restaurant in the hotel was closed on Monday nights, so we had to venture out to find food and, needless to say, we picked the one with the huge open fire. Of course we ordered seafood. Although we had experienced many French seafood dinners before, this had an array of shellfish that we had never seen. As we neared the end of the meal, we were tempted to leave behind the small shells because we couldn't be bothered with them. However once we tried them we couldn't leave them alone.

There are churches everywhere, small ones, big ones and even bigger ones. I find the cathedrals fascinating. My husband would say I find all cathedrals, basilicas and churches fascinating. He says the same about me with châteaux, palaces and mansions. He would often stand outside and wait for me; I didn't want to miss anything.

The French seem to be the most prodigious builders of châteaux. Some are extremely old and have been added to many times over the centuries. The older they are, the more likely they look like fortresses. Newer ones from the Renaissance were built more for opulence. Châteaux are located all over France, but the Loire Valley, known as the Valley of the Kings, seems to have the largest and most famous. The Loire River is beautiful and being close to Paris it was an easy ride for the many kings' hunting parties.

We stayed in Tours in the Loire Valley just before Christmas one time; we rented a suite in a *petit château*. It was a curious B&B, with round end towers and a wobbly circular staircase that was unsupported on the inside edge. When I climbed the staircase I needed to hug the wall, frightened that the staircase would fall. It had very comfy bedrooms, tiny bathrooms that were retrofitted and located under the staircase or in storage cupboards. The château was set on sweeping lawns that ran down to the river. I wondered at the time how often the river rose over the lawns. We had previously seen this river in full rage. The day we arrived we got to spend time with some other Australians from Melbourne who worked in Dubai. We wondered later how long they had been in Dubai because at this time we were in the middle of the Global Financial Crisis and many expats had needed to leave.

There are many grand châteaux in the Loire such as the Chambord, with its double helix staircase thought to be designed by Leonardo de Vinci. It was a hunting lodge where *Francis I* would usually spend six weeks hunting with the full nobility in tow. They created so much mayhem and destruction during their stays, it would take the servants months after they left to repair the damage. The day we arrived it was snowing, the château was so large and open that the guides were all huddled close to fireplaces. The fireplaces were almost the size of a large car. It was so cold that we were very tempted to step into the fireplaces. Even the large logs that fed the fires took two people to lift, not that it had any impact on the warmth of the large room, let alone the whole château.

We visited many other famous châteaux: Blois, Fontainebleau, Chenonceau, Chaumont, Villandry, Amboise and of course Versailles. We also saw small ones with amazing world heritage gardens. Some were near troglodyte caves, some unfortunately were close to nuclear power stations; some were furnished and some were not. We soon realised we couldn't possibly see them all unless we stayed there. Now that was a tempting idea and it has fermented in my brain for many years.

One night, still in the Loire Valley, we stay in Blois so we could see the château that had been overrun and badly ruined in the French revolution. The restoration work managed to save some gargoyles, decorative cornices, the exterior stone circular staircase and the throne room. We were initially alone when we visited the throne room and my husband decided to try out the throne. He was already standing by the time a lady from security raced into the room. Fortunately for us, she caught the next tourist who had copied him.

We decided, as we were very tired from seeing so many châteaux, that we would eat in the hotel dining room that night. The meal in itself was not memorable but our surprise company was. We were seated by the window, so we could watch the world go by (and the river). Our chattering attracted the attention of a man seated behind us.

'You are Australian?' he asked in a strong accent.

'Yes, we are.'

'I did my PhD at Canberra University, may I join you?'

How could we refuse? We chatted all through dinner. He was at the hotel for a conference and had decided to skip the conference dinner. A large multinational company was hosting the conference and he was there for training. His wife was heading up a new division of the company in Romania (they were Hungarian) and he was to be the product development manager. He told us that his father was extremely disappointed in his career change, having trained as an astrophysicist; he was now to be in charge of developing perfume for women's sanitary pads!

In the morning we'd had enough of terrible hotel scrambled eggs and salty bacon so we decided to have breakfast along the road on our way to Versailles. We drove until we came to a small village called Marchenoir and by then it had started to snow. We found a little café and ordered espresso to warm ourselves (coffee with milk was too hard to pronounce for our limited French). The café was packed with local people. We enjoyed the warmth and the chatter. We were on a mission to see our next château, even though my husband was again showing signs of châteaux fatigue. We headed out into the cold to be chased by the waiter returning my gloves that I had left behind.

We decided to spend several nights in Versailles. Our hotel was a 15th-century coach house with thick exposed black wooden beams that had been in-filled with lime mortar. The bedroom was furnished with heavy red velvet drapes, flock wallpaper and an iron four-poster bed. Later on we went in search of dinner but the restaurant of our choice nearby was fully booked for a birthday celebration and not interested in squeezing us in. We headed off to look for the next best thing and found a place in a dark corner of the square near a tiny park. We assumed it was a small family-run restaurant, because we were greeted at the door by two little girls who started to take us upstairs, but we were quickly shooed downstairs again by the parents. The restaurant was almost full and as we were directed to a table in the corner, I heard a woman say a little loudly, 'OMG, they're from across the ditch!' (A colloquial expression referring to the Tasman Sea).

The New Zealanders had to be talking about us. Even so we shared the next two hours in pleasant conversation about how they were using a friend's VW combi wagon to tour France with the occasional night in a hotel as a treat.

So many castles, so many palaces and so little time! But over the years we have made a good go of seeing as many as possible.

We have spent considerable time over the years travelling through Germany, Austria, Switzerland, Norway and the UK as well as France. There are many palaces in Germany and Austria built by or used by the Hapsburgs, the royal family, such as Schönbrunn, Maximilian's Palace and Nymphenburg. Many of these palaces are extraordinarily extravagant and painted pale yellow in the style of the time, which was Marie Thérèse's (mother of Marie Antoinette) favourite colour.

On our quest to see more castles one trip we drove from Munich through southern Germany into the beautiful valleys of Austria, past Imst and countless snowfields; we were momentarily distracted by a sign to a castle in the mountains which we thought we would detour to see. We diverted off the freeway and attempted to find the castle, which proved to be elusive. We didn't know if we had missed the sign but we found ourselves in a motorway tunnel. We didn't think much of entering a tunnel in Austria. After all a tunnel was an easy way of getting from one side of a mountain to the other. However, after driving into this long tunnel, unable to turn around, we came out to find ourselves in Switzerland! So we ended up in St Moritz, which definitely hadn't been on our agenda.

Everyone thinks that St Moritz is gorgeous and we were no exception. It was a beautiful October day with bright blue skies, but the weather changed quickly and it also snowed that night. Everything was covered in a dusting of snow. It looked as though the world was covered in lace.

Next day we drove over the Julian Pass where the road traffic people were installing their six-metre poles to indicate snow depth on the sides of the roads. The naked hills were also dusted in snow on our way to Liechtenstein, chasing the original castle that my husband had wanted to see. The landscape was breath-taking.

Liechtenstein was tiny. We drove through it in twenty minutes. It was also narrow. We searched and searched for the castle. There was no fairytale castle. We stayed at Füssen, a lovely medieval town as we decided that this would be a stepping-off point to see Neuschwanstein. This was the castle my husband really wanted to see, the castle we have driven half way around Germany, Austria and Switzerland to find.

We have often driven backwards and forwards and around looking for places. It is one of the many reasons why, on the whole, we don't do tour groups. We like to go down the road less travelled, see the things that others don't see, get lost, find ourselves on a detour for road works and generally have to work out for ourselves what's next. We often end up somewhere totally unexpected.

We arrived, parked the car and boarded the mandatory tourist bus up the mountain to the Neuschwanstein Castle built by King Ludwig II. It was believed he was completely mad and rumours had it he was eventually murdered by one of his family. We had finally reached the castle which was located in the heavy forested hill. Ludwig had demolished a 13th-century medieval castle to build his new castle. Many of the rooms were a tribute to his excesses. One of the reception room's ceilings was painted a rich royal blue and decorated with gold leaf fleur-de-lis. The walls were decorated with paintings of hunting parties and picnics as well as members of the family. He also had local artisans spend many years carving a timber bed with an intricate pattern and story; it took up a large part of the master bedroom. The detail of the carving was astonishing, but most people considered it a waste, like most other things he did. Ludwig had apparently lived there alone. Neuschwanstein is the castle credited with having inspired the Disney castle of Sleeping Beauty.

On another trip to France we eventually got to see the Musée d'Orsay, a magnificent former train station. Its structure was a huge arch with an iron frame and glass. The staircases were marble and the overall impression was of a huge cavernous space dotted with large-scale statues and smaller anterooms filled with paintings from the masters. It was a beautiful cathedral for the train traveller in an earlier time as were Gare de Lyon (with an exclusive restaurant, Le Train Bleu), Gare de L'Est, Gare Saint-Lazare and Gare du Nord built by Napoleon III.

On this trip we had some fantastic surprises and we also had some *désastres*, such as catching the bus to Orly airport near our apartment in Denfert-Rochereau. We were directed to get on a bus that took us past the local university. The French driver told us to change buses, which we did, luggage in tow. The next bus took us back to where we started. The third bus driver directed us to the correct bus to Orly but because we were last on and the bus was packed, we had to sit on our suitcases for the journey.

Many times we used hire cars, although driving in France after a lifetime of driving in Australia was nerve-wracking for the first few kilometres. Then you settle in, especially if you have a capable co-pilot or navigator *moi* who alerts regularly when on the wrong side of the road and reminds continually which side to stay on in the roundabouts.

After all the driving around France, I have come to the distinct conclusion that the majority of French drivers are crazy or they go crazy when they get on the motorways. They drive too fast, often in clapped-out tiny cars, they overtake in the most peculiar unsighted corners and when they have an accident they do it in spectacular fashion. French driving fatalities are enormous compared to ours, partly because they are allowed to drive twenty kilometres above the speed limit (130kph) before the police stop them and they used to be allowed to drink and drive. When they do have an accident they are mostly killed outright, and accidents can cause traffic to bank up for ten to twenty kilometres. JT's host father would comment, 'At least we are free,' whenever I commented on this phenomenon.

We were always so confused at the expressway tollbooths in France, as to whether to take a ticket to pay later or to pay in advance. We would set our sights on the green colour 'T', which hopefully meant the ticket machine was green for go. On several occasions, both in France and Spain, we went into the tollbooth to discover it was an e-toll and naturally we didn't have the right cards. We are slow learners, as things seem to happen to us several times before we get it right. The French and Spanish probably swear at us in their cars but we have never experienced road rage. No horn honking, no fingers out the window and no swearing.

We have also learnt while driving around France, Switzerland, Spain, Germany and the UK to play spotto for traffic cameras. In France many cameras were in boxes (like letterboxes) on the side of the road, not on poles as in Australia. Our most unsuccessful attempt to spot the camera was in Spain where we ended up with three speeding fines. In Germany, cameras were hung from fences, poles and overhead wires. To our surprise in rural Germany there were both speed cameras and police cars patrolling the quiet country roads.

We have used French and German trains frequently and love their efficiency and speed. They arrive on time and leave on time (the Japanese are even more precise if that's possible). We love having the space to move around and they are always so clean, even with the many dogs under seats and in their baskets. In France when we travel by train, we always hear the SNCF's French music that introduces an announcement. It's interesting as when I heard it the first few times it didn't grab me, I just thought there would be some useful information following, but now I hear it in my head all the time beckoning me back.

We were in Provence for my sixtieth birthday; we booked a large two-storey stone house (mas) in Beaumes-de-Venise for two weeks so that my family and friends could visit. Our children with their husbands and several friends came from Australia, and another friend and her sister arrived from Switzerland. The house was perched halfway up a hillside amid olive groves and vineyards. When we drove up the road to the house, we needed to cross irrigation canals with deep potholes in the gravel roadway. The house faced towards Avignon. The weather that September in Provence was spectacular and every afternoon during our stay we would sit outdoors, gazing at the brilliant orange sunsets, often eating fresh baguettes with cheese and ham, and drinking the local wine we had gathered from the various markets scattered throughout the area.

Beaumes-de-Venise was a small, quaint town set on the slopes of a large wine growing area. It is named Venise because of all the irrigation canals for the olives and grapes. Whenever we went out for our daily shopping we were held up on the roads behind tractors laden with freshly picked grapes. The harvest that season was one of the earliest picks they had ever had due to the extremely warm weather.

The valley was spectacular and the Dentelles de Montmirail mountain range behind us (meaning lace) protected the house from the fierce mistral winds. Nearby was Mont Ventoux with its permanent cap of white limestone that looked like snow.

Mont Ventoux was not on our agenda but it was on the agenda of one of our family. So one day we headed off with them to drive the mountain that was so famous for cyclists and Tour de France enthusiasts. It was sunny and warm as Provence can be in September. We drove up the hill with five of us in our little rental car. When we set off it was around 20 degrees with beautiful blue skies. The drive up the mountain was pleasant with forests and picnic areas along the way. We passed many wannabe Tour de France riders doing the forty-kilometre round trip. Onwards and upwards we went, passing other French drivers hurtling down the mountain. As we pulled out to go around cyclists on our side of the road, the oncoming traffic would do the same around their cyclists. We were often perilously close to each other on the not so wide road. It became more of an issue as the road narrowed and the cyclists became tired and wobbly and we found ourselves in cloud. The visibility dropped dramatically as we reached the summit. Then we popped through the clouds but the wind had picked up so much by then that cyclists were being blown over. And by then it was a freezing two degrees.

Provence was an area that we could have explored for many more months. The wonderful fresh food markets popped up on a daily basis across the region. There were bigger more famous markets at Carpentras and Saint Rémy. They were always so crowded but they did have amazing cheeses, salamis, honey, many types of lavender and every variety of chilli imaginable. We visited a different location for lunch every day during our stay, from Fountaine-de-Vaucluse and its water wheels, L'Isle-sur-la-Sorgue and its antique markets and canals to the pirate restaurant in Vaison-la-Romaine which had the largest Roman archaeological dig in France. On one occasion we lunched in a little mountain-top restaurant in Gigondas, simply because everything in the district was closed. We sat under the huge plane trees in the shade on a glorious afternoon and were served a magnificent three-course lunch by the most attentive French waiter of all time, and the meal only cost us 100€.

One of our more memorable evening meals was in a restaurant in Beaumes-de-Venise under the church bells where Muscat was the local speciality wine. Beaumes-de-Venise is apparently credited with having secretly hidden many vintage French wines from the Germans during WWII.

Provence and the nearby areas had amazing Roman architecture from the past as it had been a Roman province and stronghold for their legionaries; hence the name Provence. Nearby were many fascinating roman ruins, the 2000-year-old Pont du Gard, the Pantheon in Nîmes, the commemorative arch in Orange similar to the Arc de Triomphe in Paris but built in 50BC, and the coliseum in Arles.

Surprises are usually the highlight of travel. For us there is no fun if everything is thoroughly planned and organised. It leaves us no room to change our minds.

The day we decided to drive to Sarlat-la-Canéda was a spur of the moment decision. As we made our way around the many country roads and along one of the tributaries of the Dordogne, our journey took us up and over rocky escarpments and into highly forested areas. We had seen a signpost to a château and drove onwards and upwards. After several kilometres we started to worry. We really became concerned after twenty kilometres that we had missed the turn off. We turned back to Sarlat to discover directional road signs in the area only have information on one side of the post. We eventually found the car park for the château. There was a stone cottage and it was totally deserted. The road was so rough that it was hard to imagine that in high season this area would be full of tourist buses and people queuing to see the château.

We looked for evidence of life, but there was no ticket office, and no sign pointing to where we should walk. If it had not been for the appearance of a tail-wagging canine friend who seemed to have a mission to show us around, we may never have ventured down the steep rutted track that took us to the château. Commarque was a set of buildings built in the 13th century by Protestants who wished to avoid the local Baron de Beynac, who was Catholic. The medieval stone buildings were built from the local light yellow limestone and were rediscovered in the 1960s under a mass of overgrown trees and vines. It was obvious that this was a good setting for hiding, as the buildings were set deep into a valley. The stone walls in the valley and below the château had large square holes carved out to support thick beams which acted as both supports for roofs and for floors above the ground. The village would have been substantial in its time and we could only imagine what this place must have looked like originally. As we returned up the rough track we felt as though we alone had done this walk and found these ancient buildings.

Seeing La Roque-Gageac topped our visit, followed by a wonderful lunch in a lovely country restaurant filled with local farmers in all manner of clothing. We were behind the tractors going back to our cottage and managed to get stuck in another traffic jam because of a passing yacht on a trailer that had to be lowered and raised depending on bridges and power lines. As we settled into our beautiful stone cottage that night next to the *boules/pétanque* patch, we decided we could live there.

Sarlat and the Dordogne were places that will particularly stay with us because of the many châteaux, walnut groves, wineries, fortresses plus the Lascaux caves. Some of these caves hid the French Resistance in WWII as well as hiding the Huguenots who were expelled from northern France. Summer is not really the time to go as it is too crowded and the queues for everything are frustrating.

We also often visited the Sunday market at Saint-Cyprien to buy our supplies during our stay. We always noticed when we were there that many Frenchmen were having their first morning glass of red at the local café, while waiting for their wives to complete their shopping.

When you travel to new places you compare many things like the weather, the people, the transport, the food and usually the water. You compare the experiences like boating down the Seine with boating up the Canal Saint-Martin. One is not better than the other – just different – and we have found it's always worth doing both if you have time. The Seine has views of the Eiffel Tower, Notre Dame, France's Statue of Liberty, and the Louvre. The Canal Saint-Martin was built by Napoleon to provide water for Paris; some is underground and has eight locks all with different designs. We were not amused after the Canal Saint-Martin trip to discover that it was a one-way trip. This meant we had to find our way home afterwards. Just as well we never left home without our map.

If you are looking for comparisons you look subconsciously for similarities, such as, how could I relate to this environment? Could I live here? Is it too different to what I am used to? Is it as good as what I already have or better? My mind never stopped working on these issues, especially with all my experiences of so many new people, so many new ideas and so many new, fascinating and often strange places.

I have compiled my own list of the criteria that makes a place liveable. Usually similarities and differences are what it comes down to and what occurs on a macro and micro level. At a macro level, I ask myself: 'Could I live in Paris?' The answer is definitely, 'Yes.' 'Could I live in Berlin?' Again the answer is, 'Yes.' 'Could I live in Moscow?' 'Definitely not.' It is often based on how you feel when you first arrive in a place, and if you were tired, cranky, or if you were jet lagged.

At a micro level, it is often based on accommodation experiences. Was there a shower? Was the shower big enough? Did I have to run around the shower to get wet? Was there enough hot water? Why did they put the toilet roll holder there? But the criteria are not infallible. For example, our apartment on the Seine was not perfect. The bathroom was a little small, the bed was uncomfortable, the kitchen was a little grotty, and the floor ran backwards from the windows to the front door so you were almost running downhill. But it was perfect. We were able to watch the people walk past, the Palais de Justice start up every morning, the *Bouquinistes* open their stalls with their books and magazines, and see the boats that went past every hour.

Then of course there is the very ordinary. Being in a city or country apartment rather than staying in a hotel. Having a house or apartment means you have to find out how the washing machine and TV work, then the plumbing, and noticing the squeaky floorboards that drive you crazy when you get out of bed in the middle of the night to go to the bathroom, or putting up with noisy neighbours who bounce down the stairs two at a time at two in the morning. Being near restaurants whose patrons want to party until the small hours, watching and listening to buskers in the metro, and having lunch and listening to peoples' banter and laughter even when you cannot understand the conversation. Then trying to get your hair cut when you don't speak the language and learning how to post parcels back home to lighten the luggage. It's all so ordinary but in the end it's how I would decide if I could live in a place.

Similarities are good because when observed consciously, they allow you to identify things. For example, there is a common perception in many countries of what a school, restaurant or bread shop looks like. Our apartment in Denfert-Rochereau in the 14th *arrondissement* where we stayed during the time I was in Paris in 2012 for the writing workshop was one of those lovely surprises. The apartment was one of those beautiful French Haussmann properties with many French doors, a typical narrow winding staircase and a lift so small you had to breathe in so the doors could close. Downstairs was a man selling hats, gloves and bags from a large barrow and just around the corner were all manner of food stalls, fresh markets and restaurants. I felt like never cooking again as long as I lived. In the *boulangerie* close by I learnt the French words for all the different breads and for all the various types of cakes and slices and the myriad tarts.

Because we stayed in the apartment for three weeks, it meant we were able to explore an area of Paris more than we normally would. We visited the Catacombs across from us, a delight to see one of the earliest Parisian tourist attractions if not a little macabre. On one afternoon walk we discovered La Santé, both a domestic and international prison. La Santé had high walls and barbed wire making it obvious that it was a prison. However, it was different for a number of other reasons. It was in the middle of a suburb, a leftover from when the area wasn't so popular. There was only one street sign indicating that it was there, it had only one entrance and in the 1940s was the location of the last French public beheading of resistance fighters by the Vichy government. The only sign on the gaol was a commemorative plaque to these people. On the outside in the rue de la Santé was the last remaining *pissoir* in France and I watched in amusement one day as a man went to use the convenience. Further down the street was a green iron water drinking fountain introduced by Wallace, an English Francophile who wanted all Parisians to have access to fresh drinking water.

During our travels many things often did not turn out as we may have wished, but if there are no ups and downs you don't get to appreciate the things that are wondrous, plus most experiences leave us with good stories to tell.

It's these stories that keep us chasing the next experience, and the next people with whom we will interact. Castles and the cathedrals fascinate me always, the mountains and the rivers are wonderful, but in the end it's the people, the stories and surprises of our experiences that we really remember.

I love flying in across the harbour when I come home to Australia, over the Harbour Bridge and the Opera House. I love walking into my home, I love shopping and restocking the cupboards and buying in many of our unique foods that are hard to find in parts of Europe. Then a few weeks later I'm restless and ready to go again.

My travels have taught me many things: stay longer, don't go to so many places – less is more, don't always plan, don't always book, research the history and geography of a place before you move on, let my senses dictate where to go next, listen, talk, watch and don't judge too quickly. Shut up sometimes and take loads of photos for reflection.

I seriously hope that one day my grandchildren will wave farewell to me on one of my trips as I did with my grandmother, way back then, and the act of the farewell and the anticipation of where I will be going will excite and enthuse them to also travel to parts unknown, especially to France, my passion place.

Passion For Paris

Louise Wawatai

Louise Wawatai

Louise was born in Sydney in 1957 and grew up on a farm in NSW's Hunter Valley. She spent a lot of her childhood and teenage years outdoors, either wandering around in search of what she called 'treasures', or helping with manual labour on the farm. She moved to Newcastle to study English and Psychology at University, but left for a job in banking in Sydney and then moved into work in IT.

Restless, and feeling caged, she left this job to pursue creative interests of pottery, weaving and candle-making. During this time she and her husband moved to the Blue Mountains west of Sydney. There she worked with the St Vincent de Paul Society for eleven years. She has lived in the mountains for the past thirty years and feels at home in the natural beauty of her environment. It is from her interaction with the natural world that she takes her inspiration for all things creative, including her writing.

When I turned fifty, a friend gave me a little card with a verse entitled 'Follow Your Dreams'. Reading these apparent words of wisdom, I realised I had no dreams and hadn't had anything resembling a dream for a very long time. Perhaps even all my adult life. Here I was then, in the midst of my menopausal era, my life fairly empty and dark. It was time, I thought, to invent a dream.

I think now the fifteen-year-old inside me gave me the prompt and I decided I wanted to travel to Paris. Yes, that would be my dream! I put the word out, asking everyone I knew to come with me. Alas, no one seemed interested. Out of fear I would not travel alone unless on a tour, I waited and researched; and waited and researched and kept my dream alive. Like the Eiffel Tower, this dream was a beacon in my half-lit world.

Then in 2011, my quest led me to a website advertising a memoir writing workshop in Paris. Oh yes! That was it! My clever little fifteen-year-old self had wanted to be a writer. She had led me to this all along. So then there were two dreams to occupy my mental wanderings. To tempt me. To light up my life. I held her hand and walked with her and continue to do so to this day. For she is my dreamer. She is the singing bird in my heart. She knows my passions and now she is free.

As luck would have it, there was a memoir writing workshop at Varuna in the Blue Mountains that very year. I decided to enrol in the class so that I could get a feel for the teacher and to see if the then fifty-four-year old me actually wanted to write. It turned out that I did indeed want to write. Well, at least to dream of writing.

So it came about that I booked my trip to Paris in October 2012.

I then nurtured the seed that had lain dormant in unfertile soil within me for way too long. I had certainly conjured up a dream. I began my countdown to the trip with 251 sleeps to go. My excitement grew daily, moment by moment. I practised my writing and found myself in a new world. It was a place where words and sentences spilled over and stumbled onto the page from somewhere inside. Like a small child fumbling with words and clumsy sentences as she learns to speak. It was as if they had been waiting desperately for release and it seemed they had some stories to tell. Some images to describe. Some healing to impart.

Paris is the city of my imagination. I am writing here about my visit to my city of dreams. My stories are more about the essence of who I am, rather than a commentary on her. After all, this is about my passion – what it is that excites me; what moves me; what inspires me.

The instant I heard the beautiful harmonics of the French language at Charles de Gaulle airport, I was enchanted. I was in a beautiful dream. When my eyes first spied some of the buildings and monuments in the old city as our taxi neared the apartment where I was staying in the Latin Quarter, I was enraptured. Completely and utterly smitten with awe and wonder. I couldn't wait to be out there wandering amongst it all. My fifteen-year-old self, free to skip and dance in the streets. My fifty-five-year-old self, feasting and absorbing deep into her soul. My passion for Paris and walking her streets was born. Or *peut-être*, re-born.

Paris 2012

One of my first walks in Paris was from our apartment in rue Descartes, in the Latin Quarter on the Left Bank, to our writing classroom in rue Quincampoix, near the Pompidou Centre on the Right Bank. During this walk I formed an idea that Paris was one large museum, art gallery or '*cabinet de curiosités*', having passed by a curious little shop on rue Saint-Jacques with a window display that included a sculpted human hand and a shoe made with what looked like the lacy, waffled, translucent shed skin of a snake. The shop's sign read, 'Cabinet-de-Curiosités.com'.

On this day my first stop was in a little street called Place Paul Painlevé just off rue Saint-Jacques. It was the museum I'd passed by many times already, but had not yet entered into its hallowed space. Inside the Musée de Cluny (or Museum of the Middle Ages, or officially Musée National du Moyen Âge), I was drawn towards an ancient piece of broken sculpted torso and saw Braille writing; I walked over to touch it with my fingertips and to read its translation. I wondered how this museum would be for one who was blind; indeed how this whole City of Light might be. Straight away I inhaled the dry chalkiness of the limestone torso and felt its softness with my hands; then the smooth leathery-ness of a Pietà carved in alabaster. Upstairs I marvelled at wooden statues hundreds of years old and desired desperately to feel their smooth carved softness. Up there too were the magnificent red-backgrounded woven tapestries that are 'The Lady and the Unicorn', with their dozens of images woven finely with woollen thread in the sixteenth century and symbolising the five senses. My fingers were urging me to touch the wondrous cloth and I imagined it to feel prickly against my sensitive skin. I yearned for just one touch, as if to greedily sup on its lusciousness, taste its beauty, smell its history.

After the museum I headed for the *quai* of the Seine on the Left Bank near my beloved Notre Dame. On my way I passed a man pleading for money for food in a crowded cobblestone street where the aroma of cooking meat and other exotic and spicy morsels wafted into the air and had me hungry too. I was to pass by many a street-dweller, as I did every day, and I sent each a silent blessing as it was the only way I was able to freely walk on. I felt almost unable to bear the heaviness their presence brought me. They and their pets, many of them. They and their physical disabilities, many of them. Why were these people there in my dream?

Walking along the *quai* I heard: 'Bloody cold here.'

'It's coming off the water.'

I turned my head as I recognised the Australian accent of two men following me and chuckled to myself.

The man in his wheelchair who had two short stubs for legs was in his usual spot on the Left Bank's entrance to the Pont de l'Archevêché. I had developed great respect for this man as he seemed to me to be the least intrusive street-dweller I encountered. I had often wondered where he slept at night, until on one of my earlier morning walks it was revealed to me. He slept right there, with his head cushioned in his folded arms that leant on the sandstone pylon of the Pont.

I was heading for my favourite street musician whom I'd first heard the week before, plucking the beautiful and haunting notes of 'Lady D'Arbanville' on his guitar and wafting the sweet-smoky aroma of his cigar into the cool air. Since then it seems I had been stalking this man, having passed by him many times. I found him there at the Notre Dame end of the same Pont as usual, singing and playing, this time a French folk song. I was still too shy to stop and linger to listen, although his music and his presence were alluring to me.

Over to Pont Saint-Louis where there was an American with his guitar and a large chrome microphone, playing and singing 'I've Got You Under My Skin'. There I did linger, listening, watching, breathing in the crisp cold air. The sunlight danced with the water below the Pont and their union became a pink, purple and orange metallic, swirling iridescent liquid. Mercurial. Seagulls rode the little waves. Their orange legs dangled, penetrating the surface of the water, and I remembered how the sun's rays had done a similar thing a couple of days before. Rods of orange in the early morning, stabbing through as if being pulled down into the murky liquid to somewhere deep and dark, to light it up.

I had another idea about this city of light and it was about that light itself. It was a place of half-light, I thought, as if someone had dimmed the master switch. Crepuscular. As if it was always dusk or dawn. As if the light was being pulled down below its surface and didn't reflect back upwards to illuminate further, but rather was consumed greedily by the depths. Or was it that the light was filtered through a large black lacy veil. A funeral veil. A funeral veil of all its history. Or perhaps a giant stained-glass window, I wondered.

I encountered a piano parked on the Île Saint-Louis end of the Pont and beside it a cello. Or was it a double bass? A man wearing a grey leather jacket sat at the piano and began to tickle the keyboard whilst his companion, dressed in denim jacket and jeans, played the double bass. An easy jazz melody perfumed the air. The area was crawling with people. An ant colony, swarming, busy with the busyness of tourism. A woman dressed in all white sauntered by. She wore white shoes, white stockings, white dress, white overcoat, white scarf, gloves and hat. A balding man in a green suede jacket made eye contact with me; I noticed dandruff sprinkled like snow on his jacket.

I looked up and saw the wispy vapour trails of jet planes and heard the nasally calls of my friends the carrion crows. At other times I saw the long stone gargoyle-like necks and growling faces of the *chimères* lurching up and out on the upper sides of buildings in rue Saint-Jacques and on Notre Dame. As with the crows, I felt safe, protected because they were there. They were my Guardian Angels.

Down along the *quai* on the right bank heading in the direction of Pont Neuf, I saw a sign that read 'Animalerie'. I dared not enter, not wanting to see little furry and feathered creatures encaged. It was a Parisian pet shop, with an exotic and delicious name. I passed by a man and woman deeply entwined in the ecstasy of a kiss. They seemed as one. One dancing organism and I remembered how deeply a kiss such as that could take a lover into her mate.

The air blew cold across my cheeks and I felt enlivened by it as I came at last to Pont des Arts and sat down to soak in the sun's gentle warmth, to rest and to write. The bridge is for pedestrians only and is wooden underfoot. I could see the pointed end of the boat that I thought Île de la Cité was and then across to Pont Neuf. I watched two coated and scarfed men in the sacred act of attaching their 'love-padlock' to the already heavily padlock-encrusted railing of the Pont. An American tour guide and his accent sounded even more exaggerated in this place of the melodic and poetic French language.

I saw Bob Marley's face on many a poster, a poem called 'Les Chats' by Baudelaire and a fly dressed in a corset at the vendors along the *quais*. I went to the little winding rue Galande where the buildings seemed to be leaning backwards and would surely topple at any moment. There I found the gem of a shop called Pays de Poche. I had walked by this little shop of handmade curiosities a couple of times in the previous week but had to be content with window gazing. It seemed to me to be only open at the oddest hours. But that day, to my delight, I found it open and I entered. I bought three little brooches, so fragile I wondered how I would get them home. They were a butterfly, a dragonfly and a fly. Their tiny wings and eyes were made of a delicate shiny paper-like material and outlined in the finest pewter. They would be gifts for a couple of loved ones. I left this little treasure cave feeling light and happy as the beautiful woman proprietor, who was no doubt the maker of these tiny treasures, nodded smilingly and bid me *bon après midi*.

As I walked along Boulevard St Germain, the light filtering through the black lacy branches of the leafless lime trees and the metal fence danced on my face across my left cheek and I squinted my eyes to see a kaleidoscope made by the same diffused rays and my movements through them. I watched a pigeon fly at eye level all the way down the curly, cobblestoned rue Valette.

Walking in the Place du Panthéon I encountered a chicly dressed woman who seemed to be staring into my face. As we approached each other I smiled at her, the biggest smile I could muster. To my delight, her lips began to curl and her cheeks rose ever so slightly, as she almost smiled in return. Like the Mona Lisa, I thought. Like the promise of a smile. I was happy with this small encounter, this tiny breakthrough.

I rounded the corner into the street that was my home for this sojourn in Paris, rue Descartes. The scent of orange blossom left in the air by some earlier passer-by caressed my senses and infused on up into my regions of delight. I smiled at my own good fortune to have shelter in this beautiful city of curiosities, city of my dreams.

Another silver-grey day in Paris, but more importantly, *it was my last*. I had a list of things I wanted to do on that auspicious day, and perhaps not enough hours and minutes to do them all. I set out heading for my first destination, the Musée d'Orsay. I walked briskly, the cold morning air brushing across my face. I strolled down Boulevard Saint Germain and turned right into rue du Bac, fascinated all the way by the shops and their window displays. The huge chocolate-sculpted hippopotamus and gorilla in the windows of chocolatier, Patrick Roger; beautiful displays of violets in the perfumery and gift shop, Fragonard; and in rue du Bac clothing and home-wares unique to my eyes. It was too early for any of these to be open; it was only about 9.15 am and most of the shops didn't open until 10 am.

I passed by the teeming Café de Flore and Les Deux Magots, and imagined every patron to be a literary giant. In rue du Bac I also came across the famous taxidermy shop, Deyrolle, shut with its display windows curtained so I was unable to see inside. I felt cheated by this, but delighted that there was at least a little treat for my eyes. There was a bee, tail facing me, as if the tiny creature had flown into the curtain. It was a small preview of a current exhibition.

Down the bottom of rue du Bac I turned left and followed the signs to the Musée d'Orsay, walking along the Quai d'Orsay. There she was, the façade with its magnificent clock, the old railway station that is now a famous gallery of art. Not only there she was, but there it was! An enormous queue of people forming a massive river that flowed up and around into the street, flooding it. As it was my last day in Paris, I hadn't time to spend waiting in a queue such as that. I just wanted to be in there and then back out into the open air again; I had many other items on my 'to-do' list for that day. I hesitated, cleared away the intention to enter the Musée d'Orsay then walked onwards, crossing the Seine by way of the footbridge Pont de Solférino, now

They Met in Paris

renamed the passerelle Léopold-Sédar-Senghor. I looked towards the Eiffel Tower and decided instead to walk through the Tuileries, back in the direction of the Louvre.

I felt freed, like a bird flying from her cage and set upon the air; with the wind at my back carrying me onwards. I spread my wings and inhaled, recalculating how this part of the day would be spent, and exhaled all trace of ever wanting to be in the confines of a building such as the Musée d'Orsay, awe-inspiring as it may well have been – but a little sad not to have seen the small bronze ballerina sculptures of Degas. Today this little creature would fly on into the cold damp autumn air. I wanted to fly close to the Seine, I decided. I looked over her lithe form, winding her way back towards the city centre, adorned with the *ponts* and ancient buildings and spires that flanked her. I marvelled at her presence and how she was the life-blood of this city. She is its main artery, or rather her main vein. Her murky dancing waters weave and wind their way, dividing the city, feeding the vessels that branch from her. The *rues* and boulevards, *ponts* and churches, cafés and shops. The rows and rows of little green tin lock-ups that the Bouquinistes trade from on sunny days and weekends, selling used and antiquarian books. Her banks teem with life all day and night. She carries us all. Feeds us all. Inspires us all.

The Tuileries Gardens were not quite what I had been expecting, but then I was not in their heart, instead merely skirting them, in the vicinity of the Louvre. As I entered the grounds of this palace I felt its enormity. Prior to my visit to Paris I had no idea of the size of this grand building. I was intent on absorbing some of its magnificence by standing and slowly walking, looking up and around at its structures, its architecture, grand palace that it is. I was content with idling over its courtyard cobblestones and admiring its many pillars capped with sculptures of stony statues of those other winged creatures, the angels. I photographed some in an attempt to steal away with me some of their beauty for myself. But I soon abandoned that activity in favour of just gazing, mouth and heart gaping open in awe of what I perceived all around me. I expanded up and out into it all; I united with it; became part of it. I lost myself, or rather, gave myself up to it and seemed to have slotted in like a tiny piece of some thousand-piece jigsaw puzzle or like the tiny drop of water that dissolves into the vast ocean; I bathed in the glory of this huge, three-dimensional picture I was in.

Back down at ground level, there were young African men with giant key rings holding dozens of tiny replicas of the Eiffel Tower, swinging and clinking them, looking desperately anxious to sell their wares. To lighten their loads, their lots in life, I thought. I felt their desperation in the air but dared not buy anything from them, half afraid that exposing my purse would attract some clandestine thief; the other half, not wanting to unveil myself as a tourist. There were tourists from all over the world. The place crawled with us. Swarmed. Gushed. Flooded. Many wore giant cameras around their necks as their badges of honour and clicked away wildly at times and then more mindfully when one of their group posed, statuesque atop one of the many stone plinths that seemed to be there for that very purpose. Their photos would be mementos to show family and friends at home. Mine would be in my memory. In my words. In my heart.

I saw before me the glass Pyramid of the Louvre and thought how out of place it seemed in this landscape, but I remembered coming across it only days before when the late morning sunlight beamed down and bounced off it, splitting into beautiful rainbow rays. I wondered how it would be at sunset, this giant crystal.

I decided to venture underground and headed down into the small shopping mall called the Carrousel du Louvre. I indulged and visited their *toilettes* and paid one euro fifty for the use of one. Money well spent! Each throne was cleaned after every use and cubicles were complete with aromatic reed diffusers. Not only did they smell pleasant, but were meticulously clean. With items like patterned toilet papers and perfumed candles for sale, these WCs were more like a boutique.

My next stop in this haven for tourists was the shop called Fragonard. It was a gift shop selling French goods, but in particular, its own perfumes and soaps produced in France's Mecca of the perfume world, Grasse. There I bought a small set of tiny bottles of perfumes for a friend and embroidered serviettes for another. I sprayed one of the perfumes on my wrist. It was called Fleurs d'Oranger. Hours later, after sniffing its sweet true scent many times, I realised I couldn't live without it. Alas though, with the passage of the day, I was unable to get back to Fragonard to buy a bottle of that glorious-smelling fragrance.

I ascended the stairs out of this underground shopping cavern and headed along rue de Rivoli in the direction of the Marais, which was a fair walk away. Rue de Rivoli had been a major landmark and grand thoroughfare for me on the Right Bank during my stay in Paris. I walked and walked till I reached the famed up-beat Marais, little winding streets with gems of shops at every turn. Clothing shops, toy shops, home-ware shops, shoe shops, cafés, perfumeries, *papeteries*, galleries. Many seemed not to have names; there were many things that I would never see anywhere else in the entire universe. My eyes were feasting and it seemed that if I had imagined a city, then all I saw in these little boutiques would be there. 'It is my city! It is of my making!' I shouted at the top of my inner voice. I didn't venture inside any of the little beauties but was content with seeing the delicious things they had displayed in their windows; at times with a stretch of the eye into their inner sanctums. 'This is my museum, my art gallery; out here on the streets!' My joy was unbounded.

Time was running out and it had started raining, so I turned on my heels, upped my pace and headed back towards Notre Dame and my rendezvous with Diana at the iconic Shakespeare and Company English bookstore. To do this I needed to cross back over to the Left Bank again, so I scurried down rue de Rivoli and turned into rue du Pont Louis Philippe, another tiny street with many curiosities. I passed by a petit jewellery shop with earrings and necklaces made with coloured filigreed butterflies and flowers and dragonflies. I wished I had more money. I wished I had more time. Much, much more of both. Down past a couple of stationery shops. One was called

Mélodies Graphiques. Its window displayed a violin and cello that had been decorated with black and white etchings of landscapes. Another *papeterie* had a tall glass cylinder with floating jellyfish sculpted from the most delicate, almost translucent, white hand-made paper.

I quickened my pace as the rain fell more heavily and it was getting cold. I was on Île de St Louis and before I crossed completely back to the Left Bank I wanted to walk up rue Saint-Louis-en-l'Île to the beautiful gallery of Central Asian textiles, jewellery, rugs and furniture called Galerie Bamyan. It was there that I had bought a unique moonstone ring the week before and where Judith had remarked about a purple hand-woven silk coat-dress from Uzbekistan hanging up high on one of its walls: 'It is the kind of purple you could look into forever.' And it was; I saw it again and will see it forever. Not far from here in another tiny boutique selling Central Asian things, I bought Judith a small fabric purple heart in memory of all this.

I left yet another beloved street in Paris and crossed over to Île de la Cité via the Pont Saint-Louis; I walked past the buttresses behind Notre Dame and around to the Pont de l'Archevêché where my favourite street musician usually played his beautiful guitar music that haunted me. But it was too wet for him and I missed my opportunity to see and hear him one last time and to fulfil a promise I had made to myself, to buy a CD from him. I walked over the bridge which was also heavily hung with love-padlocks and over to the Left Bank. The man with two small stubs for legs who usually sat at this end of the bridge in his wheelchair was also missing. I was happy to think that he must have had shelter somewhere.

I headed then in the direction of Shakespeare and Company to meet Diana. I found her in the gem of a place overflowing with people and a playful air energising it on that cold wet afternoon. One of the women serving was welcoming a customer into the 'gingerbread house'. I smiled and joined in the fun. We ventured up the stairs and found more magical rooms up there. In the section for children there was a young English couple sitting on the cushioned bay bench against the wall. She was reading him excerpts from *The Little Prince* and we listened in on their little interludes and the reading, thinking how 'at home' they seemed, lounging back together there. It is how that place is. Just like home. Behind this couple on a pin board were the notes left by itinerants, dozens of them, who have stayed a while in this little bookshop at various times in its existence. In the reading room through the doorway was a woman asleep in an armchair and others sitting and reading, not only on chairs but also on the floor. We lingered, looking at children's books, and then wandered back downstairs. Two books, both out of their places, vied for my attention and I decided to buy both. One was a little hard-covered memoir called *Woolgathering* by Patti Smith. The other was a novel called *The Snow Child* by Eowyn Ivey.

I left Diana there and said *au revoir* to the beloved bookshop as the time was approaching 3 pm when I believed I had a date with destiny. So I headed over to the front of Notre Dame, intent on joining a ceremony that was carried out there on the first Friday of each month. I stood for a few minutes to bask in a small window of sunlight and watched a man feeding bread to the pigeons. Flocks of the silver-grey birds flew in noisily from all directions and greedily and frantically feasted, then vanished in a frenzy as quickly as they came. I was reminded of the song and scene I love from *Mary Poppins* called 'Feed the Birds' about the old street woman sitting on the steps of Saint Paul's Cathedral in London doing just that, and pleading with passers-by to buy her bags full of crumbs for tuppence a bag.

Another amazon of a queue flowed in both directions from the entrance to the cathedral. 'I will never get in for the ceremony!' I gasped. But something insistent inside me urged me on. I decided to push in, to jump the queue. So with a clear vision of myself sauntering over and melding in with the group closest to the door, I did just that and no one noticed. I did it. I pushed in. I walked with reverence, not with the bulk of the people who were gushing into this grand dame, but into the rows of pews where other worshippers were awaiting the main event, the Exposition of the Relics held by this Cathedral. They were purported to be the crown of thorns that Jesus wore as he was crucified, a piece of wood from his cross and a nail from it. When I had heard of this ritual only the week before, I had felt something inside me stir and tears overflowed from that place. It was then that I made my date with destiny to attend.

'Silence, s'il vous plaît!' A gentle but strong male voice, magnified by a microphone, echoed out in an attempt to hush the masses flowing into the cathedral and wandering around, looking and chatting ceaselessly. His command had little effect on the throngs on the periphery, but my focus and that of those now sitting in the pews was on something else. Something steeped in ritual. In mystery. In the sacred. Candles sitting in tall silver candlesticks up and behind the dressed Communion Table were lit by an altar server with a very long taper; incense smoke wafted into the air and entered my nostrils and deep into my soul. As I inhaled the aromatic stuff, a beautiful soprano voice filled the air with its glorious music and rose above us all. That too filtered through to my very depths. Then I saw it.

The procession of priests and acolytes and lay servers all dressed in a mixture of beautiful silken-satiny, golden, green, purple and white robes and garments. Then the relics themselves, in a kind of carriage. They walked right in front of me. I got goosebumps all over. Tears welled up, spilled out and rolled wet and salt-soothingly down my cheeks. Joy and grief overflowed together. It was a feeling I was almost unable to bear. Heartachingly painful and yet gloriously freeing and light. I saw the crown of thorns (or what is purported to be it) encased in an ornamental brass and glass round vessel that made it appear like a true king's crown. I gasped and almost sobbed. I asked myself where this immense feeling had come from and why it was I so strongly believed in the authenticity of these venerated objects. Why was I present at this sacred ritual in this dark, yet comforting place? What was my part in it? I was unable to participate in the prayers or the singing as I did not understand the words, yet I mumbled something and I hummed a tune in harmony with the rest. I was drawn into the heart of the ceremony. I surrendered into it. Breathed it in. Sang it out. I was participating.

I didn't stay for the duration of the ceremony, but decided to leave after about forty-five minutes. When I walked back out onto the street, it had begun raining again, this time quite heavily. As I made my way back over to the Left Bank and up Boulevard Saint Michel, the rain became more of a deluge and I, along with dozens of others on the street, was soaked from my boots up. I wove my way up the street as quickly as my legs would carry me. I had planned to buy some cards from one of the *papeteries* on the street, but they would only have been drenched and I couldn't really bring myself to enter a shop selling paper goods in my state of wetness. I arrived at the turn into rue Soufflot and made my way towards the copper dome of the Panthéon one last time. As I had promised, I did go into the Picard Surgelés on Place de Panthéon to buy our last dinner in Paris for Diana and myself. I chose a frozen cannelloni and two small chocolate gelatos. I left loaded up. On over to the steps of Saint-Étienne-du-Mont, then down the little cobbled lane that was always littered with dog droppings, then left into rue Descartes and into number 17 and up the stairs, squelching underfoot all the way.

Home now. Where would I be without my eyes to see, I wonder this evening; this early summer evening, as I look to the pale blue sky, washed-out-blue of the dusk light and wisps of pinkish clouds, almost translucent as the last rays of the setting sun, slowly drift by. I look down and around to the tea tree bushes, dozens of them, all a-flower; hundreds of white-green (or is it green-white?) flowers that adorn them.

How would I be, I wonder, if I couldn't see or hear the little thornbills forming a background harmony to the rustling of leaves in the treetops? I feel the gentle breeze that moves them across my face and bare toes and lifts my skirt a little. I smell incense, rose-flavoured, on that breeze, and hear the distant screeching of a mob of sulphur-crested cockatoos and the singing of some other bird I'm unable to name; having not spied it and with no memory nor recognition of its song. I look out into the canopy and see the gum leaves dancing in that same movement, in that cool and gentle current of air. It's an elegant ballet they seem to perform; as the slender long lacy branches sway, bending back and forth, up and down, twirling and swirling them. It's as if the branches are the male dancers and the skirts of leaves at their ends are the females.

The clouds turn even pinker, more luminescent, as the sun moves lower in the sky and behind them. The horizon seems to glow more brightly and illuminates the paling sky. It's a brilliant soft light, but down here on this earthly plane amongst the gum trees, the colours of things are darkening. They seem dense and dull as the night sneaks in. A beetle flies by and then another and another. The horizon becomes a bright blazing ember in the sun's final parting gesture and with the breeze gone, the dark silhouettes of the trees before me make it seem like some giant paper cut-out. The 'galung galung' of my beloved currawongs echoes across the airwaves from somewhere not too far away and a chorus of crickets ring out to welcome the night.

Then it is half-light, that dulled, greying light that is evidence of the sun's passing below the horizon; of the imminence of the dark of night. I remember the light of Paris and how it always seemed to be a dimmed light, even on the sunny days. Now that I have returned home the reverse seems true. I was surprised at my own response to that greyness, not being a fan of grey days and the night, particularly. Like the light I have before me now, it was soft and gentle and it was easy to blend with it, to join with it in its liminal space.

The light of Paris seemed non-reflecting; it appeared to sink deeply into everything and in some cases to become fluidly dense, like mercury. But then there was so much to absorb all the light in that city; so many buildings; so much stone and metal and wood; centuries of it; nothing to bounce off. Even the waters of the Seine were murky and dull and had a thirst for the light; nothing crystal clear there. It was as if all that was there and that had been there, made by man and woman, soaked it all in; drew it all into itself. As if there was a giant organism living within and below all the history and the evidence of it, and that being was a vital part of the living organism that is Paris. It had to be fed as much light as it could get, so as to keep the city warm in winter and sustained always.

I had another idea that somehow in Paris the light was filtered through a veil, above in the heavens. Everywhere around me in the streets, on the buildings, inside buildings, amongst the trees, I saw replicas and symbols of this light-filtering-system, this lacework, this filigree. It was there in the black wrought iron of the hundreds of balustrades of apartment balconies up and down the Seine and out into the boulevards and *rues* of the Haussmann-designed parts of the city. It was there in the intricately patterned iron-work of huge ancient doors on Notre Dame and some of the older buildings on Île de la Cité. I saw it in the old street lamps on many a corner and in that gargantuan labyrinth of underground Metro stations and platforms.

It was there in the black metal fencing and gates along parts of Boulevards Saint Germain and Saint Michel and the Jardin du Luxembourg and in the black lacy branches of the leafless lime trees everywhere. It was there at Père Lachaise Cemetery in all the above forms and in the black cats and the carrion crows that inhabited that miniature city of the dead up on the hill. I saw it represented on postcards, with the black lines and symbols of musical notes and then thought that, perhaps, the street musicians brought this to life and that music must be part of the light of the city. Part of its softening; its diffusion; light in another form; light filtering back up and out from somewhere deep down. Metabolised perhaps by that hungry creature below, transformed, transubstantiated and offered as Holy Communion for those who came with hungry souls.

I saw it in Pont des Arts, which had a network of black metal lacework on either side of it and the padlocks of lovers that it now held, hundreds of them; they subdued the sun's rays rather than reflected them. I think also that some of the light these padlocks reflected had been altered in the symbolic gesture of throwing their keys into the waters of the Seine, liquidising it.

It was there in the beautiful Chantilly lace that adorned the neo-romantic and semi-Gothic handmade garments in V.O. Boutik in rue Mouffetard. I saw it in the black lace of arm and leg stockings and little black-filigreed mittens and women's black lacy underwear in many boutiques along rue de Rivoli.

I saw it in the huge grills in the pavements along the *rues* and boulevards everywhere, where the light had become warm air beaming up from below, from that subterranean filtering, feeding and transforming organism. I thought that if I lived on those streets I would take shelter on those grills to keep me warm at night and on cold lonely days. What a wondrous city. Even the streets were warmed in cold weather.

I saw it in the magnificent stained-glass windows of Sainte-Chapelle, filtering light as they rose up and up and seemed to me to be the perfect replica of the cerulean blue of the sky. I saw it and felt it inside Notre Dame Cathedral, with her immense domed ceiling and stained-glass windows way up high and strangely the darkest place I had entered. I trod her giant warm, time-worn stones and it was there I felt that organism that was fed on the light. I felt it draw me downwards, gently and with warmth I'd not experienced before. As if in entering her, I was entering into the very heart of that being below – of the city herself; of her soul. It was a nurturing, welcoming, softening feeling; a feeling of belonging, of being at home, at home at last, perhaps. I think now maybe I was in the heart of my own soul – its womb, incubating, being fed a lifeline, nourishment, expanding upwards and outwards and down, deeply into it. Uniting with it; becoming it.

The symbol of Paris herself, the Eiffel Tower, is homage to this light-diffusing lacework and for me perhaps the grandest symbol of it, with its criss-crossing woven metal form. It is also the ultimate beacon of the soft light: luminosity. It is interesting when the tower is lit at night and the huge beam radiates out from its summit and is rotated three hundred and sixty degrees and can be felt and seen all over the city, bringing light to the dark of night. Half-light. Is it a lighthouse for lost souls, lighting their way, our way? Or is it our searchlight, our greatest inspiration, or the sign of it?

The Shakespeare and Company bookshop, is also a symbol of that gentle light with its immortalised carrion crow in the window, its bold sign atop the front of the entrance, its rows and rows of bookshelves crammed with hundreds of books, with the black and white pattern of the printed pages inside those books. The history of the shop is a tale of the light of creativity and the loving-kindness of the human spirit.

Every time now when I see anything that resembles those patterns of silhouettes, of lacework, of filigree, filtering and gentrifying the light, back here in my daily life in the Blue Mountains, I am reminded of that soft gentle light that I saw and felt in Paris, La Ville de Lumière.

I saw it in the dragonfly that was perched on my front gauze door when I arrived home from work just recently, in that beautiful lacework of its wings and then its whole appearance on the mesh itself and even the woven wire alone.

I see it in the shadows cast on the white walls of my cottage; shadows of things I have around the place, like the leaves of an aspidistra, or the image of the tall lamp on my bedside table, or the little fly and grasshopper on the veranda lamp. I see it in the images of the gum leaves dancing on the back of the curtains in this room, fluid, moving like the waters of the Seine.

I see it in black wrought-iron gates and fences and garden ornaments, in the old lamps that stand in Hyde Park in Sydney. In the Harbour Bridge. In the currawongs. In black and white photos. In the printed words and musical notes on a page. In the picture of a black and white lace parasol. In the silhouettes of tree-tops and the shadows they cast on concrete pavements and roads on days when the air is still. Wherever there are black outlines and spaces in-between and shadowy patterns.

I see it especially in the soft silken half-light of dusk and in the gentle touch of the kindness offered to me by others – and in loving gestures made by humans everywhere.

Passion for Reading

Judith Bunn

JUDITH BUNN

Judith Bunn is a romantic, passionate woman who is a voracious reader with an intense love of literature. Judith was born in Melbourne and grew up in its eastern suburbs. At university, as a mature age student, she undertook an Arts Degree majoring in Literature and Media Studies. She then went on to The University of Melbourne to do a Postgraduate Diploma in Creative Writing.

She still lives in her beloved Melbourne and leads a very busy life there. She works in the Health Sector and has travelled extensively. In 2013 she won the 'Grace Marion Wilson Award' for Emerging Writers (Creative Non-Fiction section), an award offered through Writers Victoria. She is currently working on a number of projects, including a memoir about trying to become the main character in your own life after a lifetime of accepting unwanted secondary roles. Her dream is to one day spend a year writing in Paris.

Passion for READING

I'm sitting in the forecourt of the Shakespeare and Company Bookshop in Paris waiting for a book reading by a recently published author. The evening is humid for October. There is the merest breeze caressing the trees in the forecourt. The light is a sepia pink colour that could place you in any era. Over my left shoulder stands the lovely lady, Notre Dame, bathed in the pinkish hue. There are people everywhere, talking, walking, holding each other loosely or tightly, eating and drinking in nearby cafés. There is the tinkle of glass and cutlery, the ripple of laughter and the chug of boats on the Seine.

I see a most beautiful woman standing by the bookstore door, ethereal, her blond hair catching the last of the day's sun. I'm told it is Sylvia Whitman who now runs Shakespeare and Company, the daughter of George Whitman, the eccentric one time owner. I can see people inside the bookshop scanning shelves, reaching up and bending down. Many are reading in that half prayer-like stance with the top right hand corner of the page pinched between forefinger and thumb. There are others scattered around outside with their new purchases, sitting on concrete bollards, on the wall along the river, or on the iron and wooden chairs set up for the evening's event, reading, in their own worlds that the books are helping them create. There are all nationalities, all ages, all experiences, all orientations, all at this place dedicated to reading. After all the planning, all the anticipation, all the reading, I am here. My eyes well and overflow. I feel like I am at the Mecca of reading, a supplicant home at last.

Why do I love to read, what does reading afford me, why is reading my passion? I've thought long and hard and I've made a list: comfort, security, warmth, adventure, emotion, belonging, identification, friendship, education, imagination, succour, enrichment, challenge and the sheer beauty of the words themselves. I've always just taken my passion for granted. Books and reading are as familiar and necessary to me as breathing. I do not think about breathing until a breath is compromised.

There was a period of time, some years ago, when I could not read. Reading for me is like being transfused so I now call that period of my life the *anaemic time*. During this state I would pick up a book and listlessly leaf through the pages, flit over a paragraph or two, sigh, and then throw it aside, onto the pile of its discarded mates. It was as if the pages were mostly blank and the words just black scars etched into their surface. My mind was so clogged with the grinding white noise of grief and misery that there wasn't room for my words. Words did not dance and sing as they had always done. This scared me more than anything had in my life. I know now I was suffering from acute-on-chronic depression sparked by a relationship breakdown with the person I had loved most in the world and couldn't imagine living without. This was on top of an already slow-cooking depressed state. I felt my ballast was gone, my only enduring comfort – reading – taken from me. I was bereft. But soon, a year, two years, I can't remember now, I started, slowly and tentatively, to read, to read books about what I was going through with titles that resonated with me: *Dark Nights of the Soul* by Thomas Moore, *Malignant Sadness* by Lewis Wolpert, *Following Your Own North Star* by Martha Beck, *The Noonday Demon* by Andrew Solomon. These books were interspersed with mega doses of Kinky Friedman's *Raymond Chandleresque* detective oeuvre and the complete series of Janet Evanovich's *Stephanie Plum* bounty hunter novels. These books brought reading purely for fun and escape back into my life. The on-going characters were constants in a shifting world. And word by word, page by page, I began, if not exactly to heal, to at least reach a point where I could think moderately clearly. My books held me by the hand and led me over the rocky ground. The words whispered to me gently and lovingly, encouraging me back to them. The effect was like aloe vera on sunburn. The third-degree burns to my soul had not healed but the lancinating pain had abated. Once again my books had come to rescue me, to comfort me, to be my friends, as they had all my life.

I was born. I think that's where much of the trouble started. For those interested in dates, times and places, I came into this world on Sunday, February 5th 1961 at 12:25 in the afternoon, in a yellow room at St Andrew's Hospital in East Melbourne. It was a screamingly hot day that also happened to be my father's thirty-first birthday. The obstetrician had come from church in her Sunday best to deliver me. My mother said the bells of St Patrick's Cathedral were chiming, or was that just a charming fantasy, the first of many fairytales?

The decade into which I was born was a tumultuous one. It was a confusing time, one of contradictions. It was time of the space race where boundaries were broken. It was the time of the construction of the Berlin Wall where barriers were erected. It was a time of freedom and of subjection, excess and restraint, all intermingling. Those of us born in 1961, the upside-down year, are children of the flux. The first stirrings of the Vietnam War began in 1961, *Breakfast at Tiffany's* was made, Menzies was the Prime Minister and Barbie got a boyfriend. It was a time of bombs and Beatles, contraceptive pills, Catch 22s, Mocking Birds and a Bay of Pigs. The sixties was a cacophonous decade on so many levels but to me the sixties was a peaceful time; a time of innocence, fun and security.

The suburb to which I was taken home after my birth was semi-rural farmland, still dotted with market gardens. My parents built their house in Bruce Street, Mount Waverley, and moved there in January 1956 with their eighteen-month old son, my brother. This new suburb was almost at the end of a railway line and, as far as my mother's parents were concerned, the end of the world. When Val and Laurie started building there were only a few other houses in the street. Their block of land, according to my mother, was a *dust bowl.* My parents built their house and its garden up from nothing. My mother often relates the story of how she was yoked up like a bullock with a railway sleeper suspended on the end of two ropes. She walked around and around the back yard, levelling the ground in the criminally hot weather that she hated. She would also add it was one of the best times of her life. Cicadas must have been throbbing with their sick insistence, the gum trees, menacingly abutting the back fence, would have been frying in their own oil, hissing and snuffling, and the dust must have been thick in the air from the unmade roads. My parents planted lots of trees on their quarter-acre block, amongst them a Virgilia tree, chosen, I am sure, because of its quick growth habit, hence its nickname of *Tree-in-a-Hurry*. It would have acted as screening against the wind and, thus, helped settle down the dust.

I walk past a Virgilia tree on my way to and from the railway station each morning. I always say hello to her as I walk under her branches of greyish/green pinnate leaves. Sometimes I will reach my hand up into the foliage and let the leaves run through my fingers or, if I think no one is watching, I will rub her trunk, the bark of which is a misty green and smooth because she is still a young tree. Later in life the bark will turn grey, thick and gnarly, as I suppose we all do! Virgilia is loveliest in spring when she is festooned in blossoms. The flowers individually look like hanks of mauve bouclé wool. You feel you could gather it into spools and knit a blanket to drape around you to keep you warm, forever. But it is the scent of the Virgilia's blossom that makes me swoon. It smells clean and spicy, not cloying, with a hint of peppery sweetness. When she is in season I push my face up into her bunches and breathe deeply. I am at once enveloped and transported. In the time it takes to breathe in its powerful aroma I am pulled backwards eons and wind up in the only place where I have ever really felt truly happy or peaceful – that house in Bruce Street, Mount Waverley. Home.

The scent and feel of Virgilia is inextricably linked with books and reading. As a child, I used to sit at her base and lean my back up against her trunk or sit akimbo on one of her branches and read and read, travelling far afield to foreign and exotic places but all the time grounded by Virgilia's loving presence.

The trouble with a happy childhood is that you are always in the process of sailing away from a safe harbour. The last time the world made perfect sense to me was in January 1966. My mum was at the kitchen sink, my dad was in his shed and man was in space. January 1966 was the idyll in my life, the quiet before the tempest. I was in the last month of my fourth year. I see myself sitting on Virgilia's outstretched arm on a hot humming day. I'm singing out loud and swinging my legs. I hear the burr of motor mowers murmuring in the distance throwing up the intoxicating smell of freshly cut grass and perhaps there is the smell of rain in the air and the promise of thunder. Me, a supple-limbed child in a homemade cotton shift dress on a summer's day, pulsating with life.

In the early sixties I was only afraid of the things you should be afraid of: strangers, bogeymen, groups of people, other children, steam trains and the dark. There was no future to be afraid of and a barely discernible past. All was this intense moment. I was completely myself, un-selfconscious, not worried. Content. My life consisted of Billy carts and scooters, homemade cotton frocks, thongs and shorts, red mohair jumpers, tartan skirts and gumboots, creeks and bushland, Clarke rubber pools, Holden cars, rows of houses on quarter-acre blocks with a few empty lots in between, like missing teeth. There were those ubiquitous lawn mowers, transistor radios chirping out football games or cricket matches, neighbours talking over back fences and Bellbirds. Depending on the clearly defined seasons, there were leaves in gutters or the chinka-chinka-chinka sounds of circular sprinklers throwing out great arcs of water that caught the sun in its flight, making mini-rainbows. All was cherry earrings and necklaces made from daisies.

I was an introverted, shy, internal child with a vivid imagination who was happy in my own company with a small circle of real people who constituted my world.

At around kindergarten age, my mother began to actively

encourage me to love books and I owe her a huge debt of gratitude for giving me such a priceless gift. She bought me books and read to me every night. When she took me shopping with her she would invariably buy me a Little Golden Book that cunningly lay in wait at the cash register (now replaced by chocolate bars, gossip-filled magazines and choking hazards). The books had a distinctive gold spine and were heavily and gorgeously illustrated, tantalising for a bookish child such as myself. As well as the de rigueur fairytales, I remember titles such as *The Sailor Dog, The Saggy Baggy Elephant, The Lone Ranger and Tonto, Baby Dear, Bible Stories of Boys and Girls,* and *Little Black Sambo.* (I cringed when writing that title but this is not a revisionist sociological critique.) I would be enchanted by the fact that my mother could read the words, never suspecting that I would be able to do that one day myself, even though she promised me I would when I went to school, whatever the hell that was.

My mother's tenacity for us to be readers is all the more admirable when you consider she came from a family of non-readers. I remember my maternal grandparents' house as being totally devoid of books. There were bookshelves in Nan and Pop's house but they had china ornaments on them, not books. The only reading materials in my grandparents' house were the 6"-square pieces of newspaper in the outside dunny used as toilet paper. My grandparents, I feel now, were in awe of books. One of my special bookish memories, ironically, involves my maternal grandmother, Eunice. One day Eunice came to me with a small book in her hands. She looked like one of the Wise Men with frankincense in hand, approaching the baby Jesus. She handed me the book: *David Copperfield* by Charles Dickens. She said to me, in a sepulchral voice full of import, *Never give this book away*. And I never have. It sits beside me now as I write. It was old at the time Eunice gave it to me. Now its pages are brown and brittle, its cover frayed at the edges. I flipped through the book and came upon page 193 where the following paragraph had been underlined:

Every night, said Mr. Peggotty, as reg'lar as the night comes, the candle must be stood in its old pane of glass, that if ever she should see it, it may seem to say, 'Come back, my child, come back!'

I try to read a posthumous message from my grandmother in those words.

My paternal side, on the other hand, were voracious readers. There is a family folk tale about one of my father's aunts who would read from the moment she woke up in the morning. She would read at the breakfast table, taking her eyes off the page only long enough to kiss her husband and children goodbye as they went off to work and school, and they would find her still sitting in the same position, still reading, when they came home in the evening, still in her dressing gown, the breakfast dishes still in the same position. I love that story of a woman who got her priorities so right!

I still have a few books handed down to me from my grandfather. They are all hardbacks, being from the 1920s and 1930s. They hide their secrets with totally blank covers in dung brown or forest green. I still have his set of the Geste series of books, *Beau Geste, Beau Sabreur and Beau Ideal*, written by P C Wren, dealing with derring-dos in the French Foreign Legion in Northern Africa. Once they were inadvertently sent to the op shop after a family house clean-up. I was terror-stricken that someone else would buy the books and send them to a foster home instead of remaining with me where they belonged. I went in search of them, scouring the three op shops in our area where they could have gone, frantic ... but there they stood, lonely and abandoned, on the bottom shelf, looking at me reproachfully. I gathered them up, paid for my own books and took them home where they belonged. After about fifteen subsequent house moves they are still with me, read and loved, with my grandfather's name written on the inside covers.

One morning my mother dressed me in a blue and white checked dress with a matching belt, a white Peter Pan collar and red sandals. Wow! This was a nice new outfit. My long hair was pulled back into a ponytail with a scarlet satin ribbon. We set off for a walk. I held her hand and skipped along beside her. We reached a large area of open asphalt where there seemed to be hundreds of other girls dressed just like me (I thought there must have been a sale at Coles) and boys in grey shorts with white shirts and scrupulously polished black shoes. OK, here was a situation I didn't like immediately; lots of other children milling and running about, squealing. But it was OK. Mum's hand was still there.

A bell rang and immediately all the hordes of children ran to line up in single file at the bottom of some stairs, waving goodbye to mothers who seemed to be set to walk away. My mother would never do that. Hey, wait on, what's happening here? My mother was trying to extricate my hand from hers and was gently pushing me towards the other children. My mother was actually pushing me away and making as if to leave. I wasn't having that! I clung to her as if to a lifebuoy in rough seas. I must have been crying and screaming and clawing at her. I didn't realise it was possible to even breathe independently of my mother.

At that moment a small, grey-haired, stern-faced woman, aptly named Miss Fox, came to the top of the stairs looking like Mussolini about to deliver a speech and surveyed the scene I must have been creating. She brought a megaphone to her mouth and yelled at my mother to *take that child right down the back of the playground, she's upsetting the other children!* I was grasping at my mother, wide-eyed and sobbing. I had never been yelled at in my life up to that point, let alone in front of a swarm of eyes.

I don't know how I got through the rest of that day. I can't remember. But, after what must have been an interminable amount of time my mother was waiting at the gate for me. Ah, salvation! What utter bliss. The crisis was over. I may not recover from that trauma for a long time but all was well. Whatever cruel punishment that was, it was over now and I could go back home, to my kingdom, my Little Golden friends and Virgilia. But you know what? It all happened again the next day and the next day and the day after that. And every day I cried as if my heart was wounded, which I think it was, and it never really healed or, if it did, there was a fault line running through it forever more. There was born on that first day of school a sense of homesickness, or grief, like the pinch of a pulled stitch, which has never really left me. I turned five on the Saturday after that first week of school. Could I read yet?

The first book I picked up to read by myself was *John and Betty: The Earliest Reader for the Little Ones* in 1966, the Education Department's primary reader of the time. This book also sits in front of me now as I write. Its flimsy orange cardboard cover has my name written on the front of it in the tongue out, over-large scrawl of a five-year-old child. This was possibly one of the first attempts to write my name. The letters are uneven, wobbly and of varying sizes but it was my first stamp on my first book, my first foray into ownership of words. I don't remember being taught to read. I don't remember learning my ABCs. It was like an osmotic process. It seemed that one day I couldn't read, then the next day I could. School changed for me then. It meant access to the wonder of words, books and reading. I had found a niche at last.

My favourite thing at school was being read to by our teacher. I remember sitting cross-legged on our little maroon school-issue cushions in a circle around the teacher who would be seated on a wooden, high-backed chair in a haze of chalk. I would sit with open mouth and eyes as she read the book side-on to her face so we could see the pictures as she read, following the words with her finger. One of the books she read and I loved the most was *Charlotte's Web* by E B White, a tale stating that little friends may indeed become great friends. I was mesmerised by the story of talking animals and I also remember howling at the end of it. I think it was the first time I was completely overwhelmed by the power of words and story to evoke emotion.

My father would take me to the library every Saturday morning for a pile of books. I was astonished that they would give you books to take home by simply showing a small piece of cardboard. In return

I got the maximum allotment of books allowed. I can still hear the sound of the date stamp as the librarian indelibly thumped the return date inside the back cover on a little piece of white paper where other dates from past borrowers lay stark in their chronology. I was afraid of the date because it meant I had to return the books and if I did not do so we would be charged a *fine*. I didn't know what that was but it seemed a bad thing.

Without really noticing, I had begun to read on my own. I could at last read my Little Golden Books and instead of my mother reading to me, I would read to her. At that age, I think around eight or nine, I was obsessed with Aesop's fables. I trawled my way through every one of them and learned the lessons and the morals they had to teach and the sayings that have been used since Aesop wrote them around the 6th century BC:

Appearances often are deceiving; familiarity breeds contempt; slow and steady wins the race; one person's meat is another's poison; things are not always what they seem; never trust a flatterer; beware the wolf in sheep's clothing; little friends may become great friends.

Ah, I could relate that back to *Charlotte's Web*. I could see there was interconnectedness between books.

Books are also responsible for leading me into a life of petty crime. I used to *borrow* books from the school library and, er, neglect to return them. I didn't see it as stealing. I felt I had a God-given right to the books. No one would love them as much as I would, no one would understand them like I would, they would only be happy in my hands, the power of the words could only be unleashed by me. I still have these ill-gotten gains on my bookshelf.

For him that stealeth, or borroweth and returneth not, this book from its owner, let it change into a serpent in his hand and rend him. Let him be struck with palsy, and all his members blasted. Let him languish in pain, crying aloud for mercy, and let there be no surcease to this agony till he sing in dissolution. Let bookworms gnaw his entrails… and when at last he goeth to his final punishment, let the flames of Hell consume him forever.

– Anonymous curse on book thieves from the Monastery of San Pedro, Barcelona Spain

Oh my! I'm going to burn in hell but as long as they have books there, I'll be OK. Hell to me would be a place without books.

The most profound reading experience I have ever had, and am ever likely to have, was reading C S Lewis's charming set of books constituting the Narnia series. I was so bewitched and enchanted by these seven books that I first read when I was about twelve. I thought that they were written just for me. I remember distinctly having a moment of great awareness when I understood the allegory inherent in the stories. I also was touched by the religious fervour they invoked. I spent an inordinate amount of time jumping in and out of wardrobes trying to reach other worlds that I was positive were there, if only I could break down the barriers. Peter, Susan, Edmund and Lucy became my companions and my friends. There was always a fifth in their adventures, me, tagging along behind, hanging onto shirt tails, listening in to conversations, being privy to a world beyond my own. I became lost in the world they depicted. I was transported by the feelings Lewis's prose evoked, the cold, the fur coats, the musty cupboards. I also fell in love with Lewis's use of words, even down to the gorgeously named third book in the instalment, *The Voyage of the Dawn Treader*, and the majesty of words and the visions they conjured. I had the same feeling of complicity with *The Secret Garden*, a surface story of a neglected girl and an equally neglected garden but with the palimpsest story of regeneration.

These books also led me to re-enacting their stories in my back yard. I had pretend friends, like Dobbin from *The Secret Garden*. I used to love to read sets of books: *Anne of Green Gables* by Lucy Maud Montgomery, the tales of an orphan on Prince Edward Island, Nova Scotia, the *Billabong* books by Mary Grant Bruce about life in the

Australian bush, the *Poldark* series of books by Winston Graham set in Cornwall. I liked the stories of continuity and connection they depicted. I also liked that I got to live lives in other countries and other settings than my own. It was heady stuff. Characters became friends; they stepped out of the pages and into my life, fully fleshed. Coming out of a book was like emerging from a cave into strong sunlight and I would reach behind to pull the characters out with me too.

I suppose I should have started with a confession, or perhaps codicil would be a better word. I am a middle-class, white Anglo-Saxon, Protestant, heterosexual, third generation Australian from the eastern suburbs of Melbourne. You may already have picked that up! I am not sure whether I am a Baby Boomer or a Generation X-er. According to sources I have read the divide is generally agreed to be around 1960. Therefore it would appear I stand right on the cusp, or as it sometimes feels, right on the quakeline.

As a product of my upbringing and the zeitgeist in Australia, I didn't know anything about indigenous politics, I didn't know anything about feminism, I would not have had the least idea of what 'gay' meant, except in its literal colourful sense, and the closest I got to multiculturalism was a Greek kid call George Georgioupoulas who came to our school in 1966, and the local Chinese food restaurant where we thought it was terribly cutting edge to take our saucepans to be filled with chicken balls in sweet and sour sauce with 'special' fried rice. Mine was a suburb of young couples bringing up young children. Everyone was going through the same life experiences at the same time as their peers: building homes, making gardens, the men taking the 8:12 into the city, the women doing the housework and talking over the back fence. I didn't know anyone's mother who worked outside the house, I didn't know anyone whose parents were divorced.

As for 'cultcha', we were considered ever so slightly posh because my mother took me to the ballet. I had no concept of life outside my suburb other than for the brief forays into Preston and Sandringham where my grandparents lived. Looking back now, it all had a bit of a Stepford quality to it. It certainly had a homogeneity about it. But for me, books were the set of keys to the wider world and of worlds outside this world.

My high school education was ostensibly a Leavisite one, based on the canon of English literature. We were the retinue of dead white males. I had an English Literature teacher in my HSC year who did her very best to extinguish any possible flame of joy you might possibly derive from literature. Luckily her best was not quite good enough and I managed to retain my love of books. This paragon of pedagogy would sit at the front of the class and say, 'Right girls, open to page 1 of *A Tale of Two Cities* and underline the following lines.' That was all we did all class, and consequently thirty-five years later I have a large proportion of the canon of English Literature almost completely underlined. She would give us her interpretation of the underlinings and we took that interpretation as gospel.

We never studied contemporary texts and we studied very few Australian texts. There was very much a high culture/low culture binary opposition in my high school education. I still learned nothing of multiculturalism, gay literature and, most interestingly in a girls' school, there were no feminist critiques of any kind. But, hey, it was the seventies, perhaps one of the most male-centric decades in Australian and world history.

There were 'school books' which you had to read as they had a lesson to impart, and there were books you read because you wanted to: escape books, weekend books, and it was to these that I turned, slightly guiltily, outside of school hours.

At the age of fifteen or so there was a craze for the Susan Howatch books, *Penmarric*, *Cashelmara* and *The Rich Are Different*. They were sweeping family sagas which completely swept me away. I also had a real penchant for (cue the cringe) Mills & Boon. I was set on fire as a teenager reading these books.

I would get caught up in the milieu of books. I went through my flapper/jazz age phase after overdosing on F Scott Fitzgerald, my mad, moody, moorland phase after reading all the books of the Bronte sisters, my Regency rage phase after reading Jane Austen, my World War I poetry phase, being in love with Siegfried Sassoon, Wilfred Owen and Rupert Brooke. Once I get my teeth onto the teat of a subject I tend to milk it for all it's worth. I became obsessed by the books and the eras depicted, and would read around the book I was reading. I would read everything I could find on World War I, including Vera Brittain, Erich Maria Remarque and Robert Graves. I would immerse myself in topics and be in a fog for the duration of that particular obsession *du jour*. I would almost take on the persona of the times. I believe I conjured my Byronic/melancholy temperament into being through choice of reading matter. I was enflamed by books and read myself into a heightened sense of romanticism. My love of books turned into intense interest in their authors. I sometimes liked the authors more than their books and would read books *about* authors instead. I longed to be part of the Algonquin Round Table.

I started work when I was eighteen and became a train reader. I distinctly remember having to buy a handbag (dark blue with a tassel) and a book (*All the Green Year* by Don Charlwood) for my first day of work. Work was a hideous experience. I was young, green, naïve, gullible, unsophisticated. Get out the Thesaurus and find all the adjectives you can for a child/woman who was really just uncooked dough. I was a sparrow set amongst a group of feral cats. I suppose, looking back, I was bullied. I was certainly ridiculed and belittled with no coping resources at my disposal. Books became even more important to me at that time. They were a refuge and they were the friends I was so lacking in this new stage of my life. The office overlooked an oval and I used to look out and imagine the characters of my books sitting out there waiting for me. They would wave at me, encouraging and comforting me. I couldn't wait for 5 o'clock when I could leave work, get on the train and, ahhhh, read.

One of my most loved train-reading experiences was *Zemindar* by Valerie Fitzgerald, a kind of *Pride and Prejudice* set in 1850s India at the time of the Raj. One buttock cheek was perched on the edge of the seat trying to avoid the touch of the person next to me, difficult given that the carriage was at capacity. It had been raining and the paraphernalia associated with a wet day was strewn around. Used umbrellas lay defeated on the floor, wet coats were steaming over cold bodies giving off a mildewy odour, there was the murmur of conversation and an occasional ricochet of laughter, and the insistent chorus of sniffing and coughing. A day like any other. But I was in the far north of India, hot and sweaty, on the edge of a rebellion, desperately following the love affair between Laura, an Englishwoman sent to India as a companion, and Oliver, the arrogant, proud, worldly landowner of a huge estate in the district of Oudh.

A friend once asked me which I preferred, watching movies or reading. To me they were much the same thing, the only difference being that with a book you may not have written the script but you are the director, the casting director, the location spotter, camera operator, and the main character all rolled into one. You have a movie in your head that you create as you read. I have read *Zemindar* several times since that first reading on the train and I still get the same visual and sensory setting that I did all those years ago; the only thing that may have changed slightly is an understanding of the relationship dynamics and the politics surrounding India in 1857. It is a big book, running to almost 800 pages, but every time I've read it, it has only taken me a few days, so seduced am I by Valerie Fitzgerald's writing and the story. I love those times of utter involvement that a book gives you, when all you want to do is sneak off in a corner and read until you get a headache.

I still read on the train. It is one of my favourite times of the day. One day, not so long ago, I was running late for my train to work and realised I didn't have anything to read on the journey, being currently 'between books'. In desperation I shuffled through my shelves and grabbed a copy of *A Difficult Young Man* by Martin Boyd, a book I first read thirty-five years ago and had not touched since. As I read it on the train, I remembered the powerful feelings I had for the main character, Dominic. It dawned on me then that my heroes have always been mythical, literary, arising from a television or cinema screen, or between the covers of a book, and always of a certain ilk: dark, dangerous, brooding, difficult, Byronic, but with barely hidden vulnerability.

I think my first literary love affair was with Achilles from Homer's *The Iliad*. I became so infatuated with him that to this day I can still remember the romantic, near impenetrable, bubble I was in for almost the whole of my fifteenth year. And it has been this way with so many forays into literature. My other loves have been Raskolnikov, Mr Darcy, Heathcliff, Mr Rochester, Sidney Carton, and my sympathies always lay with Judas. I was drawn to the misunderstood bad boy.

Now I have a greater affinity with the gentle equanimity of a Dobbin or a Bingley. I now respect and admire the patience and fortitude of a Ulysses whereas once I preferred the quick tempered impulses of Achilles. I preferred melancholy to joy. I was heady with the romance of melancholy, which I believe would later contribute to my descent into depression. Now I can't imagine living with Heathcliff or Achilles. It would be too exhausting. These heroes don't seem to be the type to talk about house insurance, low-fat milk versus full cream, or who should go into the chemist to buy the haemorrhoid ointment. These were the things of the future, a future I couldn't countenance. Now I am living that future; days of one foot in front of the other. But, oh, in the night these heroes circle at the edge of consciousness and lie in wait on the outskirts of Arcadia.

Books have also, frighteningly, sometimes acted as fortune-tellers. I had a moment of clarity reading *Gone with the Wind*. It was like a pre-emptive strike on the future. I remember, at the age of fifteen or so, crying bitterly in my bed at the end of *Gone with the Wind*, when Scarlett has her epiphany that indeed Rhett was the man she loved and she had been piss-farting around, breaking her own heart over the feckless, married, Ashley and had mistakenly thought her friend Melanie weak and mealy-mouthed when, in fact, she was the strongest character in the book and the best friend Scarlett would ever have. It was a precursory warning of what was to happen in my own life thirty years later but I didn't know that then, of course, but I felt the enormity of the concept when I read that book when I was about fifteen.

I started to travel extensively in my twenties and I turned into a toucher and a stalker but before you edge away from me and determine never to make eye contact, you are completely safe, that is, unless you are a dead and famous writer. If you are a dead and famous writer, you are fair game. I should warn you that the authorities and museum curators will not like what I am about to say and I hasten to add that I do not condone this behaviour, but I make an exception in my case because, well, it's me!

It all started when I found myself alone in a room in Jane Austen's house in Chawton, England. I was compelled to touch a piece of patchwork quilting that she and her sister, Cassandra, had worked on in the 1700s and which was hanging on a wall. My touch was not a stroke, just a quick poke and run, expecting all the time to have my shoulder tapped upon. Flushed with success, later, on a trip to North Yorkshire I leaned over and petted the leg of the couch upon which Emily Bronte had died at the Haworth Parsonage where the family had lived. But here I came to grief. An almighty alarm started to scream, followed by a very polite English voice coming over a loud speaker ... *We are not going to ask who touched the exhibit but we would like to remind everyone that it is strictly forbidden to touch anything behind the roped off areas. We thank you for your cooperation.* Oops. On a walk up to Top Withens (supposedly the location that inspired *Wuthering Heights*) later that same day I sat on a large smooth rock called 'Emily's Chair' where she used to sit to rest on her many walks on the moors. I felt it would give me inspiration. I think it only gave me piles. But I was thrilled that my bottom had been where Emily Bronte's bottom had been. Er, is that ever so slightly creepy?!

That brings me, somewhat circuitously, to my university education. I did not go to university until I was in my thirties, having gone, as I have already stated, straight from school into the workforce at age eighteen. I always wanted to get a degree in English Literature and I suppose when I came to university I was expecting to receive a classical education where I would walk around the honeysuckle-covered quad quoting Tennyson and pontificating on the merits of Eliot, Trollope, Dostoyevsky et al., and where I could finally indulge my passion for Jane Austen and the Brontes. I got something completely different. One of the books we were set to read was Christos Tsiolkas's *Loaded*. Boy, did I get the education I missed out on in the seventies! It was a book totally out of my sphere. I was blasted out of my safe, soft little literary bubble and that bubble became a blister but, in the words of the Rolling Stones, you don't always get what you want, but sometimes you get what you need.

In the 1990s when I went to university books were *on the turn*. We were studying the advent of the internet and its impact on literature. Whilst in itself a fascinating topic, it was not quite what I was envisaging. I saw the collapse of high culture/low culture distinctions. The two now lived side by side, a more true reflection of life itself perhaps. There was an inter-disciplinary approach with spillage between disciplines. Film, cult TV and pulp fiction were no longer things of the private sphere, guilty pleasures; they became things to be studied in their own right.

My reading horizons were certainly broadened. I was 'forced' to read things I never would have chosen for myself. I started to read science fiction, a genre I had never before touched. I got heavily into all of Philip K Dick's work, *Snow Crash* by Neal Stephenson and *Neuromancer* by William Gibson. These books really messed with my brain, but in a good way. I realised that in essence I had returned to the fantasy, make-believe world of my childhood, yet in an adult vernacular, and I was no less swept away by these books as I had been by the Narnia books forty odd years before.

In 2002 I studied full-time for a year (a luxury I could afford due to a redundancy package from a job I'd long begun to hate), doing a Post Graduate Diploma in Creative Writing. It was in this year that I found my new, and abiding, reading passion: memoir and creative non-fiction. I was reading about people and in turn reading about myself.

I started to do many courses about writing memoir and started to read memoir voraciously but I still felt somewhat jaded. I didn't believe any book would have the capacity to 'blow my mind' anymore as had those books in my childhood, adolescence and early adulthood. Of course, I still loved reading and enjoyed some things more than others, but middle age sometimes brings a gentle fading. I had lost the capacity to be truly astounded by anything.

That was, until I read Geoff Dyer's book. It was set for us in a writing class where we were dealing with creative non-fiction, still a relatively new genre in my reading repertoire and one quickly gaining hold of me. From the first paragraph of *Rage* until the last page, I believe I had my mouth open the whole time, so awed was I by the writing style and content of Dyer's book. It was as though this man had crawled inside my head and swept out the detritus onto a page. This writer's thinking processes were mine, his savage humour was the kind I liked most and this writer had the shape and course of depression so very right. His descriptions of procrastination had me howling with laughter and recognition.

In an essay called 'The Last Book I Loved, Out of Sheer Rage', Kathleen Heil wrote the following:

> *What Dyer does in this book, and does remarkably, hilariously well, is document inertia, frustration, boredom, indecision, insecurity, loneliness, despair, and a host of other shitty, very human emotions which we are almost always too proud or*

scared to admit to feeling to other people, or even to ourselves. He lays them out on the page and, rather than seeming the way they usually feel inside our scattered synapses, which is pathetic, embarrassing, shameful, or terrifying, he makes them, well, funny. Really, fucking, hilariously funny. Dyer makes comedy of the various ways we torment ourselves with our doubts and failures big and small. If I were French I would probably try to argue that the heart of Dyer's comic touch is the very darkness we suffer in our saddest hours, but I am not, so I'll just say I'd much rather be laughing with Dyer than crying alone.

With my reading passion reinvigorated by the new genre of memoir, I went on a trip to Paris, ground zero for all my passions. One of the loveliest days of my life was a brittle-sunned autumn day in Paris, sitting in the Café de la Rotonde on the Boulevard Montparnasse in a shaft of sunlight with a glass of wine, a *croque-monsieur*, a notebook and a whole day at my feet, just to myself. The Café Rotonde was where many of the great writers and artists, amongst others, used to sit during my favourite *siècle*, the 1920s. Simone de Beauvoir was born in a room upstairs. I had spent the morning in Montparnasse hunting down the houses of some of the literary and artistic greats of the era: F Scott Fitzgerald, Gertrude Stein, Ford Maddox Ford and his wife, the Australian painter Stella Bowen, and the photographer Man Ray to name but a few. I also found and photographed the cafés they frequented: Le Select, La Coupole, Le Dôme, La Closerie des Lilas and the Dingo. To see these places was beyond ecstasy for me.

I love to stand, sit and genuflect in the shadow of greatness, to walk where the writers I admire have walked, to breathe where they have breathed, to take up the same space they have occupied. I touch door handles, bar rails and door steps and, at times, I have cried with the overwhelming emotion of these experiences. I get excited to think that my hand has touched something that my literary heroes have touched. I suppose I am hoping greatness will rub off on me.

I can't get away without voicing an opinion on 'new reading', that is, reading in the new digital age. Books are now under siege from the new technological age. The closing of book shops, on-line publishing and e-readers are threatening a bibliophile's safe, clandestine life. As I write here in my study, my books stand sentinel around me, arranged in their platoons, protecting me. I love to fossick in op shops for the chance of finding a gem. There are treasures to be found and I revel in the thrill of the chase.

To me, a screen has no personality. Books have personality, especially second-hand or 'pre-loved' books. I like to find a book in a second-hand environment that is dog-eared, tea-stained, be-crumbed, slightly wrinkly from being cried over, written upon, dedicated to, slept with, thrown across the room. I like the sense of continuity that a book gives. Someone else has read it, enjoyed it (or not) and lived it before it comes to me. I recently read a lovely book by Rebecca Mead called *The Road to Middlemarch* about her love affair with George Eliot's book. In it she relates the experience of going into the New York Public Library to see a notebook of Eliot's from 1868. Mead says:

> I opened to the first page, and as I did so I became vaguely aware of a slight scent in the air that was at once out of place and oddly familiar: the smell of a spent hearth. For a moment, I wondered if there could be a fireplace in the adjoining room – a silly thought, quickly dismissed. But then it dawned on me that the smell was coming from the notebook itself ... I inclined towards the notebook and surreptitiously inhaled. There was something there beyond the usual mustiness of an old, infrequently opened book, I was sure – something that smelled like the lingering trace of a fire burning in a long-cooled grate.

Try replicating that, Mr Apple!

The generic nature and homogeneity of books now available for e-readers bothers me. Best sellers do not always constitute the best of reading, not that I want to engage in a high brow/low brow debate about what constitutes a *good* book. Reading is reading and what people read for enjoyment is not up for debate. Heaven knows, in times of dire need for reading material I have been known to peruse the back of air freshener cans in the toilet *in lieu* (pun intended) of something to read. People's choice of reading material is not the issue here, rather that people continue to have a *choice* of what to read. So much in life now is narrowed down and being rendered devoid of personality: packaged food; music, where the commercial channels play the same top ten songs on high rotation; TV, where channels cross promote their own shows and people; drop-in pitches in cricket, taking away the individuality of the conditions in the different states to create uniformity, *terroir* as the French farmers call it. I'm not going to get into the whole reading in the bath debate between books and e-readers. I hate baths anyway. My beef is more about content than usability and the fact that I'm sick of a world mediated by a screen. Call me a technological luddite, but to me screens mean work and bondage whereas books mean play and escape. The new technology seems to create a 'sound bite' mentality, everything must be in small digestible units, with the inherent threat that attention spans will be hitherto measured in nano-seconds. As Dr Maryanne Wolf and Dr Mirit Barzillai ask in their essay 'Questions for a Reader (Stop What You're Doing and Read This)':

> *... will the omnipresence of innumerable distractions for attention, coupled with the sheer volume of information available, contribute in our young to a mindset towards reading that seeks to reduce the massive information to its lowest conceptual denominator as quickly as possible? With too much before them to grasp, and a set towards immediate feedback, will today's novice reader learn to want things simple, quick and explained by others?*
>
> *A book to me will always be an oasis from this*

information-fraught world we live in. I worry about children in this new technological era. Do they take the time to read and then re-enact the stories in their imaginations or their backyards as I did? Or are their imaginations cued in for them and explanations a mouse click away? Do they passively accept rather than explore?

A pivotal question in today's historical transition is whether the more time-consuming demands of [these] deep-reading processes will atrophy or, in fact, never be fully formed in children raised within a culture whose principal mediums for reading increasingly advantage speed, multi-tasking and the processing of the next 'new' piece of information.

I'm sure Kindles are wonderful for travelling, being able to store innumerable books in them, but I believe I would miss the worry of how to carry home the myriad books I find on my travels that I simply can't live without. I would miss the security they give with a pile sitting on my bedside table when I'm otherwise feeling lonely in a B&B in an off-season English seaside village. I would miss going into a bookshop in a foreign country and finding the English section. I would miss the validity a book gives you when you're sitting alone in a café or restaurant. If I have a book in my hand I never feel compromised. A book is a sign saying *I'm OK, I don't need the world, I have the world in my hands, all the company I need*. A book is the finest of companions.

When I began to write this piece, the first thing I did was to write a list of the books I have loved and that have had a profound effect on me throughout my reading life, from five to fifty. The trajectory of that reading is most interesting to me and I wondered whether reading makes you what you are or whether you read what you are. Is reading horses for courses? The first thirty years of my life seemed to be made up of fiction and fantasy reading, the next twenty-plus years have been all about non-fiction.

They Met in Paris

I was a child of wonder. Everything fascinated me in this world and others. My childhood reading was magical, mystical, full of fantasy. Aesop's words were the mantras to live by. My teenage reading gave me the florid romanticism and Goth-like personality. I think I read myself into a dark place, but read myself out again in my forties. University reading perhaps gave me what I needed: a hand grenade to blast me out of that veiled world. In my forties and fifties I discovered memoir and creative non-fiction.

Now I read for the person I am or the person I would like to be with the life I would like to have. I love reading May Sarton for her gentle observations about life and living singly in this Noah's Ark world. She writes of flowers in vases and the way sunlight plays on a table. I like to read books on how people get through life, how they survive the maelstrom. I read now for the comfort of the shared life experience, to know that I'm not alone. I read more to learn now than I ever did. I have read myself into a good place.

A B C D E F G H I J K L M N O P Q R S T U V W X Y Z. I find it incredible that these twenty-six letters in myriad configurations constitute the world, my world, books, reading, words. Books have accompanied me on the journey of life; they have led me at times, followed me and certainly pushed me. Books have taken me out of myself and books have brought me back to myself. Books have allowed me to hide, and books have allowed me to be found, and for that I am profoundly grateful.

Passion

For

Food

Carole Lethbridge

Carole Lethbridge

Carole Lethbridge is an author, designer and sculptor. She is the mother of two and grandmother of five. She lives a very active life and resides in the Australian Blue Mountains 100 kilometres west of Sydney. She was born in Maitland NSW and grew up in Newcastle. In the 70s she worked with a Slimming and Nutrition magazine as an adviser on dieting for their readers and she also ran the magazine's first slimming clubs in NSW.

She had originally trained as a lettering artist and by the late 70s her creative skills led her to a very successful career in advertising, reaching board level before leaving Australia to live in Milan, Italy, for five years. She still travels extensively and has a love of Paris and most of Italy. She has just completed her first book about her three years experience with internet dating. In her leisure time she still loves to work on her sculptures which are timber assemblies, mostly in antique Japanese boxes.

It was my third visit to Paris.

This visit I was in Paris to invest time in my writing skills. While I was there most of my writing centred around food; the essay I wrote to summarise my time in Paris was titled: 'The taste of Paris'. I was in Paris to study memoir writing so I was really surprised that I'd chosen to mainly write about food.

Why food?

It was during my time in Paris that I realised I had really wanted to write about food for many years. Was it being in Paris surrounded by the most sublime, magnificent, marvellous, heavenly, divine out-of-this-world seafood, poultry, cheeses, breads and desserts that had made me choose to write about food while I was there?

I thought at the time that maybe later I should write about specific food groups, such as the amazing desserts I'd had in Paris. Desserts like the *tarte au citron* at Le Dôme located on the Boulevard du Montparnasse, or the *tarte aux myrtilles* at Le Camille on the rue des Francs-Bourgeois. Also several years prior, during my time in Italy, I had done extensive research on the food customs of the Northern Italians where many consume rice rather than pasta. I thought perhaps this would be suitable as part of a story on food.

I had written restaurant and café reviews a few years ago but I'd been told that no editor would ever publish my reviews as my writing style was far too honest. I was told off the record that a food writer couldn't be too honest or too critical, because advertisers have to be considered above editorial. The advertisers only want their products presented favourably. If a writer were to say in a review that the restaurant served Vittoria coffee and it was disgusting, this would affect the brand and subsequently upset the advertiser.

After these experiences I decided that if I were to write about food, I would write as I wanted. I now think that writing about food while doing a memoir writing course stirred up many memories of the food issues I had with my mother during my childhood.

So this story is not about the wonderful food in the restaurants and cafés that I experienced during my travels through Paris or France or Italy. It is about how parents can shape a child's lifelong attitude to food.

There will be no recipes in this story and the memories of food I write about will be in no particular order.

During my lifetime I've seen many, many changes in relation to food. Not so much the food itself but to the way it is brought into the home, how it is prepared and how it is stored.

When I was a child, our milk was delivered in the early hours of the morning direct to our home. My mother used to leave a green enamel billy can at the side of the house with the money. The milkman used to fill our billy can from a large milk urn in his truck. Some years' later, milk became available in glass bottles, sealed with silver foil tops. The cream was so thick at the top of the bottles that to get the milk to start pouring out of the bottles, we had to push the handle of a teaspoon through the cream. My mum used to wash the silver foil tops and save them, although I can't remember now what she did with them.

Bread came in two versions: a round loaf or a square loaf. White only. Bread was also delivered to our homes. It usually arrived mid-morning. We loved school holidays because we were home for lunch and could have same-day bread. Other days our packed lunch would have bread from the previous day. Then day-old bread was quite dry, no preservatives in the bread in those days. I still remember our bread man. His name was Mr Mason and he also baked the bread. We could buy full loaves and half loaves. If we wanted a half loaf, the baker just pulled the loaf apart with his hands.

Meat was purchased from butcher shops and cut to order from a butcher wearing a navy and white striped apron. Mostly my parents would buy a side of mutton and have it cut, as they wanted it. The cuts of various pieces and the cost would then be shared amongst our grandparents and family. There was no domestic refrigeration, so meat couldn't be kept for more than two or three days. We had ice chests in our kitchen which held large blocks of ice. An iceman delivered it directly to our house. He usually carried the block of ice on his shoulder, protected with a hessian bag. We also had cabinets with sections that were ventilated with holes so the cool air could circulate; these were called 'safes'. They were kept in the coolest place in the house, usually on or near south-facing verandahs, or hung under the roof eaves by a large hook. Most housewives went to the butchers at least three times a week and always went to the same shop; they were well known to the butcher. Our butcher, Mr Harris, used to give my mother free lamb shanks, tripe and other offal to help stretch her limited budget. Meat scraps and bones for the dogs were also given free. There was no such thing as tinned dog food. Even our animals ate natural foods then without the preservatives and food colourings their foods are loaded with today.

A fishmonger supplied our fish. He would drive around the suburban streets with the fish he'd usually caught himself. My mother would choose what she wanted and the monger would scale and gut the fish in the street. He would slap the cleaned fish onto the plate my mother had brought out. Packaging didn't exist. We weren't Catholics but we always ate fish on Fridays. I think it was a family thing or maybe a hangover from the English.

Bought fish and chips were a luxury but I do recall occasionally having them. Mostly they were sold from Greek milk bars that sold other things like hamburgers to go or mixed grills to eat in. The fish and chips were usually wrapped in second-hand newspaper. Can you imagine that now? My grandchildren have never ever purchased a newspaper and the way things are going my great grandchildren won't even know what newspapers are.

Fruit and vegetables were also sold around the streets from a horse-drawn cart. Because of the variety the Fruiter had, I'm sure the produce would have come from a market somewhere in town. Of course, only seasonal fruit and vegetables were ever available. No imports or out-of-season luxuries flown in from overseas in those days. No packaging either – women took out their baskets, and what they bought was put directly into the basket. Plastic bags were yet to be developed.

The main reason everything was hawked around the streets was that women at home with families had no form of transport and most families didn't have cars. Women were usually locked to the house doing their daily chores. No vacuum cleaners, no washing machines, so everything required much more time and manual labour.

Arnotts biscuits were popular and available at our corner store (no supermarkets). They were called 'bought biscuits' because prior to their availability, women baked their own biscuits. To have 'bought biscuits' was very special. They were sold in bulk by the pound. The storeowners would take them out of the bulk tins with their hands and put them in a brown paper bag and weigh them. Then they would twist the corner of the paper bag and swing them until the corners tightened and sealed the paper bag (no such thing as sticky tape). They also sold bags of broken biscuits to us kids for a penny or so.

I know it is said that all we can really rely on is change. But I wonder if all the food changes my generation has witnessed have improved our quality of life?

Many people have issues with food that has shaped them as adults. I'm definitely one of them, as food throughout my life had been both my best friend and my worst enemy. Food contributed to who I am, and my childhood to why I eat what I do today.

We all know a child needs a healthy diet to develop and achieve, but unfortunately my parents had witnessed dramatic food shortages in their lives. Therefore, my early eating habits were mostly formed from my parents' traumatic experiences of not having enough food during the Depression, and for periods during World War II when my father was unemployed.

There are many foods I'm extremely passionate about and there are other foods that I passionately dislike. Having been born during the war, during my formative years I was made to eat whatever was available. I also had to stay at the table until I had eaten everything that was put in front of me, including bread and butter and of course dessert. I was made to eat far too much which has had a permanent lifelong damaging effect on me, making food both my comfort and my combatant.

These experiences from my childhood dramatically affected my relationship with food and with my parents.

A homemaker who prepares food three times a day makes at least 1,095 meals a year.

For the many millions starving in third-world countries, food is often out of their reach. Many are lucky if they eat once a day. Even then, for many of them it may only be a cup of rice.

In contrast, in the Western world there are many millions of people paying millions of dollars or euros to help them *not* to eat. Expensive, drastic gastric bypass surgery is now commonplace, and undertaken by many to curb their appetite and reduce food volume intake.

In our world, people eat everywhere. They eat walking; they eat in parks, on transport and in cars. They eat at airports to fill in time while waiting for flights, and then eat again after boarding because food is there and they are bored again. At times, passengers have to book two seats on an aircraft because they are too obese to fit into one seat. Some airlines are even now considering charging passengers by their weight.

Eating is sheer pleasure for many. For others, overindulgence of food has created dramatic health problems. People eat passionately

They Met in Paris

due to habit, social events, family pressures, stress and many due to food addiction. Food brings families together to celebrate events, which often lead to people overindulging.

Holidays often lead to many people overeating. For many, a holiday on a cruise ship becomes a passionate food-a-thon. Often, after their trips, holidaymakers can roll off their cruise ship carrying ten plus kilos around their girths.

I could write forever on smorgasbords and what has been witnessed at these eating events where people make pigs of themselves, often going back many times to refill their plates.

The elderly structure most of their day around meals. Those in hospital are cheered up when meals arrive. Food can bring happiness to the lonely and the depressed.

Food is part of our social life. Restaurants offer degustation menus of ten or more courses, where people eat nonstop for two to three hours and drink a variety of wines to accompany the many courses. Many business deals are discussed and won over meals, even if the diners have consumed copious amounts of alcohol. Men ask women to join them for dinner as an entrée into the bedroom.

Others at the opposite end of the scale starve themselves to be thin – models so that clothes hang on their bony frames better; teenagers starve themselves to fit in and be popular; and myriad other complex medical reasons.

Dr Phil often describes overeating as people having a party in their mouths.

Food is as diverse as it is complex. Take the simple hen's egg, for example. The egg as a food source is universally accessible to all socio-economic groups. The way a hen's egg can be used is amazing. For many, it's best in its simplest form, boiled or poached in water, or fried in a little butter.

Or for a quick meal, eggs can be scrambled with the addition of butter and cream, garnished with fresh parsley and cracked pepper, and served on a slice of buttered sourdough toast.

Then there's wonderful French toast – a thick slice of white bread dipped into whipped egg, and shallow fried in butter until golden then served with a drizzle of treacle or honey.

Or a tasty quiche Lorraine that takes the humble egg into brunch or lunch. The eggs are whipped together with fried-off bacon pieces and placed into a cooked pastry base then baked in the oven to set and brown.

And the egg can move to our dinner table, sitting atop an elegant Caesar salad, with shaved parmesan and a light sprinkling of cracked black pepper.

The uses for eggs are endless. Really, this whole story could just be about eggs.

Is there anything better than the smell of bacon sizzling in a pan, wafting from a kitchen in the morning?

Pork wasn't as readily available in my youth as it is today. I can't recall having bacon rashers, as we know them today, prior to the 1960s. I have to confess I adore bacon. My favourite is grilled strips on top of a pile of creamy scrambled eggs on toasted sourdough. It is the easiest meal to have at any time of the day. I've been known to often have this for dinner. Add some wilted spinach and it's a balanced meal.

If a café serves all-day breakfast, they have won me. But I'm a little mistrustful of restaurants with all those hidden kilojoules, and often opt to have bacon and egg on Turkish rather than having some tricked-up item off a menu. If you're watching your budget, it's also usually economical to order bacon and eggs in a café.

When storing bacon, I wrap the rashers in portions of three strips and freeze them. I tend to panic if my store gets down under a couple of frozen portions.

Rice is a very important grain to billions of people worldwide. It stores well and is simple to prepare. In the Western world we mostly utilise rice differently than in the East and third-world countries.

When I was growing up, the only way rice was served was as a sweet (dessert). My mother used to make creamed rice with nutmeg sprinkled on top. We also had sweetened baked rice pudding cut into portion-size pieces and we used to add brown sugar. I can't recall ever eating rice with a protein and vegetables as we do today.

When I worked in advertising, I was involved in the marketing of a rice herbicide. The product I worked on was flushed through the rice field at the three-leaf stage of the rice plants' development. The aim was to produce a better yield per hectare by ridding the area of weeds. I became fascinated with the project and ended up speaking on the subject at many conferences for our client. My writer on the project was a young Peter Carey. We even travelled to Griffith in NSW several times for briefings.

Some twenty years later. I became fascinated again with rice when I lived in Milan, Italy. The use of the Arborio variety of the rice grain was used extensively in the popular Northern Italian dish *risotto*. At the time I did extensive research and some writing on Arborio rice and its uses. The variations of making risotto are amazing. One of my favourites became *risi e bisi* which was rice with green peas. Champagne risotto was another favourite where champagne was used in lieu of stock.

Risotto wasn't eaten as we do here in Australia. It was mostly eaten more like a light snack for lunch. Eaten on the run, as we would do at McDonalds or KFC. In the north of Italy, business people would turn up at a bar (café) where they would be served up a medium-sized plate of risotto. They would eat it while standing up and then take off back to work.

I have to admit after all my research I make a mean risotto.

I look back now on some of my early family experiences in relation to food and it makes me sad to think that if food had been introduced to me differently, how my childhood could have been so much better.

And I'm sure as an adult my relationship with food would have been healthier.

I remember vividly my appalling family experiences with many foods such as pumpkin, beetroot, choko, liver, tripe, offal and prawns. Recently when I was staying with my son, as he served up the baked dinner he had just cooked for his family and me, he said, 'You don't eat pumpkin or sweet potato, do you, Mum?'

Almost instantly I was back at the green laminex table some time in the 1950s with my mother standing over me saying, 'Hold her nose and I'll push it in. That will show her not to defy me'. My father held my nose and my mother tried to force the pumpkin into my mouth, pushing to try and force it through my clenched teeth.

My father said, 'Be careful, you may break her teeth off.'

'So what?' my mother said. 'That will teach her to eat what I tell her to.'

'You know it makes her puke. I don't know why you persist.'

My mother replied, 'My mother made me eat what I didn't like. She's going to eat anything I want her to when I want her to …'

My son repeated, 'Mum, did you hear me? Do you want pumpkin and sweet potato or not?'

'Absolutely not,' I said, and it felt good for me to be able to say it.

I now wonder if, back then, pumpkin had been introduced to me in a different way, whether my relationship with this versatile vegetable would have been better.

Beetroot is not one of my favourite foods. It was introduced to me when I was a small child, cold from a tin. In those days it was readily available in tins. My mother used to put it on salads and the bright red juice ran all over the other food on the plate. I used to plead with her to put it on a separate plate so the horrible red juice wasn't on everything. It made me ill just to look at it. No. Of course she wouldn't. So my aversion to beetroot and anything red and runny developed.

In later life, it extended to anything I couldn't recognise in a runny sauce. Anyone who knows me well knows I don't eat what I now call camouflaged food. I usually don't share in Chinese, Japanese or Indian restaurants so as to avoid discussing my food foibles.

When serving food to my family, including my grandchildren, I always put each type of food that may have any juices on separate plates. I never ever serve or eat beetroot.

Oh my God, chokoes. My father used to bring them home, having picked them from over someone's fence on his way back from work. They were slimy, pale green, disgusting things with prickly skin that my mother boiled for far too long until they were almost mush. Again more family drama. More holding of my nose. More screaming at the tea (dinner) table. Naturally, my sister loved them.

I managed to eat them, but I hated them. It was only as I grew up that I realised my parents really only ate them because they had so little money. I'm rather ashamed of myself now, because even though, due to their treatment of me I was very damaged, I realise they were only doing their best.

I never see chokoes in our supermarkets nowadays. I imagine they are still used as a vegetable in some places, although I understand that they are often used as fillers in manufactured goods.

> *'Your sister is such a good girl. She eats anything we put in front of her.'*

Doctor Weston asked me, 'When do you think your reliance on eating to push down your emotions first started?'

I told him I was force-fed from as early as I could remember. Because my mother spent her childhood hungry, I was never allowed to leave the table until I'd eaten what she dictated I should. I was always forced to eat stuff that I hated. I was made to eat bread and butter with every meal even if I'd had enough and was full. The payoff was dessert, even if I didn't want it. I was always praised when I'd finally eaten everything.

Then I continued with a huge sigh, 'I now think that eating carbs is some way of saying to myself I'm OK, and I'm now a good girl. Maybe I think it will make things better, and she would love me if she was still around.'

'Is it your mother's voice that you hear in your head that is trying to convince you to keep eating?' Doctor Weston asked.

'I don't know.' I replied. 'Perhaps it is her.'

The Doctor continued, 'What do you think you could do to stop eating when you hear this voice?'

'One way is to go to bed.'

'Does that work for you?'

'It has at times.'

'Then you should try to do this if convenient.'

'OK, I'll try. At least living alone, this won't be too hard.'

'Your time is up today. See you next week,' he said, then added, 'Call me anytime if you need to discuss anything or you're having trouble coping.'

Sure, I thought. So I can get your answering service and you won't call me back.

Like most children, I hated, hated, hated liver. When I was a child it was given away for free. So naturally it was on our family table at least once a week. Even holding my nose and trying to force it down my neck didn't work. As soon as she pushed it into my mouth, I started heaving and up would come anything I'd eaten before being forced to eat the liver.

After many dramatic attempts, my mother actually gave up on this one. Not that I fully escaped. I was allowed to have eggs in lieu of liver, but they were fried in the same pan as the liver. Naturally, the dominant taste of the liver overtook the flavour of the eggs.

Surprisingly, I now often eat liver, especially in hotels for breakfast, fried up with bacon. I also like paté although I don't make it myself. Even when I do eat liver, I have flashes of that drama in my formative years over this food, and wonder if I eat it now just to spite her.

Tripe (lining of the cow's stomach). My mother took so much time preparing tripe – she'd cut it into slices and soak it for ages before boiling it, I expect to tenderise it. She then made a white onion sauce for it and braised it for an hour or so. My sister hated tripe, so I escaped the trauma of being forced to eat it. I loved it when my sister rejected food, as the focus was off me for once. I can't remember what we had to eat when my parents had tripe. It was probably eggs again.

I'm told many upmarket restaurants have tripe on their menus. As there are so many other wonderful foods available, I can't understand, given that it can require so much preparation, how it is practical for them to use. I won't even write about what other offal they served up on a regular basis. It makes me feel sick and upset now to even think about it.

Prawns. I think my childhood experience with these crustaceans was quiet unique: I came to hate Mondays and Thursdays because they were the days my father went prawning after work. He would come home after dark with huge buckets of the disgusting things.

… Those evenings my mother used to say to my sister and me, 'Your father will be home in about an hour with the prawns. So both of you hurry up and have your baths.'

As soon as he got home with the prawns, they were cooked straight away because we had no freezer storage for them. My mother would have the copper, where she boiled the water for our baths and the weekly wash, filled with boiling water ready to boil the prawns. Afterwards my father would transfer them to our bathtub to cool them off. Naturally the stench went right through the house.

When the catch had cooled, the distribution would take place, with neighbours and our extended family. Most people only had ice chests to keep the catch fresh, as again it was long before refrigeration was in the domestic home.

All through my childhood in my parents' house, all I could smell was the sickening stench of boiling prawns. It penetrated everything, even my long hair. One of the most embarrassing things was that I was made to take prawn and lettuce sandwiches to school. I would try to hide my lunch because if the other kids saw what I had, they would taunt me, saying things like, 'Look, she has pink animals on her sandwiches again.' All I wanted was to be like everyone else, with vegemite or peanut butter sandwiches. This went on for most of my primary school years.

For many years I couldn't look at prawns without it triggering bad childhood memories. Then when I was around fifty, a friend served prawns as an entrée at a dinner party. Rather than having to explain yet again, I decided to try them. And I was really surprised that I quite enjoyed them.

What amuses me is that what was peasant food in the 1940s and '50s is now seen almost as a luxury food item. Nowadays I eat them often.

Time changes many things.

In our working-class family in Australia in the 50s, dessert and sweets were used as a bribe for us children to eat our meat and veggies. The psychiatrists now attribute these post-war habits to the issues many baby boomers have with obesity and food addiction problems.

Processed sugar is now seen to be as addictive as many banned substances. Unfortunately, sugar is in almost every processed food manufactured today.

Caramel for me is bliss. My mother often made me caramel meringue pie or caramel slice for my birthday. It was one of the only times I though she maybe liked me a little. Caramel slice on a biscuit base topped with thick chocolate, and heavenly caramel meringue pie with short crust pastry are my favourites.

I also love the old-fashioned Fantales lollies, a square of luscious hard caramel covered in chocolate. Snicker bars are another favourite, a combination of caramel, nuts and chocolate. Caramel Magnum ice-creams are to die for and now Woolies sells them in a pack of four for under $10. I buy them often for my grandchildren.

My two adult kids don't eat sweets or desserts. This is hysterical, given that I can hardly leave them alone. Both of them are savoury eaters; they love salami, cheese, olives and so on.

Even for their birthdays they don't have cake. For my son, I do a leg of ham with candles. For my daughter, I usually do a large round of camembert cheese with candles.

I now wonder how this came to be. I didn't ever encourage them to have savoury foods, or discourage them from eating sweets and desserts. Maybe it was subliminal?

They are both slim and fit. So whatever I did, it worked.

Tim Tams were on special at Woolworths. I thought I would buy a few packets for when my grandkids were visiting. Who was I kidding?

Then the voices started in my head again. 'Why put temptation in my way? Remember what Doctor Weston advised a few sessions back when I told him that I had a container in the basement where I stashed stuff away from myself.'

He had asked, 'Why buy them? When you know that if you get in a mood, you'll get at them, no matter where they are.'

I thought once again, I'm an adult woman; why in the hell can't I control what I eat?

I arrived for my doctor's appointment in North Sydney. The receptionist said, 'Your appointment was for 12.30, wasn't it?'

'Yes,' I said, knowing she was going to tell me he was running late as usual.

'I'm so sorry but Doctor is running late. Can you come back in an hour? We can give you a coffee voucher and you can go upstairs to the café and get a tea or a coffee.'

Great, I thought, and be surrounded by people stuffing themselves as usual. But I just said, 'OK, thank you.' After confirming I'd return by 1.30 pm, I took the voucher and left the surgery.

I had planned my appointment at 12.30 during the lunch break to take my mind off food. Now I needed to kill time. I thought maybe I could be strong and just have a coffee. So I headed upstairs to the café.

Temptation. Temptation. Temptation.

'Can I help you?' The waitress said.

'A flat white please.'

'Would you like anything with your coffee?'

'No ... ah ... yes, I'll have one of those caramel slices with the chocolate, please.'

Bloody hell, here I go again trying to please her, I thought.

'Your sister is such a good girl. She eats anything we put in front of her.'

Oh my God, who doesn't love chocolate. Chocolate is heaven to a chocoholic. There is a feeling of euphoria at the first bite of a chocolate bar, or the first mouthful of a liquid chocolate drink.

The cocoa solids contain alkaloids theobromine, phenethylamine and caffeine. These have physiological effects on the body, which are linked to serotonin levels in the brain. Serotonin is responsible for the feeling of wellbeing.

The Europeans often sweetened and fattened the cocoa by adding refined sugar and milk. Then in the 19th century, John Cadbury developed an emulsification process to make solid chocolate, making the chocolate bar we know today.

In my opinion many psychiatrists may be better advised to have their patients eat chocolate, rather than resort to Valium or other antidepressants.

Professor Newton told me, 'It will be better after your surgery if you eat only small amounts. Patients who have five or six small snacks a day do much better. It's less for your system to cope with at one time, especially with your disability.'

'OK,' I said knowing that I would take no notice.

The doctor asked, 'Would you like to see a dietician to discuss this with?'

'That won't be necessary. I'll check it out on the internet.'

All I could think about was what was I going to eat as soon as I got out of the surgery. Maybe the café down the street would have those wonderful large pistachio shortbread biscuits coated on one side in chocolate, or caramel slices with a thick layer of chocolate on the top. I always felt better after indulging in these.

Why always biscuits, caramel and chocolate, I wondered again. Was it really because my mother had made me caramel slice for my birthday, if I was good?

Did having caramel and chocolate make me feel finally that I was OK?

I could eat fish every day. I really love it. My favourite is salmon fillets pan fried in extra virgin olive oil and served with a simple salad. I also love barramundi cooked on a grill and served simply with a drizzle of oil and loads of lemon juice. I now live in an area where fresh fish is not readily available. But when I eat out I always try to choose fish – that is, if I trust the restaurant.

When I was a small child my dad used to take me fishing on our annual holidays to get me away from annoying my mother. Over the years I became extremely good at fishing, and many times I would be the only one in the boat who would catch any. It continued into my early teenage years. Not only did I catch the most fish, I mostly also caught the largest. It became a family thing that if they wanted fish for tea (dinner), it was mandatory that I should go with them.

Even though my parents didn't cook it the way I liked, it didn't take away my love of fish. Pleasant memories around a food can live with one forever.

And bread baking. Isn't the smell of bread baking just wonderful?

Given that most bread is made from the same simple ingredients, it is amazing what varieties are available.

There is a bakery close by in the small village where I live in the Australian Blue Mountains. Depending on the direction of the wind, I can smell bread baking early every morning through my west-side bedroom window.

I love bread, even though I was made to eat the two mandatory slices at the end of each meal when I was young.

When I lived in Italy in the late eighties my love of bread increased. The fashion then was the Rosetta roll that was served in all the restaurants. The Rosetta roll had indentations so it could be broken into pieces. In the centre was a round piece which was just heaven. Unlike us Australians, the Italians eat their bread without butter.

When I'm in Paris I love the tradition of buying a fresh baguette several times a day. All I can think of when my flight is landing at Charles De Gaulle airport is the bread I'm going to enjoy during my stay.

Even though I can almost trust myself with bread, when I buy my latest favourite yummy no-preservatives-and-no-food-colourings Lawson bread, I freeze it just in case I lose control.

And scones. I love, love, love scones. They have to be warm, preferably direct from the oven. Scones remind me of my Gran, whom I loved dearly and she loved me as well. I think. Whenever I travel in Australia I'm always drawn to cafés that serve Devonshire teas. For those unaware of this English tradition, it's usually two warm scones, served with strawberry jam and fresh cream in separate little dishes.

In the main street of Oberon in NSW there is a café that does wonderful Devonshire teas. Also at the Sydney Royal Easter Show, the Country Women's Association (CWA) serve basic but good Devonshire teas as well. I can't make scones but I do intend to master making them one day.

And damper. I haven't had damper now for at least forty years, but I can remember the taste like it was yesterday. It's an unleavened loaf that was traditionally cooked in the ashes of a fire. The first Sunday of every month my grandmother and her sister, my great-aunt, used to visit us. They came from Maitland to see our family in Newcastle (NSW), travelling by train to visit for the day. They both loved damper. My mother used to make it especially for morning tea before our traditional baked dinner (for lunch) with apple pie and cream for afters. She used to place the hot damper on a wire rack after it came out of the oven and cover it with a tea towel to keep the steam in.

I would be sent to Hamilton railway station to meet my gran and my great-aunt. My task was to carry my gran's bag for her. In her bag would always be some home-made goodies for our family, usually a slab of her wonderful butter cake and, if she had been preserving, some jam. After greeting them, I would always love telling them that mum had made a damper and it had just came out of the oven before I left to meet them.

It's amazing how memories relating to food can bring back so many sensations. Even as I'm writing this I can still smell the damper in my mother's kitchen all those years ago.

My son tells me that when he is camping, he makes damper for his family over the campfire with the three simple ingredients: flour, salt and water.

The tradition lives on.

Caesar salad is a salad consisting of cos lettuce, croutons, bacon and anchovies served with a dressing of olive oil, lemon juice, raw egg, Worcester sauce and seasoning. It was originally named after Caesar Cardini, the Mexican restaurateur who invented it in 1924.

I passionately love Caesar salad.

I love that it usually comes in a huge bowl.

I love the colour and the crunch of the cos lettuce.

I love the saltiness of the parmesan cheese, the bacon and the anchovies.

I love the crunch and oiliness of the croutons.

I love the poached egg perched on the top.

I love the creamy rich dressing drizzled all over.

I once loved passionately the man I was married to thirty years ago with whom I shared my first Caesar salad in the San Francisco Grill at the Sydney Hilton.

I love my son and daughter with whom, during their teenage years, I shared many Caesar salads at the MacLeay Street Bistro in Kings Cross.

I love my five grandchildren for whom I now make Caesar salads when they visit.

I'm happy that I never shared a Caesar salad with my mother.

I now know why I love Caesar salad.

I was at a buffet at the Country Club. I knew that I had to be very careful at these types of dinners as I can lose control and overindulge.

I looked around at the people already returning to their tables with their food. The slimish people were having a small bowl of soup first, obviously pacing what they were eating. The average-sized people were having a large bowl of soup with a few pieces of bread. The overweight and obese people were giving the soup a miss, and piling just about anything that would fit onto a dinner plate. They'd put the mini-spring rolls and the other bits and pieces meant for entrée on the plate first. Then on top of that they loaded chips, wedges and potato bake. Then baked potatoes, prawns, chicken legs, ham, lamb, pork and balancing on the top of it all, as many pieces of bread that would fit. In the palms of their hands were pats of butter for the bread.

I felt for the obese people that night. What had made them turn to food for comfort? Did any of them have a mother like mine, who made me feel that I was only good if I ate and ate and ate?

I was a little worried as I approached the buffet area. I thought to myself, just have a small entrée and go back to your table.

As I was returning to the table my mind went back to my early twenties ...

They Met in Paris

By then, my parents were occasionally going out for meals. One night when I was visiting them, they invited me to join them for dinner at the RSL club on buffet night. I thought at the time that this would be a test. My mother was OK in public. But my father was nothing but an embarrassment. On this night, not only did he fill his plate to overcapacity, but he went back at least four times. When he had completely had his fill, he started putting the excess food in his pockets. Then he wrapped up other bits in napkins and made my mother put the food in her handbag.

I sat down with my entrée. An obese woman at the table in front of me had taken out a takeaway container from her bag, and she was scraping food off a second plate into it. I wondered what her childhood had been like and why she needed to do this.

Dessert was being served on a side table. A great rush ensued. The overweight and obese almost fell over themselves to get there. I looked around at those who had returned from the dessert bar and most of them still had mounds of food left on their dinner plates. They were obviously worried that if they waited until they had finished their dinner, they would miss out getting a mound of dessert.

I returned to the buffet and selected some veggies, potato bake and roast pork with applesauce for my main. Even though I'd had enough to eat, the old voice in my head convinced me to have some dessert. I went towards the dessert table. It looked like a war zone, mess everywhere, and almost nothing left. The waitress was trying to clean the area up.

I said to the waitress that I would like some dessert.

She told me, 'If you want dessert you have to grab it as soon as it's served. Otherwise you miss out.'

'And look like these other pigs at the trough? No way.' I said.

As I was leaving I thought to myself, it's best if I stay away from this place.

These experiences have made me more determined not to give up the struggle to control my weight. I live in fear of ballooning out in middle age like many of the women I see around me.

⚜

My Italian lover in Italy was slim and he ate very moderately. He also loved to cook. When I lived with him in Italy I became terribly aware that the portion sizes of my meals in the past were far too large.

An example of his moderate eating was when we were having lamb one night and he bought two 100-gram cutlets and served just one cutlet each with vegetables for the evening meal. I was in shock. It was nothing for me to have served up three lamb cutlets per person at home in Australia.

I have to admit I was starving most of the time when I first went to live with him. Many times I would go to bed with my stomach rumbling but in time I did get used to the moderate amounts of foods, and of course I became very slim. It was a great example of how most of us overeat.

Now I almost can't remember the last time I felt hungry.

Recently I was diagnosed with cancer again and after surgery required radiation oncology treatment at a hospital in Sydney. I was very angry at having a repeat bout of cancer, and I was letting loose on all those around me. My specialist in the treatment room took me aside and he told me that the staff were concerned I wasn't coping. I told him I was just angry. He wanted me to see a counsellor and said he would check out who was available. I just agreed. But I had no intention of starting all that again.

That night, I was rummaging through my shelf in the freezer at the patient accommodation where I was staying during my treatment, and I came across a caramel Magnum ice-cream that was left from my grandchildren's visit the previous Sunday. I scoffed it.

To my surprise, within minutes of eating the Magnum a feeling of euphoria came over me. I was amazed. I knew about serotonin and the effect chocolate can have on the brain, but I'd never experienced the effect of it as immediately as I did that evening.

When I went in the following day for treatment the nurse took me aside again. She told me that they had made arrangements for me to see a counsellor the following Friday. I thanked her. Then I told her that for the time being I was on chocolate to cheer me up and make me smile. I knew that my weight may increase with continual chocolate consumption, but to stay away from the counsellor I was prepared to diet later.

I did put on a few kilos, but once home I talked myself into going on the popular 5:2 diet to shed the weight.

Food Colourings. Preservatives. Emulsifiers. We have yet to know the long-term effect of what the food manufacturing industry has really inflicted on those born in the last forty or fifty years with all the additives in packaged food. I have my suspicions that children with food allergies from peanuts are just the start of what we can expect to see in coming years.

Once milk was just milk. Now fresh milk available in our supermarkets comes as full cream, organic full cream, low fat, organic low fat, skim, organic skim, semi-skim, buttermilk, soy and rice. I could go on forever but I'm sure you get the message.

Then we have the UHT heat-treated milk, with long use-by dates. What has been done to milk to take it from a shelf life of around two days and make it last 365-plus days! We just pick up the carton and trust that the supplier has our best interest at heart. In my opinion they don't, because we still don't know the long-term effects of the treatment they are doing to this simple staple food.

When I was a child, there were only three or four ingredients in bread at most. Now, the standard white sliced loaf of bread has a list of up to fifteen ingredients. This allows our bread to be kept for up to five days or frozen for up to four months. Courtesy of emulsifiers 481, 472a and 471. Of course the average person has no idea what these emulsifiers in our bread are, or many of the other ingredients.

My gran used to often make us a wonderful simple butter cake. The ingredients were, from memory, flour, sugar, butter, milk, eggs and salt. Today packaged butter cake mix is used and the contents are: wheat flour (thiamin, folic acid), sugar, vegetable fats and oils [emulsifiers (soy lecithin, 471, 477), antioxidant (320)], raising agents (500, 450), dextrose, starch, emulsifiers (471, 475) (soy), salt, flavour (milk, soy), vegetable gum (xanthan), colour (beta carotene). And after these twenty-two additives, you will still need to add: 60g soft butter, two eggs and 190ml of fresh milk! So the twenty-two additives in the pack replace only the flour and the sugar! This gives the pack a twelve-month-plus shelf life and allows the manufacturer to charge four times the price of the required simple ingredients. And anyway, most kitchens would have flour and sugar as a staple.

When my mum needed breadcrumbs to add to her beef rissoles, she went to the breadbox and took out the stale bread she saved for crumbing. Now the modern mum takes out her box of packaged breadcrumbs with a shelf life of twelve-eighteen months and sprinkles out the quantity she needs for her recipe. And guess what tumbles out: wheat, thiamin, foliate, rye, barley, yeast, iodised salt, soy flour, gluten, vegetable oil, vegetable fibre, wheat soy, vinegar, sugar, emulsifiers 471, 481, and 472c. (Eighteen ingredients).

And oh my God, breakfast cereal! When we were children all we knew as breakfast cereal were simple oats boiled until soft in milk and served with natural brown sugar and extra whole plain milk. We now have at least sixty varieties of sugar-laden cereals available and this doesn't include muesli!

The contents of one of our best know cereals: rice, oats, wheat (49%), fruit (12%) humectant (glycerol), food acid (330), sunflower oil, sugar, wheat gluten, almonds (5%), wheat flour, wheat bran pieces, minerals (calcium carbonate, iron, zinc), vegetable oil, salt, maltodextrin, honey, barley malt extract, niacin, vitamin E, vitamin B6, riboflavin, thiamin, foliate, rosemary extract.

Today many packaged foods which are sealed with long use-by dates rot extremely quickly once opened. This has made these packaged foods that we have for our convenience much more costly as there is at times so much more wastage.

I often wonder, if we weren't paying for food packaging how much less would an average grocery shop of $200 cost?

The amount of packaging on meat that we are paying for that is thrown into our bins is horrendous. Meat in the supermarket comes on poly tray bases. Then there is the absorbent black thing under the meat to sop up the blood drainage. Then the outer plastic wrap, the manufacturer's sticker, the supermarket sticker and often a promo sticker as well. All these items that get removed and dumped in our bins have a cost.

Frozen dinners are usually in an outer box with a zip open end. The dinner is sealed with plastic; you peel the corner back before you zap it in the microwave. Half way through the heating process you peel off the sealed plastic totally and stir the contents to make sure the zapping can penetrate though to the middle of the contents. You can eat it direct from the plastic tray and then you just dump all the packaging elements in the bin.

Yes it's easy. But what are we doing to our environment and ourselves?

Then there is the home delivered food service that supplies a week's calorie-controlled food. It's usually delivered in a foam chiller box in separate plastic bags for the fridge and the freezer. The bags for the fridge hold seven other bags for breakfast and seven for lunch. The bags for the freezer hold seven more bags for breakfast and seven more bags for lunch. The dinner bag for the freezer comes with seven frozen dinners and they are in the standard boxed packaging. Without counting the packaging within each of the freezer and fridge bags for breakfast and lunch, we have thirty-three plastic bags. God knows how many other trays, dishes, cello bags, plastic bags and bits and pieces of packaging is involved in the whole seven-day delivery. I was too scared to work it out exactly but it's probably 200-plus pieces of packaging!

I'm not bagging this type of service, I'm just commenting on the volume of inedible packaging involved.

Breaking the cycle

Although I still retain many of my childhood food dislikes, hopefully most of my family trauma around food is buried away in my subconscious memory. Despite my bad childhood experiences, I've still had some wonderful, unusual and amusing experiences relating to food. I've eaten at many of the best restaurants around the world and I'm a huge fan of two of our great chefs in Australia, Tetsuya and Neil Perry.

I hope with my own children and grandchildren that I have been successful in breaking the cycle of physical and emotional abuse that I suffered during those thousands of meals with my birth family. When my son and daughter were growing up I would always say to them: … 'I don't mind what you eat. I'll put everything on the platter and you take what you want.'

As I said this, I would always reflect on just why I allowed my children to eat only what they wanted. Maybe I was too relaxed with them, but I didn't ever want them to experience what I'd gone through during my childhood.

I would mostly serve large platters of carrot sticks, green beans, tomato, chicken, ham, olives and chunks of bread and place it in the centre of the table, for them to help themselves. If we had a roast or a BBQ I would do the same. If we had takeaway Chinese I would put the food in wonderful Chinese bowls in the centre of the table, we'd have Chinese tea and I would play Chinese music. I did the same if we had Japanese or Indian. I wanted to make all our meals special, and an entertaining and pleasant experience for us.

Both my son and my daughter would always reach greedily for bits of everything off the platter or bowls. I would always smile to myself as I mostly only placed on the table what they liked anyway. The most important thing for me was that they were able to make their own food choices. I also allowed them to make their own career choices. Even today with my five grandchildren I always serve food on platters for them to make their own choices.

They Met in Paris

My generation is probably the last to have grown up with totally natural foods. Even though I now travel extensively and dine in many different places, I still remember fondly how food was when I was growing up. I'm now happy to have my food memories of how things were – the good ones at least.

Burnt Fig, Honeycomb & Caramel Ice Cream – yum, how tempting.

Passion

for

Romance

Valerie McCrae

Valerie McCrae

Valerie McCrae has a diverse background in teaching, counselling, community corrections, group facilitating, life coaching and massage therapy. She is a skilled and qualified counsellor and is now involved in her local area with a school program that teaches Ethics to primary aged schoolchildren.

She has a passionate love of literature and is an avid reader; she now writes interest pieces for an Australian national website. Val was born in the small island of Guernsey in the Channel Islands in 1947. In 1971, she immigrated to Australia with her young family and settled in Sydney, where she later went to Teachers' College and University. Now remarried with two adult children and six precious grandchildren, she lives in Warrimoo NSW, a village in the Australian Blue Mountains. Val is an active part of the local community and a keen bridge player. She is still a romantic woman with a love of Paris which she hopes to visit again soon.

Passion for ROMANCE

'To practice any art no matter how well or how badly, is a way to make your soul grow. So do it!'
– Kurt Vonnegurt

Eleven women meet on a memoir writing course in Paris. Yes, we were all at least interested in the art of writing. Some of us were no doubt passionate about it too. But I think I might safely say that all of us were feeling passionately about being in Paris for three whole weeks and the experience did not disappoint. Our exuberance on this Paris writing adventure I think fulfilled (most of the time) one of the definitions of passion to be found in a dictionary – and that is 'boundless enthusiasm'. This is what we felt and shared – excepting perhaps for moments of fatigue and those times when we may have sensed that our writing was drying up or not living up to our hopes. Unusually, in my experience, more than a year after the course ended, we were all still keeping in touch by email, talking about our writing, our reading and anything else of interest in our lives. When one of our group, proposed this project – that we should all write about some aspect of passion in our lives, I can only describe the response from ten out of eleven of us as immediate and wholehearted.

Having set out in my memoir writing to tell the story of my life – my childhood, being brought up on a small island, marrying young and moving to Australia – I was a bit nonplussed to find that a lot of my writing was about episodes of love in my life – romance, friendships and family. And the Paris experience filled me once again with thoughts of romance. It seems to be firmly in our minds that Paris is 'the city of romance'. This idea may not need too much explanation to anyone who has visited, or even just seen the movies that are set there, let alone heard the music, seen the art, gazed at the depictions of the monuments, pored over its fashion and its style. From its history-steeped buildings to its tête-à-tête cafés where many famous artists may have sat to discuss their work, their loves and the way of the world, Paris evokes a yearning for the past, for the exotic, for the richness of life. Picture, if you will, a saxophonist playing a melancholy tune on the banks of the Seine, two lovers holding hands as they stroll the cobbled streets, young parents on the metro with their arms clasped together around a new baby, a shiningly dark-skinned man with his scarf thrown nonchalantly around his neck, a glamorous and beautiful older woman still chic and sexy, in her tight suit and high heels. Paris embodies romance. Its sights, its smells of pastries, wine, street traffic and even sweat, its sounds of music, lyrical language and the rumbling metro, all remind us of life, no matter how blasé we think we may have become about cities in general. Paris embodies – for me – *la vie en rose*.

This is why, in this story, I have chosen to explore the topic of romance, to understand what it has meant to me in my life and how it shows itself in ways that are perhaps not that commonly associated with the word. Both passion and romance are often identified solely with significant other relationships – sex and lust – but both have also much wider and more varied influences on our lives. So with this in mind, I am intrigued to have an opportunity to combine my love of writing memoir with the pleasure of connection with fellow writers, and the wonderful topics of love, romance and passion.

A definition of romance from Wikipedia: 'Romance is the expressive and pleasurable feeling from an emotional attraction towards another person associated with love; In the context of romantic love relationships, romance usually implies an expression of one's strong romantic love or ones' deep and strong emotional desires to connect with another person intimately or romantically'.

My own feeling is that our experience of romance may be far more varied and inclusive than the attachment to one significant 'other' which is concerned with attraction, love and desire. Hence my wish to explore the concept from a mixture of viewpoints and experiences, and to understand the part it plays in my life … and perhaps in yours too?

The importance of literature in my own life seems to be an obvious place for me to begin. There may be a reason why, if I am asked, 'What is your favourite book?', I usually reply '*Anna Karenina*'. And perhaps it's because I read it in my thirties, when I was married with two school-aged children and at a stage when my heart needed something to fill an ever expanding void. Something in my rapt reading of this classic novel touched a part of me that seemed to have lain dormant for a while, but was gnawing for recognition. At that age and stage, I could explore the many possibilities of what was being stirred and touched. And I wonder – if I re-read this book now, would it still be a favourite? Or have time, experience, a change in attitude and age taken away that special something? Because at the time, I think that 'special something' would have been described as 'romance'.

But how do I define the meaning of this word for myself – and for you to understand? How very unfortunate indeed that our heroine in *Anna Karenina* – as in *Madame Bovary* and *Romeo and Juliet* – ends up dead almost as if that is the only solution to such a passion. Marriage might, after all, kill the romance and what sort of ending would that be? Many classics of literature have endlessly explored the topic of romantic love. In fiction, there is usually great conflict and obstacles to be overcome, and sometimes there is a happy ending – Rhett and Scarlett fought and argued through their story, hiding great passion. One could not help but wonder what their ongoing relationship would be like once the 'romance' and passion had ended (which it invariably does) and they were back to disagreeing. There has been academic analysis done of the supposedly 'true love' between Heathcliff and Catherine in *Wuthering Heights*. In their story, are they soul mates? Well, it seems they do have an irresistible attraction for each other – but this may not be a happy thing. It also appears that they may both be searching to fulfil their empty soul, by completion with another. While their love seems to be on a higher plane, it may be of no earthly use. Some have described this fictional love as a 'life force' type of love. This indeed starts to explain the desire and pursuance of romance – but does this have to be found only in some other person? Indeed, is it possible to find it at all in another person? Are these two ill-fated lovers trying to create a meaning in life through each other? Catherine suggests this might be the case: 'If all else perished, and *he* remained, I should still continue to be; and if all else remained, and he were annihilated, the Universe would turn to a mighty stranger. I should not seem part of it.'

It would seem that their love is an attempt to break down boundaries between the self and another – to somehow transcend the aloneness of the human condition. There is a desire to be 'as one', merged, absorbed with the other. Freud explains this urge as 'a natural part of romantic love'. At the height of being in love, the boundary between ego and object threatens to melt away. Against all the evidence of his/her senses, a person who is in love might declare 'I' and 'you' are one, and is prepared to behave as if it were a fact. Jung also talks about love being the search to find 'the other half' – to merge the animus and anima to make a soul complete. (This tends to leave out the idea of gay love somewhat, but we get the general gist.)

Well, for those of us who read a lot of literature and poetry and love to listen to classical music while we dream, it is hardly any wonder that we grow to adolescence with a somewhat dreamy sense of wanting to find ourselves in the form of another – a romantic love object who will complete us. Or anyway, it seems that is what *I* may have done! And bearing in mind that this is not an academic essay, nor merely research on the subject, I will recollect and lay bare some of my romantic experiences, some for the first time.

At home, which is where we all start to be influenced by our very first experiences of love and romance, I think the latter was quite lacking in my own childhood home. I literally never saw my parents show affection to each other. When I look back, I think my mother felt the lack of this very strongly in her life. I remember her singing songs such as 'Try a Little Tenderness': the lyrics in this song were about women getting weary and having to wear the same shabby dresses. Given a constant lack of spare money, and Dad's rather brusque and sometimes verbally abusive communication style, that was probably how she often felt. Another of her favourite songs was 'Little Things Mean a Lot', about little things that were important such as a woman having her hair touched as he passed her chair. I never saw Dad touch Mum's hair as he passed her chair. How sad. Although, truth be told, as they got older, there was a more direct and communicated affection between them. They seemed to have found a lasting and enduring love. It had been a long time coming.

So when, many moons ago as a pre-pubescent girl, I began to read little square illustrated comic books called *Love Stories*, I soon became quite addicted to this new and exciting view of relationships between lovers. They were filled with beautiful young women, usually called something like Belle, or Cassandra or Fiona – and muscly, handsome and often quietly moody young men called perhaps Scott, or Troy, or Daniel. These stories often had a plot centred around man meets woman, they get off on the wrong foot, many obstacles come their way ... until one moonlit evening, they look into each other's eyes and love and passion dawn and they realise they are madly in love and live happily ever after – as far as we know. So, they were not likely to include family war and suicides as in *Romeo and Juliet*, but the theme still plays out.

There were variants on this theme, of course, sometimes including a rather plain young woman whose love for our hero remains mostly unrequited throughout the story, until when she has taken off her glasses and uncoiled her hair, she becomes an irresistible love magnet to the enduringly handsome man. Sometimes it could be the quite nerdy, bespectacled young man who, after performing some manly act of courage, becomes instantly attractive to the gorgeous woman. But, you get my drift. I bought these little books whenever my financial situation would allow, or when I could persuade Mum, Grandmother or an aunt to do so for me. I suppose we all thought they were pretty harmless. Kissing was the usual climax of these stories and maybe marriage – there were no blatantly sexual scenes. There may have been some insinuations, but they were a bit lost on me at that stage. When I look back through my life now, though, I think that this is probably where my penchant for 'romance' began. It was about beauty, yearning, striving and being ultimately rewarded. Not exactly Shakespeare, I have to say – he came later – but really, what more could a young girl want?

And so I come to my own first experiences of romance and the memories they stir up. I was about fourteen when I first tasted romance's sweet fruit for the first (and very innocent) time.

My Early Romance

Long ago, it was the smell of Old Spice shaving lotion mixed with a new leather jacket. Or maybe the taste of mint on his tongue from the gum he chewed to cover his nervousness. Or perhaps that slight smell of lager on his breath as he breathed up close to my face. There was the woolly smell of his favourite jumper, the shampoo on his curly blond hair. Always the smells and the tastes were so irresistible, so vital, so evocative of the time and place and the feelings. All of these and more still haunt me to this day and throw me backwards, back to the past and the incredible aliveness of love, romance and lust.

Then the sounds of the bicycle wheels drawing up to my door and the bike nonchalantly thrown against the wall before the longed-for knock that would cause the lurching in my stomach, as I swiftly tore out the rollers from my defiantly straight hair. The songs, the music, the tunes, each so familiar, that accompanied us all along the way, with many lyrics remembered forever, melodies being hummed decades later as if they had never stopped. There were a voice and laugh, so unique and loved, even if mainly unappreciated at the time.

And there was always my own laughter bubbling up so often and so freely.

The sensuousness of the first time we held hands. How can a hand that is so much in use suddenly feel like this new part of the body, and how can this touch be so allowable and yet so intimate? Not so long ago, I had the wondrous opportunity to hold the hand of a man who once was a boy I loved way back then. I was startled to realise that his hand was still familiar and that I had never held another one just like it since then. It seemed so small and light, somehow more feminine than I had remembered. It conjured up a host of other memories and reactions that I thought had been long put away.

Where does one begin to try to reveal the many facets of a word that is bandied around and yet means different things to different people, at different stages? Is it a feeling? Is it something tangible? Is it something one can see or hear? Is it eternal or fleeting? Is it only for the young? Is it only about being 'in love' or is it much more? Or much less? So many questions and I am still excited as I look for clues in this writing process and in the remembering.

Another quote from a writer, this time Leo Tolstoy writing about Vronsky, Anna's lover: 'He stepped down, trying not to look long at her, as if she were the sun, yet he saw her, like the sun, even without looking.' Yes, this is perhaps the ultimate in romantic worship, likening the beloved to the sun around which the whole earth revolves, which gives the brightest of lights, which is our warmth, our healing and our energy. Imagine feeling like this about another person ... imagine another person feeling like this about you. And from Jane Austen, 'You pierce my soul; I am half agony, half hope ... I have loved none but you.' Here, some of the pain of feeling strong romantic feelings is touched on; the exclusiveness of the feelings and the 'exquisite agony' of romantic love are combined. There are endless quotes from the classics and even more from more modern-day writers that would fill this essay and then some!

What about the Romantic poets, the artists, the song writers, the composers? All of these contribute to our understanding or even our possible rejection of romance, that is, romance in all its shades, in all its meanings, in all its glory. When I think of all these examples, it is of course 'romantic love' that is on my mind, of which these artists and musicians and writers all speak, and that may cause us to believe and to remember or to search and to find it again.

It is in the state of romantic longing that I am sometimes moved to write a poem myself. One romantically favourite story from the classics is probably that of Mr Darcy and Elizabeth Bennett from Jane Austen's *Pride and Prejudice*. Oh, that handsome, inscrutable, moody and sometimes quite rude Mr Darcy led Elizabeth into such misunderstandings and situations of agony. How he makes our (mainly women's!) hearts flutter as we turn the pages, or later as we watch him on screen in the delectable form of Colin Firth. I confess, there was a situation in my own life where I was communicating through writing with a man from my past. The details must remain discreet; suffice to say we had a highly romantic written communication for a few months. We were far apart and we had our sweet memories to stoke the fire of our passion. It led to much creativity in the form of wordy letters and love poetry. We talked of Jane Austen in our letters and the following was one result:

Mr Darcy
Memory of my past
Love in my present
Dream for my future
Friend to my soul
Salt in my tears
Longing as I sleep
Excitement in my day
Yearning in my night
Pain in the missing
Joy in the loving

Fear in not knowing
Grief not to hold you
Hope filling my heart.
You fill all my senses
Tho' I can't see or touch you
Miss Bennett

In all honesty, when I read that now, I feel slightly embarrassed and I don't even want to share that I was not that young at the time!

I have also received poetry from others, sometimes not exactly in the style of Keats, it is true, but it is a delight nevertheless to evoke a poetic response in another.

The interesting thing about the following is that I am still not sure if HE actually composed it or if it was NOT an original. I couldn't find it anywhere, but I did not have the heart to ask as I really wanted to believe it was his own creation. If it was, then I am duly impressed, but either way, I will always treasure it for its sentiment. Although I am now a woman in my sixties, when I read this I still glow to have been thought of in this way. How could I regret anything that evokes such emotion and thoughts?

'You move through my world like the endless swell of the ocean, deep and unfathomable, bearing me effortlessly away

You are the adrenalin I've felt on a rock face, and you're the warmth of the sun on my back

You are the wild exhilaration that strides bleak Bronte moors under glowering skies

And you are the delight felt high on northern fells looking down on huddled grit-stone hamlets

You are the laughter of rushing becks in Winter, hustling and bubbling down to broad meadows

You are the promise of Spring flowers shyly and demurely welcoming Summer

They Met in Paris

> *You are the searing, cruel heat of my desert stripping me to the bone*
> *And the pure diamond white of snow reflected sunlight, probing and revealing all to your gaze*
> *You're my first love and my last*
> *My mother, sister, daughter, lover'*

Of course, as may be expected, this height of poetic romanticism had an end when a big dose of reality came into town. Enough said? Down to earth we came with a bump, but the other planet was a very lovely place to live for a while and after the bump, the yearning again inspired my poetic side to emerge in desperation and longing to return to that place.

> *Love's Sweet Paradox*
> *New Forest ponies and old English pubs*
> *Fitting together napping like old married lovers*
> *Struggling to make sense of the inexplicable*
> *With words that are always too many or not enough*
> *Remembering old times and forever exploring new*
> *Laughter and tears with love and anger*
> *Still crazy after all these years*
> *Bluebell woods, coconut gorse and pale primroses*
> *Cliff top walks and unending ocean vistas*
> *Sharp taste of salt on my lips*
> *Welcome wind rearranging my hair*
> *Adrenaline speeding up my heart as*
> *Happiness and sadness strive to win their place*
> *Warm hand in mine comforting in its sweet familiarity.*
> *Driving in the car singing along to an old tune*
> *Sudden fear to be discovered in our joy*
> *Restless movement with opposing wills*

Of the need to avoid and the need to confront
Watching once in a lifetime fireworks in the freezing cold
Your arms wrapped around me so that I feel safe
For just this moment but not for long.
Eating, laughing and sipping wine careless of tomorrow
While at times the pain of your words cuts through to scar me and
Mine shoot back to ensure you also know the pain.
When you touch me, I feel alive again and smile
When I touch you, you want me here and now
But maybe not tomorrow. We make these moments safe
And real with creamy, melting chocolate on our tongues.
You make me know the truth of opposites
That joy and sorrow and love and doubt live side by side.
Our love carries us through many months of words and feelings
While forty years of time trips us up and blocks our way
Life forever intervening to remind us of our folly
We live so far apart in space and yet we stay inextricably linked
In defiance of the laws of time and space we hold each other close
You are my true love, my nemesis, my soul mate
I am your youth, your punishment and your reward
You own me but you let me go
You are mine yet I say goodbye
History repeats itself with wild determination
And we are swept along on its wilful tide
Hope keeping us constantly alive

According to the history of romance, the concept of romantic love was made popular in Western culture by the concept of 'courtly love'. Wikipedia tells us that 'Chevaliers or knights in the Middle

Ages, engaged in what were usually non-physical and non-marital relationships with women of nobility of [sic] whom they served. These relations were highly elaborate and ritualised in a complexity that was steeped in a framework of tradition, which stemmed from theories of etiquette derived out of chivalry as a moral code of conduct.'

This idea of 'elaborate and ritualised' gestures and actions seems to provide a little insight on where ideas of romance first began. It also suggests that romance was mainly unconsummated – perhaps untainted – by actual physical, sexual contact. It starts to suggest something in the mind, or the heart, that must be expressed flamboyantly with the earthly realism missing from the equation.

With this in mind, I thought I might do my own small survey to find what my friends thought romance meant to them, so I asked them to tell me in a sentence what romance is and in another sentence what it is not. The replies were interesting and varied, covering the amusing, the practical, the cynical and the poetic. It seemed that in the main, romance was immediately associated solely with the love of a special and significant 'other'. Several respondents thought it was not to do with lust – but some thought lust had to be there somewhere! I had only a few men respond. One quoted Leonard Cohen, specifically, 'Dance Me to the End of Love'. I am totally with him on this particular song, when Cohen invites the listener to dance to beauty. I find the sentiment of the words is completely romantic and seductive. Other responses included: 'Enjoying a meal together, flowers on Valentine's Day, being cared for, having dinner cooked, warmth and trust', and one more cynical respondent quoted the dictionary definition, i.e. 'a picturesque falsehood'.

What romance is NOT includes: 'Being asked what I would like for Christmas, being grabbed on the arse, having an argument in a supposedly romantic situation, lust, just remembering anniversaries and birthdays'. I would gather, then, from this small survey sample, that romance is indelibly linked with the love of the special someone, the 'romantic relationship'. And our expectations and emotional experiences greatly affect what we focus on when romance is mentioned or rears its head in our lives.

But, in truth, we are influenced in our thinking too, not only by literature and art, but also by philosophy and psychology. I have selected, as a starting point, a few ideas that appeal to me, or conflict with my own views. I make no attempt to scientifically argue for one point of view or another!

Martie Haselton, a psychologist at UCLA, for instance, considers romantic love to be a 'commitment device' or mechanism to encourage two humans to form a lasting bond – so that they may have children and family. Well, that seems to me the very antithesis of what we normally think of as romance – but quite clearly describes the purpose of lust and sexual attraction. Are these the same as romance? Not in my view.

Some university research on the topic concludes that romantic love lasts for about a year and then it is replaced by a more stable form of love called companionate love. This then would suggest that perhaps romance and marriage do not go hand in hand. Many writers have supported this view. It might seem, in view of literary writers on the subject, that there is a need to be in the extramarital state and hence, the tragic endings of many romantic tales. Love needs to be unrequited, unobtainable or short-lived to remain romantic.

This gives me food for thought as I contemplate my interest in the topic from the point of view of a sixteen-year second marriage ... Is there, then, no more romance in my life? If I am never again to be in the early stages of a romantic relationship, why do I still want and need – and assume there always is – romance in my life?

Certainly, what I at the time considered to be perhaps the most highly romantic episodes in my own experience turned out to have sad endings, and to be filled with much longing and pain. The beginning was memorable for its romance and its excitement but the ending even more so for its ensuing hurt and disappointment. Not a tragic death of a body, but certainly the ending of a part of me that would never go to quite that place of fantasy again.

In retrospect, I can see that the person who was the object of perhaps my strongest and most romantically emotional involvement was, in reality, just a small part of what I had imagined him to be, and the rest was what I projected on to him from my own fantasy. Sadly, the reality took a long time to unravel and become clear. And this relationship, perhaps above all others, taught me the black side of being swept up in 'romance'. He was also a 'romantic'. He told me this in the very early days. I thought this was a positive, but perhaps this was where I was quite mistaken. Here is a piece I wrote about the light and dark experienced in the life-threatening heartbreak of romance that ends:

Swan Song

We often listened to and loved 'The Swan' by Sans Saens with its slow, floating melody creating the perfect image of the gracious gliding of these magnificent creatures. But deeper beneath the water, it evokes memories of candlelit dinners, sipping champagne, the light laughter of romantic moments, hand holding, making love. Deeper still, and the feelings become colder and harder. Now a yearning and an emptiness and darkness encloses and a void opens up that may never again be filled. I can't stay here, there is no life, only the pull from below. Gasping, struggling, I fight back to the surface, I allow the warmth and healing of the air and the sunshine and the beauty of the swan to fill my senses again. I hear the strains of the haunting melody repeating in my brain and gradually, I open my heart and let love in. Swans may be black or white and each is as beautiful as the other in its own way and in its own place, as are the joys and sorrows that provide the backdrop to life.

Having thought about some of the significant romantic memories in my own journey, the romance of literature and music, and the explanations of psychologists and historians, I realised that another concept that is forever in my heart and in my dreams, that calls to me often and for which I yearn on a fairly consistent basis, is my own island home. I was born on a small island called Guernsey which is part of the Channel Islands – little dots on the map off the south coast of England and nearer to France. As a child, I lived very close to the ocean, across the road from it, in fact. In that place, in those days, one did not have to be well off to have this magnificent view and to take sandy beaches, rugged cliffs, and an abundance of beauty for granted. At the tender age of seventeen, I left the island to pursue a career in London, returning for a short period when my first child was born and leaving again about eighteen months later to live in England and then to travel to the other side of the world, never to live in my island home again. Since then, some forty years later, I have gone back there for holidays, probably on average of once every five years. In the early days, it was with great excitement to see my parents, other family members and old friends. More recently, sadly, all the previous generation have passed on to even greener pastures and the friends I still love to see are now more limited in number, but still much appreciated for all the memories we share.

For me, also, perhaps because I left my island home so early in my life, the idea of 'home' has taken on a longing, yearning and a feeling that is certainly akin to a romance that I revisit from time to time, but is mostly unattainable. I imagine this goes hand in hand with memories of childhood and family that are long gone. I dream of my island home, I long for her, I treasure her beauty. My love for her ocean shores and craggy cliffs is perhaps comparable to the deep sense of belonging experienced by our native Aboriginals. It is a risk to confess this longing, because it is not considered 'Australian' not to feel very grateful to live in the 'lucky country' and to yearn for another; it is seen as a betrayal in some eyes. I think I may be told to 'just go back home, then'. While my adopted home in Australia now keeps many of my adult memories and holds a very dear place in my heart, the evocative calling of my own native 'home' will always remain with me. I have two homes – that is the way that it is. And of course, in true romantic fashion, I must yearn for the one in which I don't live – and which is now unattainable to me.

⚜

A Romance with Home

'Should auld acquaintance be forgot and never brought to mind' rang out as the ship left the dock in Southampton. People were waving streamers and watching their loved ones get ever smaller as they waved stoically on the shore. Yes, it is a scene from a movie, but it was real, it was happening to me. It was the first real leaving, and the only one on a ship. But, over the years there would be many homecomings and leavings.

Going Home. It begins as the plane starts to lower over the island. The shape is instantly recognisable, then the patchwork fields of variegated greens, the few odd remaining and often broken-down greenhouses, the little white and solid granite houses, and of course the looming cliffs overlooking the ever dominant foaming ocean. It is all so beautiful and so nostalgic. My stomach always starts to lurch with excitement and my heart literally flutters with a feeling that is somehow unique at this arriving moment. Stepping out of the plane, I immediately have memories of the days of the old airport, when family members would be lined up at the windows, and one could wave at them while walking from the plane to the terminal. Those days are gone now and the airport is larger, allowing for viewing from an upper storey. Also, there is now a proper luggage pick-up area and passport control. In those earlier days, Dad would somehow get into this part and greet me there. Those days are also gone. He is gone. And so is Mum.

On my last visit home, it was the very first one when my Mum would also not be there. I just could not help being overtaken by memories of earlier days and the excitement of seeing my family – and of them seeing me. The first visit home from Australia, with my two children aged nine and six and their Dad – such excitement all round, even though my Mum immediately got upset at the thought of us leaving again.

The drive from the airport begins that strange contradictory reaction of strangeness and familiarity that the early days of return always create. It all seems so small, as even the main roads are more like lanes. The big drive from the airport is not long at all but just about twenty minutes to the town. I notice it all in a kind of blurred mix of travel tiredness, excitement, nostalgia and pleasant anticipation.

On this most recent visit, I was met by an old friend who then took me to a rented apartment near the town. The climb up the stairs to the top floor was almost too much good exercise but the view was just exquisite of the harbour, the town and the church spire on which I could see the time on the town clock from my window. Amazingly, this was a very similar view to one I had had from the flat I lived in with my parents in my teens. Anyone who knew me then, commented on it. I felt really at home. I was on my own here this time, but it was so comforting and inspiring to see this view every morning, and any time I returned to it, to just gaze out at the other islands – on a clear day I could see the outline of France; on a foggy day, I could see very little. The fog and its accompanying horn were also familiar and took me right back to childhood days.

Not much of my family is left there now, the older generation having all passed away, and others such as my brother, leaving for new pastures, usually for financial reasons. But I have some nephews there, a great-niece, some cousins and some wonderful lifelong friends who welcome me still. Some family and friends have got on a plane to come from the mainland to see me, one who is plane phobic, having to endure two false landings because of fog. What more could one ask of a friend? Dinners, lunches, shopping in town, visits to homes, walks, my view. I love it. I don't want to leave. Leaving is hard and sad and keeps happening to me.

On my last day of this last visit, I have to leave the apartment by 6 am in order to catch the 'red eye', the first plane off the island, in order to get my connections by taxi, plane, train, euro rail and another taxi to my apartment in Paris where the rest of this trip is going to take place. I am a few minutes late coming down to my Guernsey taxi. All taxi drivers thus far have been friendly, talkative and one even remembered my Dad. This one, though, must have had a bad early start and he tells me off for being late, as if I were a child. I manage to tell him that his reprimand is not acceptable – but that's all it takes to set me off and I then sob quietly all the way to the airport. He knows this is happening and tries to cheer me – to no avail.

How can one keep leaving home? It is easier now because my family – my adult children, my grandchildren and of course my Australian husband – are all in Australia. I come back to my family rather than leave them now. But still, Guernsey remains home. It is the land that I belong to. It is the beauty of the island with its hedgerows, cliff walks and cobbled streets. It is the memories of childhood, the smell of the sea, the harshness of its biting winds, the green fields, the milking cows, and again, the sea. There is always the sea with its majestic presence, its dominance, its ability to cut us off from others and change its mood each day. I remember it even making its way into my childhood home during a storm and Dad and I sweeping it out of the front door. I love that ocean. I love that island. Next time I go, I think, had better be in springtime so that I can see and smell again the daffodils, irises, freesias, bluebells and primroses. My heart yearns as I see these in my mind, I can hear the cuckoo again that we heard while picking primroses one Easter.

As the plane takes off and I watch that little island get smaller and gradually disappear, I try to keep in the tears as the man sitting next to me pretends not to see me. I have another life, far, far from here. I have family on the other side of the world. I will be glad to see them again, of course, and this time I have an exciting sojourn of writing in Paris to excite and intrigue me. But part of my heart is left behind. I have to leave it still there in that place. It always has been and it always will be living there, without the rest of me. And living with a little part of your heart in another place is the true experience of migration. It affects your life forever, no matter how long you live in your new home, and no matter how hard you try to fit in and belong. It is a relief now to face this truth, not to fight the slight homesickness that has never left me, but to accept and realise that is the reality of my being, of my identity of who I am. And the romance of it is that this longing for something unattainable is what keeps it forever desirable in the heart.

Perhaps that is beginning to sound like the very nature of a romantic heart to me. That is, something personal and private that is deeper and more revealing than the everyday actions of an 'ordinary' life ever could be. It is likely to have an aspect of longing and being unattainable, producing a depth of emotion. Recently, I watched a video clip about a woman of 109, Alice Herz-Sommer, the oldest Holocaust survivor, who still played the piano beautifully until her death. She told of her great passion for music which had literally kept her alive during her days of imprisonment and deprivation and accompanied her through her whole life. The really impressive and inspiring aspect of this was seeing the great passion and vitality still in her eyes when she spoke of her ongoing and lifelong affair with her music. There could surely be no more sustaining a view of passion or romance than that which is so life affirming and enduring.

What about the present day, aged in my sixties – if there is to be no more early days with a lover, is romance faded forever? I think not. Romance for me, more than anything, means some sort of yearning in the heart and soul. It is a feeling of aliveness combined with a kind of sadness. It is an excitement about things to come which may not be quite fulfilled. This can be recaptured time and again with memories, photos, songs, music, poems, familiar sights and smells. It can be evoked in beauty of all kinds, in nature, in a new baby, in a child's laughter. The birth of my grandchildren revisited the birth of my own children and the consequent falling in love with the babies. The 'romance' of the relationships with grandchildren, though, can be held onto for a longer time, as it is more occasional, without the domestic responsibility that caring for children on a full-time basis brings. There is a longing to see those cherished beings, to hold them, to smell them, to feel their little hands in mine, to hear their laughter and soothe their tears. Being without them for too long creates a physical feeling of emptiness that is very reminiscent of the romantic feelings for a significant other. This has nothing to do with lust, though, just a pure desire for that love and closeness.

While not religious at this stage of my life, there is now a spiritual aspect to romance. There is a longing for connection, an intense pleasure in some friendships and some activities, as well as for the creativity which creates a spark of emotion, of tenderness of joy. Tara Beach, in her book *Radical Acceptance* says, 'Longing, felt fully, carries us to belonging. The more times we traverse this path – feeling the loneliness or craving, and inhabiting its immensity – the more the longing for love becomes a gateway into love itself. Our longings don't disappear, nor does the need for others. But by opening into the well of desire – again and again – we come to trust the boundless love that is its source.'

As the knowledge of moving closer to one's death approaches, so does a realisation of its inevitability that creates a love of life which can often be missing in youth, when life is assumed to be neverending and eternal. At the risk of sounding 'New Agey', I think that ultimately I am finding romance within myself and for myself. From the point of view of getting to know the person I really am without all the distractions of youth, there is a new love being kindled. There is the dawning that emotion, intensity, pain and sorrow are inside me; they are generated by me – they are not from external sources. And with that recognition, there is the acceptance that love and romance are ultimately also from within. They are not about some other person. The other half of me cannot be found in someone else – it is all part of the complexity of who I am inside. Romance can always be mine, as long as I have life and love and passion.

Deep inside now is all the love that is left behind by those who are long gone. The ups and downs of many tempestuous and passionate romances reside now side by side in my heart forever. But still, that romance-shaped hole is refilled by you and you and a special few. Its passion is inflamed by music and beauty and the written word, by the memories and the feelings. Feelings fuelled always by a need for the intensity of joy and sometimes sorrow. It is a need to hold onto all that creates fullness in a soul that has rejected emptiness. And so I return internally to my own *vie en rose*.

I end, though, with another poetic outburst about the joy and sadness to be found in the romantic love of another.

Romantic Pining …
Days of wine and roses
Nights of love and dreams
Knowing all and dreading nothing
Hope is never what it seems
Memories of warmth and kisses
Bodies close and burning still
Colours bright and never fading
Need to trust they never will
Tears so wet and filled with longing
Life goes on its own sweet way
Pain or joy we wade right in
We count the cost each day
The Gods are laughing while we play
They're watching when we cry
They wait for us to make our choice
They stand there while we die
Human hearts still search for joy
Until in the end they try
To make the choice and bear the loss
And not to wonder why.

Passion

for

Life

Anne Whaite

ANNE WHAITE

Anne Whaite was born in Sydney where she still lives, very close to the harbour and on it as much as possible. She worked for twenty years as a member of the Guardianship Tribunal of NSW and for lesser periods on both the Mental Health Review Tribunal and the Administrative Decisions Tribunal.

Recently Anne decided to change the direction of her life to focus on her passions. Although a process not dissimilar to changing the direction of an ocean liner going at full speed in the middle of the ocean, she now spends a satisfying amount of time exploring the art of writing, working with disadvantaged kids to improve their literacy and delighting in her family and friends. She is a staunch supporter of organisations dedicated to protecting both the integrity of the natural world and the sustainability of human activity.

'It is a small part of life we really live. Indeed all the rest is not life but merely time'

– Seneca, 'On the Shortness of Life', AD 49

Alaska 2008

We climb from the yacht into a dinghy with an electric motor and glide silently to the water's edge. A grizzly bear wanders out of the forest with her two cubs, both toddlers in their second summer, and starts feeding on the fertile lip of land next to the water. She must know we are here. We are only feet away but although she takes us in with her gaze, she pays us no more attention than she does the scurrying mink or the goldeneye ducks on the beach. The cubs ignore us completely; our little boatload is not perceived as a threat. We can hear the sound of tearing grass as they mow it into their mouths using their massive paws as scythes. As the tide drops, they dig for clams in the exposed mud, dextrously winkling the meat from the shells with their huge claws.

We are in far north British Columbia exploring the estuary of the Khutzeymateen Grizzly Bear Sanctuary by boat, just four humans in a community of fifty-sixty bears ranging over 44,300 hectares.

One day, on the sedge meadows at the head of the estuary Dan, the skipper, briefly allows us ashore and I mention that I would like to walk about 90 metres to where a waterfall descends into the fjord.

'You can't go more than ten metres from the boat,' Dan tells me. 'The bears can run faster, swim faster and climb higher than you. If there is a charge from the forest, you need to be back in the boat before the bear gets here.'

The days in the Khutzeymateen touch me deeply. Something

happens to time as I watch the bears; it could be one hour, it could be two. Time stands still.

Here in the wilderness the interconnectedness of all living things is manifest and with the pure joy of merging with this world comes a realisation of a goal achieved, the ability to live completely in the moment.

One of the hard won lessons I have learnt is that if I am to indulge the passion I feel for the bittersweet wonder of this life, I must, just must … be right here, right now.

Long, long ago

The blinds were drawn defensively against the heat of a late summer afternoon blazing on western windows; outside, cicadas droned sonorously in a minor key. The skinny teenager, clad only in beige short shorts and a pink singlet top, was cool in the living room but where her bare legs draped over the arm of the boxy lounge chair, her skin stuck damply to green vinyl. She shifted her position as the square edge of the chair cut circulation to her feet but continued reading, absorbed in the forbidden fruit of *Lady Chatterley's Lover*.

From time to time she looked up and stared into middle distance, trying to work out why the book caused such an outbreak of condemnation. The words that she read were a revelation; she glimpsed something intense and alive, far removed from her small world of knowing. Tantalisingly redolent of life, a life for which she had a passion.

She knew that she wanted to dive into life, grab it by the throat and push it to the limits. But this was proving difficult.

She lived in a small dark brick Californian bungalow tucked in bushland near a harbourside bay where Sydney sandstone was moulded into soft caves with marbled walls, perfect wombs for dreaming. The dining room became the third bedroom as the family expanded, and the kitchen table was the focus of hospitality; warm teacake with cinnamon topping, pikelets with butter and jam and peanut cookies baked with love by her beautiful mother. However, the idyllic surroundings and abundant love contrasted with her parents' deep suspicion of nonconformity and a paternal parenting style that mimicked the Christian control and denial to which her father had been subjected in his childhood.

It was the 1960s and the sexual revolution was happening somewhere out there, not in this neat house, although sometime later her mother confided, 'Frankly, the fear of getting pregnant was the main reason I stayed a virgin until I was married.'

She knew without being told that there was a clear path to be taken, a careful ordinary existence, exactly like the one her parents had chosen for themselves. She couldn't blame them. After an excoriating war she understood that they craved security, peace and quiet, safety and conformity, but she always felt she was the cuckoo in this nest. She yearned for something different, more exciting.

She had no idea how to make that happen, that there were prerequisites and she didn't have them. Of the barriers she was more aware.

At the dinner table one Saturday lunch, her parents were reading a postcard depicting a geometric white façade gleaming against an ink blue sea; overflowing geraniums pots completed the riot of primary colours. The words on the flipside were from the only family friends with the means to travel beyond the Australian border and were enthusiastic, amusing and not a little bit gloating. The vividness of the image, the enticement of exploration led her to enthuse: 'I'd love to visit Greece one day.'

'Yes, but what more would you expect of someone with your mentality,' came the acidic reply.

Perhaps her father was right. She decided it was prudent to keep her opinions to herself.

Ecstatic when a teacher at her high school suggested that she apply for a scholarship to study in America, she was resigned to her fate when her father refused her permission to apply.

'It's just too dangerous, look at those riots in Little Rock Arkansas.'

Of course he was right, much better to be safe. The civil rights movement might be happening out there, but certainly not in her quiet suburb.

The constant conflicting messages, her instincts versus the daily disparaging evaluation of them, ensured that she became deeply unsure of herself, lacking in confidence to know her own mind. She decided to study science at university rather than indulge her interest in literature and history, because she assumed that there would be more job opportunities available to her. Her father insisted that she study chemistry as he had done, rather than the geology that she loved. She built an inner fortress to protect what sense of self she retained and Zelig-like, projected herself as she thought others wanted her to be. She was empathic, always giving, never disagreeing, always smiling, not taking any risks, just going through the motions. An unengaged, insipid life.

Over the following years there were moments of intense experience, fully lived. One day, wandering alone in a wide sloping paddock under a huge Riverina sky, she had an urge to become one with the sound of the wind in the silence, and fully inhabit the great empty space. But she couldn't escape the sense of being constrained by her skin, so like a whirling dervish she started to spin, arms outstretched, trying to merge with the cosmos and free her 'self' from its boundaries via centrifugal force. Dizzy and giggling, she fell on desiccated grass and listened to the crows that mocked her with jaded, disappointed voices.

It was her mother's uncle's farm and she yearned to spend her holidays in the farmhouse sheltered beside the peppercorn tree and eat her aunt's simple meals and marvel at the 'largest apple pie tin in the world', a remnant of times past when her aunt cooked daily for the shearers.

Her uncle was a very attractive man who kissed her in the wool shed and squeezed her hand and told her how attractive she was to him. 'If only I was a few years younger I could go for you in a big way.' He was probably the first person who had ever referred to her femininity. Instead of being put off, she was fascinated and adoring. She mentioned it to her mother one day. 'Good grief, he used to kiss me in the wool shed too,' she chortled. 'You'd think he'd be over that by now. Did you mind?'

It appears neither of them did.

Angie, her cousin, was a few years younger. An aura of notoriety hovered around her. She had left home and was living with her boyfriend. Angie had escaped.

'We don't approve of how your cousin is living but she's always welcome in our home.' Her mother's tone conveyed the gravity of the situation.

She suspected that her father's willingness to continue to see her cousin was influenced in no small part by the fact that Angie's mother had asked the family not have anything to do with her daughter in order 'not to encourage her' and her father was not the sort of person to pass up an opportunity to annoy his sister.

Mama Cass – an imposing body clad in an Indian caftan, blonde hair hanging straight to her shoulders – was fleetingly in the room when Angie entered. Although firmer fleshed, she was only slightly less outrageous, and would drape herself like an odalisque on the nearest couch or bed and hold court. Generosity of spirit glowed in her face and one of the most delicious ways to spend time was to hang out with her.

Her story both thrilled and scandalised. 'My parents locked me in my room so that I couldn't go out and meet my boyfriend. I talked to the school counsellor who said 'climb out the window', so I did. One day they explained that they didn't want me getting into a situation where I'd be holding hands with my boyfriend. At that stage we'd been lovers for ages, for God's sake, and I realised there was no way to bridge the yawning gap with my parents so I left home, got a job, finished high school and moved to Sydney.'

Angie told her, 'One of the happiest days of my life was when I started university. I felt so proud my life had begun. I was going to be a teacher and that was what I had always wanted to be.'

At the same time that Angie had decided to follow her passion for teaching, there she was, working in the physiology department of a medical school, operating on scared possums caged in a torture chamber called the 'animal house', attempting to delineate their visual pathways. Why? Because the lecturer asked her would she care to do an honours degree in his laboratory. Why not? He seemed keen for her to work with him and her parents thought it was a good idea. Later, whenever she thought of those decisions during that time of her life, she would be humiliated by her cowardice.

She loved to move in her cousin's orbit and observe how Angie lived at the edge of life.

There were parties where lean young men flirted outrageously with each other and girls with long straight hair, wearing Indian caftans, sobbed in corners while the object of their desire was spending time upstairs with someone else. At 2 am, cast-iron fry pans sizzled vast quantities of eggs and bacon to satisfy sudden outbreaks of 'the munchies'; there were kitchen floors so sticky that cockroaches stuck to them, and late night trips to pubs in Oxford Street.

She lived life vicariously through Angie for years.

Then something unexpected happened. One day she met someone she knew, as he knew her, from the time their gaze first met.

He took a battering ram to her defences and when they started to breach, he persisted. Then he zipped open his body and took her inside himself and she wore him around her shoulders like a cloak.

'I love your dark eyes, your dark hair and I love the way you smell. You are so beautiful to me. I like you better than anyone else I know.' His face was black against a hot night sky.

What was left of the wall between her and reality melted under his gaze, sometimes soft, smoky, smiling, sometimes naked and hard with desire.

In deep moaning moments of requited love she lost the sense of being constrained by her skin and had a sense of becoming one with the cosmos, just as she had tried so hard to do so many years before.

They played together like adolescents, daring each other to charm their way uninvited to VIP events and racing cars across town in the early hours of the morning. Silly, dangerous things she hadn't previously had the courage to try; both challenging restrictive upbringings.

Eventually they stopped expressing their passion for each other and a degree of normality returned, but she knew that something was different. Now she could allow herself to be open to all manner of experiences, an essential prerequisite for fulfilling her passion for life.

It did not last. The framework of her life was poorly constructed and eventually, when confronted with a combination of health and personal issues, it came tumbling down. Happily married now and with a small baby, she plunged into an abyss of depression and struggled to continue. Her passion for living was annihilated; all feeling other than paralysing fear was extinguished. She used every ounce of her will to ensure that she cared for her child. Nothing else mattered and nothing else was possible.

Waiting to cross the road one day, she saw a bus approaching and the thought passed through her mind, 'If this is what my life will be like now, it would be better if I stepped in front of that bus.'

She was shocked by the cool, dispassionate nature of the thought and how astonishingly easy it would have been to take that fatal step.

'Suicide is not an option,' said her husband decisively. This meant that the only way out was up. There was no alternative on offer after hitting rock bottom.

Slowly, painfully with the rock-solid support of her husband and the help of kind professionals, she forged a way through the fog until she emerged into clear air. She rebuilt her sense of self on a firm foundation and emerged, ready and determined to directly engage with her life.

Now in my mid forties I had a lot of catching up to do.

The Kimberley 2006

The places that drew me were the wild untamed places. I wanted to revisit the Kimberley where I had stayed as a teenager with family friends.

I had distant memories of a pre-dawn flight from Perth in the cockpit of a Fokker Friendship, watching the first rays of the sun gilding mesa tips in the desert, gleaming bronze slashed through black. We landed at Wittenoom Gorge where the mountain range was layered in hues of purple and deep blue and Sturt peas grew in profusion, brilliant red clashing perfectly with blood-red dirt, the colour of which was so startling that I took some home in a bottle. My destination was a Kimberley cattle station, 1,500,000 acres with a community of thirty Aboriginal people and six Europeans.

'Once you've drunk the water of the Kimberley you always return,' observed one of the stockmen, who talked so slow they called him 'Flash'.

There is always the possibility that returning to a place with high expectations ensures disappointment. Not this time. That year I spent two weeks travelling with ten others on a boat from Wyndham to Broome, visiting places inaccessible from the land.

We clambered over ancient red rocks, swam in waterholes under waterfalls, visited Ice Age art galleries, caught mud crabs in mangrove-lined creeks teeming with mud skippers, surfed the horizontal waterfalls, patted sharks, saw huge crocodiles, travelled with whales, caught – and ate – barramundi and mangrove jack, met a tiny helicopter on a red rock somewhere and zoomed low over crocodiles sunning themselves on the banks of the Mitchell river.

As I opened to the terrifying power of the tides, the harsh beauty of the landscape and the humbling reality of rocks that had existed unchanged for 1.8 billion years, I felt intensely, gloriously alive.

The boat was a Tardis from which we ventured into a world where the only visible evidence of the human species was etched on rock faces up to 50,000 years ago, possibly the oldest rock art on the planet. In this terrain, without the boat I would not have survived.

I imagined being cradled in the palm of the brooding landscape and felt a glow of deep security. In these moments my passion for life was realised.

Alaska revisited

Inexorably drawn to revisit the Khutzeymateen Grizzly Bear Sanctuary, I returned in autumn when the salmon were spawning and the bears were gorging before their long winter sleep.

Again we travelled with Dan, a tall rangy concave man who was involved in the battle to save the Khutzeymateen and its bears from the relentless onslaught of human activity. In 1994 these efforts had resulted in the establishment of the first and only area set aside specifically to protect grizzlies and their habitat. Now, Dan and one other operator are licensed to take visitors by boat into the Sanctuary; about 250 people visit each year. As a result the current population of bears has never seen a sibling shot and they have not learnt to see humans as a source of food. Here in the Khutzeymateen, humans and bears warily coexist.

Travelling with Dan means hitching a ride in the place that has been his summer home for twenty-five years. We sleep in bunks in the bow of the 40-foot *Sunchaser* and when I attempt to stow my belongings, I find the drawers filled to overflowing with ropes and 'useful' pieces of metal.

When I open the spice drawer in the galley, it is jam-packed with nails; 'Someone once inadvertently opened the drawer too fast and all the nails fell in the salad,' comments Dan.

It's a boys' boat; we wriggle in and make our own space. It's an adventure!

We travel north up the coast towards the Alaskan border. My excitement grows as the yacht motors into the side channel that leads to the Khutzeymateen fjord. Once we have entered and turned inland, the entrance is no longer visible and the sense of being in an enclosed, special place charges the atmosphere. In another hour we anchor at the head of a stream that Dan calls Mouse Creek.

We are surrounded by mile-high mountains, their summits laden with deep snow drifts that blend into dense forests of towering cedar, western hemlock, Sitka spruce and bare rock slopes exposed by landslides. Waterfalls cascade into the fjord as the snow melts in the sun. We transfer to the dinghy, impatient to see the salmon in the shallows.

Salmon live at sea for several years then return to spawn in the creeks and rivers where they were hatched. The female lays her eggs in a shallow depression in the gravel of the creek bed and the male ejaculates milt onto the eggs; subsequently they both die.

Dying salmon are all around us. If they have enough strength they hang in the current with their heads facing upstream but many have lost their ability to navigate and flap haplessly in the water. One particularly macabre fish floats past, its outer flesh dead and black … Halloweenesque.

Suddenly there's a bear 30 feet away. She must have been there all the time, asleep in the long grass, and she's very lethargic.

'She's feasted for an hour and slept for four and now she's trying to wake up.' Dan's voice is low, husky with excitement.

Waking up is not proving easy; she rolls over, looks around then slumps back with a huff in the grass.

Again I am in awe of the way our presence is tolerated by 'Sweetie', as Dan calls her.

In her own good time she has a final scratch then wanders along the banks of the creek where dying salmon are floating in the shallows. Before reaching the water she digs up and eats a plant with a long tuber. Dan calls them cowslips and says they have medicinal properties, especially to rid them of tapeworms. Looks like Sweetie could use a cowslip; behind the superb condition of her glossy honey coloured fur drags a tapeworm perhaps three metres long.

In this time of plenty, no effort is required and if the fish show any resistance she lets them go. If they are too weak to struggle from under her paw she takes a bite then lets them go. She continues feeding, casually working her way upstream until the water is so shallow we can no longer follow her.

One day Sweetie is faced with an intruder. We watch her returning to Mouse Creek when another bear, unfamiliar to the area, is feeding in her territory. She approaches the newcomer purposefully, quietly. They face each other and growl. Neither retreat. They bare their teeth, rise on hind legs and, roaring, tussle ferociously. They move apart and stare at each other then the newcomer walks up one side of the creek and Sweetie up the other, ambling away as silently as they came. I realise I've been holding my breath.

That night a half moon rises over the snow streaked mountains, the reflection so perfect that reality and illusion fuse to one. I lie in the hammock slung low at the bow, shivering but unable to let the moment go. As the harbour seals float by, their little faces peering at me in the twilight and the sound of running streams blend with the cries of gulls and ducks, it occurs to me that I have never been anywhere more beautiful, either physically or spiritually. The experience of the Khutzeymateen is so far removed from day to day life that I struggle to find words to describe it.

'This is the real world out here, you can't decide you want to see a bear and just 'change channels'. You can't switch the bears on or the rain off. Nothing prepares you for the experience,' says Dan. He is right.

We leave the sanctuary at dawn surrounded in morning mist and drizzle. I am cosy in my bunk. Dan says there is no need to get up as we get under way but I must have just one last look. I am pulling on gumboots and coat over my pyjamas when Dan's excited whisper reaches me: 'Come quickly, the bear's come out to say goodbye.'

A light and lovely fog sits low on the mountains; there are no seals to be seen, even the gulls are silent. There in the cosmic stillness the newcomer is fishing lazily at the entrance to Mouse Creek as it always has and, God and human willing, as it always will.

Paris, 2012

'*Bonjour Madame,*' says the gypsy who sits with his white Pekinese dog and comfortable stool on rue du Roi-de-Sicile near the corner of rue Pavée This morning he isn't pressing me for money.

'*Bonjour monsieur,*' I reply with a frisson of delight at the improbable thought that he has come to regard me as a local since I walk past every morning en route to my writing class.

The cold autumn wind is deflected by the same purple, puffy coat that warmed me in the Khutzeymateen, but in all other respects there is a yawning disconnect. The multi-layered strata of human endeavour and folly that defines Paris is, however, no less seductive than the lure of the bears' silent world, and I crave to know both.

The experience of the wilderness has subtly but profoundly adjusted the framework of my thinking. It has rebalanced the influence of the past, soothed anxiety from the present and provided a credible framework for the future. It has also provided a perspective for exploration of the world of humans.

My writing eyrie is in the rue des Rosiers in the 4th *arrondissement* and from the window I watch the throngs drawn to the fashionable shops. Jeans and scarves striped grey and red displayed in what was previously the Goldenberg restaurant, a black-and-white-themed window in the fashion boutique next door. People queue patiently at all hours of the day and night at the kosher food outlet below, sit on doorsteps or wander along the street eating falafel folded in napkins before wiping their fingers and resuming their shopping excursion. The warm smell of falafel and matzo bread rising from the café is a reminder of the Jewish heritage of the area.

Early black and white moving pictures of the rue des Rosiers show well rounded women, their hair pulled back in buns wearing long simple belted dresses, carrying large French baskets and walking purposefully up the street while others push or pull carts laden with produce. There are horse-drawn carriages, men with white beards and long black coat and hats.

Then in the 1940s thousands of members of the Jewish diaspora, resident here since the Middle Ages, were taken away by the French police who were collaborating with the Nazis. Ultimately they went to concentration camps and few returned. I keep thinking about this as I wander along the narrow cobbled street, even as I'm distracted by a particularly fetching green wool coat in a boutique window. Has the Jewish community so integral to this place since the Middle Ages been completely annihilated by the combined onslaught of Hitler and materialism?

A plain limestone plaque outside L'Ecole de Travail is inscribed 'To the memory of the director, personnel and students of this school, arrested in 1943 and 1944 by the Vichy police and the Gestapo, deported and exterminated at Auschwitz because they were Jews.'

And another around the corner: '260 Jewish children from this school were deported to Germany in World War II and were exterminated in the Nazi camps. Never forget.'

The primary school stands opposite a building inscribed with the words *Liberté, Egalité, Fraternité*.

I also find a Yiddish Library, a temple and a group of orthodox men, proud and serious in their black suits and hats, long ringlets framing their faces.

Some of the original shops remain. Behind the vivid blue-tiled facade of the Boulangerie Murciano is a kosher patisserie that has been here for over 100 years. It sells strudel and baklava and proclaims its heritage with a gold seven-branched candlestick displayed in the window. An English voice besides me comments to her companion as she peers in the window, 'The lady at the back looks a bit traditional.' Then she walks away, Michelin guide firmly in hand. Tourists and shoppers, but is there a local community?

I sit down at a table outside the unadorned facade of the Café des Psaumes. A gentleman asks if he can join me. 'I am Jewish,' he says. 'I live far from here but I like to return every week for the kosher food and to reconnect with my people. This café is where Jewish people come for a coffee and a talk.' In an attempt to stem the tide of fashionista, this old café was reopened as a gathering place for the Jewish community in 2010.

On a cold, sunny Sunday, as I stand on my Juliet balcony overlooking the street, I am haunted by the thought of the time when the residents were rounded up and herded away. The clomp of their feet still echoes beneath the click of stylish boots and the carefree hum of the Sunday shoppers.

'Paris ... a postgraduate course in Everything.'
– James Thurber

Even in the midst of this intellectual and sensual deliciousness, contemplating the activity in the narrow street below, I register a niggling reminder of the artifice of a city. Something is missing.

Looking up, I see clouds streaking grey blue above the attic windows that jut from the rooftops. They provide the connection between this human world, the world of the Kimberley and the world of the bears. No matter where I am, it is only necessary to look up and see the clouds moving across the sky or the stars in the night sky to remind myself of the whole of which I am just a part.

I experience a strange and most agreeable sensation, my muscles relaxing and a tingling at my core: contentment. After half a lifetime of being open to the experience of living and through that connection with the world, I have developed a sense of completeness.

Here, utterly in this moment, I touch my passion for life. I sense the knowledge it brings and the questions it raises. I know it is the greatest gift I have ever received.

Passion

for

Women

Diana Wilde

DIANA WILDE

Diana Wilde is a writer, musician and photographer residing in the Blue Mountains of NSW. Born in Sydney in 1947, she completed her schooling, worked as a secretary and at twenty embarked on a journey of discovery, travel and work in England. She later lived and worked in Switzerland for six months, then travelled by bus through Europe to Nepal. Returning to Sydney in 1970, she married, raised a family and worked as a secretary in high profile positions.

Classically trained in pianoforte as a child, she completed 3rd Level of the Suzuki Piano Method and went on to teach piano and musicianship. At forty-eight, she began tertiary studies at Macquarie University, gaining a Bachelor degree specialising in English Literature, Creative Writing and Women's Studies. While studying, she took up African drumming, joining a popular and successful women's drumming group.

She now spends her retirement with grandchildren, writing, studying the clarinet and her passion for photography.

Paris beckoned again. She held out her generous, pink-tinged arms inviting me to join ten women for a memoir writing course in October 2012. The thought of being in Paris again brought back the cloying aroma of croissants and café au lait in the rue de Narbonne apartment within the 7th *arrondissement* where I had stayed in 1969. Then I had devoured the works of Balzac and Maupassant and Flaubert. At university during my forties I began to voraciously digest women writers like Jean Rhys while studying *Feminism and Literature* and *Sexual Difference*. During these days I realised I had grown up a member of Simone de Beauvoir's *Second Sex* and really experienced her *Woman Destroyed* during my twenty-year marriage. I fervently fantasised about being in a passionate *ménage a trois* with Anaïs Nin and Charlotte Rampling and yearned to exchange words at the Café Procope with Gertrude Stein.

Nine months before my departure, and only a few months after my sixty-fourth birthday, I learned something about myself that would change me forever: a secret which members of my family had withheld. A brave older cousin, Rhonda, was determined to share this secret with me before I began working on my memoir in Paris.

Our mothers always remain the strangest, craziest people we've ever met.

– Marguerite Duras, French Author

I had no passion for women growing up in Sydney's inner west during the 1950s. My mother Rita made certain of that. Passion for her was to lie prostrate and suffering on the floor while giving thanks to the

Lord Jesus. In those days I would squint my right eye over my parents' bedroom door keyhole, but saw no passion. The image looked painful and disgusting. I only saw a big lump of a father pushing down on an impassionate mother. Angry like her, I was called *Fury* in primary school. I would vigorously throw whole tree branches at male antagonists like James Bull. As his name implied, his frame hung like a prize bull parading around the show ring at the Royal Easter Show. He enjoyed pelting me with snails and lumps of mud from the creek that flowed through Girrahween Park, where I played on the way home from school. I had picked up my violent reactions from a mother who had no qualms in pushing my inebriated father through a fibro wall when he came home with a skinful of alcohol.

My mother Rita ran the household with the vigour of a fanatic. She was a cold, controlling, it is *my way or the highway* sort of woman. Born in 1921, the youngest of a family consisting of three older brothers and two older sisters, she had the beauty of the 1940s B-movie actress Ann Sheridan, and the style of the 1940s A-movie actress Rita Hayworth. She became like Medea when I answered her back or did not do as she instructed. If I played up at the house of my aunty Rose, my mother's sister in Marrickville, I would be marched downstairs into their cavernous, porcelain-smelling laundry at the back of their house, where razors sat waiting for my uncle to shave, and the sink filled with buckets of soaking menstrual rags. Aunt Rose's house sat behind the Army Barracks, and many times when I was thrown into their dark and forbidding laundry the soldiers would be marching past, their boots grating loudly across the gravel roadway. The sound of soldiers and enveloping darkness scared me so much I couldn't go into a darkened room until my twenties.

Living and growing up with Rita made me terrified of women. I longed to be held and cuddled, nurtured and made a fuss of, but my mum didn't seem capable of doing this with me. When my sister Debbie arrived two years and nine months after me, she became the one my mother held and cuddled. I would creep up the hallway to my mother's bedroom and watch her feeding my sister with a bottle.

Debbie was petite compared to me. I had a robust body and bigger than average extremities. My fingers were long and made for playing the piano, as family members pointed out regularly. My father religiously took me to piano lessons twice a week with Mrs McGeaghie, who would slap my fingers with a ruler if I missed a note, or mixed up forte with pianissimo. I didn't want to play the piano *gay and lively*. I was a tomboy. I preferred to play with dirt and would refuse to wear shoes over my enormously broad feet. My father Oscar called my feet *plates of meat* and constantly said I had a good grip on the world. For my first birthday my father bought me Tracy, my fox terrier. From that moment we were inseparable.

My father was a robust and affectionate man who smothered me with kisses and cuddles. He would always take me to the chrome plating factory which he and his family ran in Marrickville. I would sit at his desk and pretend to type on the old and battered Remington his secretary used. My favourite men at the factory were William, his accountant, and Allen, the factory foreman. They were gentle men with soothing voices.

As I got older, movies saved me. They gave me a fantasy world to escape to when my mother became too controlling. During my teens I was passionately in love with Kim Novak. I adored her in Somerset Maugham's *Of Human Bondage*, admiring the way she treated the leading man, Laurence Harvey, with such disdain and cruelty. The movies *Picnic* with William Holden and *The Eddy Duchin Story* with Tyrone Power encouraged my adoration of her.

During my early teenage years, Rita got her dream car. A shiny new beige Austin A40, with leather seats that squished under your bottom when you sat on them. It sported a column gearshift and little red and yellow indicators that popped out from the side doors between the front and back seat windows. My mother loved this car with a passion. I fell in love with it too. I got my licence in 1964 at seventeen. My father taught me to drive; he believed the only way to learn to drive properly was to drive at night without the distractions of people and other cars.

I had begged and pleaded with my mother to lend me her Austin. I had to behave like a 'lady' and do many jobs around the house such as mowing the lawns before my mother finally relented. I got up to some outrageous adventures. My favourite drive was along Kensington Road in Randwick that went for many miles, with a dip at the left of each intersection. I would drive the car at a wild pace in the dip as close to the left hand kerb as was possible without hitting the telegraph poles. At each intersection my sister and I would be hurtled upwards over the bumps and hit our heads on the inside roof of the car. We laughed so hard before each bump we nearly bit our tongues at the point of impact. Seatbelts were not compulsory and we were thrown around without any restraint.

Five years before I began learning to drive, I tried very hard to destroy my mother's Austin motorcar, which took pride of place at the back of our double garage. I was a pathological liar, never admitting to any wrongdoing, even when neighbours had seen me trying to break into parked cars to steal whatever had been left on the seats or in the glove box. I had also been caught stealing mail from neighbours' letterboxes, so my mother forbade me from going out for a month. Our local cinema was just around the corner on Homer Street and within easy walking distance. I would meet my school friends there every Saturday afternoon, and to be banned from going anywhere for a month was a killer. She also hinted that I might never be allowed to drive her precious Austin.

The following Saturday my mother went up the road to her church to prepare the flowers for the Sunday service. I was unsupervised as Dad and sister Debbie were delivering orders from his factory. Dad had taken Debbie because he knew she wouldn't dob on him if he called in to the bowling club for a few drinks on the way home. I found myself alone and decided to get back at my mother for grounding me. I calmly walked out through the sliding screen door of the back sunroom; it opened onto a back verandah that ran the full length of the sunroom and my bedroom.

The back rooms of our house faced west and the besser block

screen on the verandah stopped the heat of the afternoon sun cooking this part of the house in the humid and sometimes unbearable summer heat. Beyond the verandah was a well watered and manicured green, prickly 'buffalo' grass lawn. Pride of place was a Hills Hoist clothesline, which Debbie and I would swing on when Mum and Dad were at the church or inside the front part of the house. Just past the lawn at the end of the side driveway was a fibro double garage. Attached to the side of the entire garage wall was the laundry and my cubby house where I would hide with my dog Tracy when things got too unbearable. At the end was Dad's tool shed where he hid most of his grog amongst his work tools.

At the back of the garage stood the sacred, shiny, polish-buffed Austin A40 which I desperately wanted to drive one day. It was hot, humid and dusty in the garage. The side gates were shut. When my dad came home he would drive his lime-green cream-trimmed Holden station wagon through the side gates and park it in front of the Austin. I had plenty of time to hover and hatch my plan.

There were shelves along the garage walls filled with terracotta pots, house paint in many colours, snail bait and disgustingly smelling garden fertilisers. There were jerry cans of turpentine, lawn mower fuel and leaded petrol, lined up in perfect order. My mother had old newspapers bundled up ready for my dad to take to the factory the following Monday. The factory storeroom used the papers, especially the *Herald*, to cover chrome work prior to it being wrapped in brown paper. I had matches in my pocket, as I used to smoke used cigarette butts I found in gutters along the way to the shops. Sometimes I would find cigarette samples in my dad's dressing room, which was behind my bedroom. One of his best clients for chrome work was W.D. & H.O. Wills. My dad's mate, Johnny Page, a salesman with the cigarette company, gave my dad packets containing three Craven A cigarettes as gifts for workers at his factory. I thought Johnny only did this to get the workers to buy larger packets from him. I had been secretly smoking since the age of ten. Everyone smoked, except Mum and Dad.

I tore some paper and put it close to the petrol tank area of the Austin. I found some wood shavings and threw them on the pile before adding a dash of petrol. I struck a match and lit my little bundle. Within minutes I heard my mother's voice from inside the house. I hadn't noticed her walk up the side driveway and go into the kitchen. It was dark in the garage. I hadn't wanted to turn on the fluorescent lights to make me visible to anyone coming up the drive. I ran out of the garage and across the garden, and pretended to have been sitting on the verandah. Then I casually walked in through the sliding door of the sunroom and sat down to the salad and cold meat my mother had already prepared and left on the table.

It was exactly 6 pm. My dad and sister were still not home, but that didn't stop dinnertime in our house. I heard a man's voice yelling, 'Rita, open the gate, it's Ken, there's a fire in your garage. Open the gate! I'll help you put it out. Hurry, Rita ... Rita!'

My mother had been staring at me, mouth open in disbelief. 'What have you been up to Diana?'

'Nothing Mum, nothing.' My mother began to scream, rushing past me, nearly pushing the sliding door off its hinges. Mr Cooper had somehow opened the gate and was pulling the hose into the garage, which was by now filled with more smoke than actual flames.

Shortly after, when the fire had been safely put out, my mother came inside and began my inquisition. 'You lit the fire, didn't you?'

'No I didn't. I haven't been near the garage.'

'Don't lie to me. Stop lying.' My mother's voice got louder and louder as she continued her ranting. 'Go to your room, get out of my sight. All the things I've done for you, and this is what you do to me. You destroy everything. You don't deserve to have the family you have. I'm going to talk to your father about the girls' home in Parramatta again. I can't take anymore of this!'

I got up from my chair and calmly walked the few steps across the sunroom, through the plastic concertina door into my bedroom. I was unable to lock my bedroom door with a key. It had a flimsy hook. That's all I had for security to keep out my crazy mother. As I walked into my room I kept repeating my innocence, unable to be heard above the frenzied verbal battering I was trying to ignore.

… After a lifetime of heated verbal exchanges, my mother died on August 4th 2009. My sister and I went to the family home our mother had lived in from 1946. I was amazed there was no gas or log fire in the house named *RITAMAY* where I grew up, just a two-bar electric heater to warm the large double brick east-facing house. The name of the house was a combination of my mother's Christian names, *Rita May*, and had been created by my father. He had fashioned a metal chrome-plated house plaque. Now it sat, lonely and forlorn in the backyard atop a brick BBQ I had helped my father build in the 1950s.

An overpowering smell of Tweed perfume and musty bibles hit me as my sister and I entered our mother's icy-cold bedroom. Outside, the mid-morning rays of lukewarm sun were trying to penetrate the tightly shut venetian blinds. They had been closed since our mother had been rushed by ambulance to the nearest hospital. Debbie and I stood either side of the narrow, uninviting single bed our mother had slept in since our father died in 1984. Pulling back the flimsy pink flannelette sheets and crumpled single pink blanket, I noticed the sheets had been re-sewn in half after worn sections had been cut out.

I asked Debbie, 'Why hadn't Mum bought a new set of sheets? She had plenty of money. She could have been so much more comfortable.' At the top of the bed was a tired, padded pink bedhead.

Debbie sadly replied, 'These horrible old beds will be the first to go in the rubbish skip I ordered this morning.'

I cautiously opened up the doors of the wardrobe, which I had known intimately since childhood. The outside had a veneer of golden, honey colour with a few unusual spots every now and again. On the inside of the door was the name of the company where my dad had bought it, Buckingham's, a furniture store in Sydney. I asked, 'How old is this wardrobe, Debbie? It would have to be sixty years old, I'm sixty-two in November.' I remembered whenever Mum and Dad were out of the house for even a short time, I would creep in and search drawers for coins, or some tiny treasure of jewellery, and stash them away in my room where no one could find them. I received many beltings with a leather strap for poking into cupboards and drawers searching for treasures. I had also often seen my mum going through my dad's trousers and coat pockets doing exactly the same thing. I would see my mum clutch pound notes and scurry off to her bedroom, as my dad lay sprawled out on the sunroom floor, pissed to the eyeballs.

After my father died, I asked my mum why she went through his clothes. 'I did it for you and Debbie. Your father would have gone out and spent it on whisky and floozies, or his mates at the Bowling Club.' I knew that was true, but witnessing this at such an early age had taught me to be devious.

Continuing my search through her wardrobe I came across a beret-style hat, made of dark-blue dyed wool with embroidered stitching around the brim. The hat was in the style of the type worn by paperboys, and became popular with the movie *The Great Gatsby*. I remembered how popular these hats were while living in London between 1968 and 1970. Jean Shrimpton and Lulu wore them with tight sweaters, mini skirts and knee-high leather boots. This was the trendy hat my mother had worn to my presentation at Granville Technical College. I was being presented with a special award for Literature, just prior to gaining my Tertiary Preparation Certificate as a mature-age student in 1994. I was forty-seven and my mother was seventy-three. I remembered being so embarrassed by her presence. Family members had described my mother as *mutton dressed up as lamb*. I had told her about the special award, but she turned up when the presentation had already commenced. Almost everyone in the auditorium turned their heads to see this older woman teeter between the rows of chairs dressed in pedal pusher pants, corked high heel sandals and this Gatsby-style beret perched on Bardot-like platinum-bleached hair. I had been jealous of my mother for years, and this sudden late appearance at my award made me angry and even more jealous.

My thoughts returned to the contents of the wardrobe. I said to Debbie, 'Mum definitely had a shoe fetish. There must be over thirty shoe boxes, and I know the second bedroom wardrobe is filled with boxes of shoes.'

'Just be careful, Di. Mum hid money in those boxes. I haven't gone through all of them yet, just the ones she told me about a while ago before she got sick. Don't throw anything out until you check them all. Promise me, Di?'

'I will. I promise, Deb.'

Later that afternoon, as we examined coffins in the Parramatta funeral rooms, my mother's words flashed through my brain. She would constantly say, 'When I die I just want one of those cardboard boxes, the ones that are easy to burn, nothing fancy and no gold or silver handles, just plain and simple. The attendants pinch those handles before the coffin goes into the incinerator. It's true. Your father worked with a coffin maker. Remember Mr Agostini? Your dad chrome-plated handles for him.'

After making arrangements for the funeral to be held within a few days I asked my sister, 'How do you feel, Deb?'

She replied, 'You don't know how bad it got for me, Di.'

'What do you mean?'

'Mum demanded so much. I had to visit sometimes twice a week to do the banking, pay the bills and get the shopping. You lived further away. She was too scared to ask you. She was frightened you'd tell her to go to hell.'

'Debbie, she didn't have to live the way she lived. She was eligible to have someone come in every day to clean, change the sheets and give her medication. She refused any help at all.'

'I know, but she didn't want anyone except us coming into the house. I don't know how I kept it up all this time, Di. She nearly killed me ... she did ... she nearly killed me.' I placed my arms around her. 'When this is all over, the cremation, the memorial service, why don't you get away. There's plenty of time before probate comes through.'

Debbie opened up another stubby of Tooheys New, her favourite beer, tears pouring down her cheeks. 'I might just do that, but let's get this over with first.'

The following Wednesday the family drove to the Crematorium. The ordinary and cheap coffin, specifically asked for by our mother, now held her visible remains, and was situated in the front of the chapel. I could hear my mother's words ringing in my ears, 'See those boxes in the walls with the plaques? Don't ever put me in one of those, Di. I won't be able to breathe in them. I want my ashes scattered.'

I helped Debbie walk up to the open coffin. Our mother's body had become anorexic. We believed she had decided to kill herself by not eating, or even perhaps only having the barest intake of food to save money. The funeral house had covered our emaciated mother with plain white silk material which shimmered in the early morning sunlight. Her face was smooth. I didn't need to kiss it like I had at the hospital just a few hours after she had died. Then I had held her still warm hand while my family stood alongside me. I whispered I was so relieved she had finally let go of this world.

Rita didn't look like my passionate, fierce and awe-inspiring mother anymore. Her hair was still long, but very grey. Her prominent Romanesque nose was now even more pronounced. I noticed how large her ears were compared to how I thought they were. Debbie asked, 'Should we take some of Mum's hair, Di?'

'Yes, that's a good idea.' My father had kept a lock of my hair from my first haircut. In 1984 when he died, I had found a Craven A cigarette tin containing a tight curl of my blonde hair tucked away in the desk drawer at his office. I also found, within the tin, a small chrome-plated plaque of Australia inscribed with the address where he had lived with my mother in Brighton-le-Sands before Debbie and I were born.

The funeral usher came over and gave us two small blue velvet bags for our mother's hair. Debbie had even thought to bring a pair of small scissors with her. She proceeded to cut some hair from our mother's head and placed some in each bag. We took the little blue bags with us to the pews in the chapel and held them tight as we said our goodbyes.

Fasten your seat belts, it's going to be a bumpy night.
– Bette Davis as fading star Margo Channing, from *All About Eve* (1950)

One woman in my family exuded what I thought was real passion: Rose, the older sister of my mother. She was a tall, wiry, always-on-the-go woman, nicknamed Rosa, Rebel or Bubsy by family and friends. I only ever called her Aunty Rose and loved her much more than I loved my mother.

As soon as I knew how to escape my prison-like home by climbing out my bedroom window, I would attempt to run away. I'd take a small wooden suitcase with a change of clothes, a copy of *Tom Sawyer* stolen from the local library, a penknife stolen from the local Coles variety store and my Bible, which I was attempting to read from beginning to end. I would run to the bottom of my street, jump on a tram and get off close to where my Aunty Rose lived in Marrickville, a village close to Sydney. I would walk up the hill past the Woollen Mills, which emitted an odour of metal shavings and lubrication oil. The smell reminded me of burnt clothing, wool in particular, like when I stood too close to our coal fire. At the top of the street I'd pass the hotel, where a few of my uncles drank after work. These were the days of the *six o'clock swill* when men finished work at 4 pm and dashed to the nearest pub to fervently drink as many schooners of beer as they could before closing time at 6 pm.

My Uncle Bruce wasn't much of a drinker – it was Aunty Rose who drank. She became extremely fiery and violent towards Uncle Bruce after too many beers. I thought, at the time, this behaviour was passion. One evening I watched in awe as Aunty Rose chased Uncle Bruce around the house with a carving knife. Passion in my mind became mixed up with violent behaviour and loud rantings.

Opposite the hotel was where Aunty Rose lived, and within a hundred metres of each other, lived four families related to my mother. The 50s and 60s were a time of extended families, Friday night family get-togethers, grandparents to grandchildren, talking, dancing and playing games. Alcohol for the adults was a huge part of these gatherings. The children were confined to the kitchen and back sunroom to play gin rummy although they could hear the goings on in the front of the house. There were many angry outbursts as well as lots of uncontrollable laughter from the front rooms. Alcohol loosened many lips, telling stories of the latest scandal of the street or snippets of what was overheard at the pub the day before.

I was always seeking the truth behind the relatives who had died, or those I visited with my mother in places like hospitals or sanitariums (which were really mental asylums). I would be told a relative was a hypochondriac who took too many pills, but as I got older I realised they may have had some form of mental illness or were unable to support themselves. The truth was withheld to prevent damaging the veneer of normal behaviour.

On many occasions I would arrive by tram at my aunt's house and plead with her to stay. 'I can't go back, Aunty Rose. I hate Mum. Can't I stay with you?'

'You can stay for the day, but I'll have to call your mother, Di. She will be worried about you.' I would sob uncontrollably, knowing what would happen when I was taken home. I would be given another belting with the leather strap, which hung from a hook in the hallway cupboard. If it had been the 1990s the laboratory of Crime Scene Investigations would have found copious amounts of my raw flesh and DNA on those two strips of stained brown leather. My mother would scream, 'You always embarrassed me in front of the whole family. Wait until your father gets home, Diana.'

Aunty Rose became a sounding board, a refuge for me throughout my childhood and beyond, standing up for me and sometimes defending me when I got into trouble with my mother. Rita would say to Aunty Rose, 'Don't interfere. She doesn't live with you. I have to put up with her thieving, back-answering, and unladylike behaviour. When I threaten to send her to the girls' home in Parramatta, she runs away.'

When I answered back, which I did constantly, or wouldn't eat all my dinner if we were at Aunty Rose's house, my mother would always drag me down the back stairs and push me into their dank-smelling and cave-like laundry. I would scream non-stop until Aunty Rose pleaded with my mother to let me out. It was as if two passionate individuals, (Rita and me), constantly sparred with each other to see who could be the loudest and most animated.

After much introspection about my childhood I came to the conclusion that my mother and I were both totally dissatisfied with our lives. We fervently wanted more, and the only way to deal with our frustrations was to be vocal or throw things at walls. Mum would become so angry when Dad was teaching her to drive she would often stop the car in the middle of Newtown, get out, slam the car door and walk back to her older sister Rose's place in Marrickville. My father would then drive like a maniac to the hotel on the corner of Illawarra and Marrickville Roads, rush inside to be with the barmaid Fay, who I am sure he was having a fling with. She would later come out to the car with her breasts spilling out of her blouse and her peroxide-dyed blonde hair piled high up in a Rita Hayworth hairstyle with *Blue Bow* lemonades for me and my sister. We would sit in the back of the car sipping our drinks, checked up on every so often by Dad to see if we needed to go to the toilet. After a few hours Dad would get back in the car and swerve the whole way up Illawarra Road, through the Warren, across Cook's River at Undercliffe and up the big hill to Homer Street.

After spending hours complaining to her sister about Dad's behaviour while trying to teach her to drive, Mum would catch the tram home. When we finally arrived home, Dad would be sozzled; apologising profusely to our mother for not bringing us home in time for dinner, which always went on the table at exactly 6 pm. The daily timetable was as sacred as the Sunday church service and could never be changed, no matter what happened. We didn't mind because while we waited in the car for Dad we were usually plied with treats. Dad's favourite barmaids would even at times pop up the road to buy fish and chips or Chinese fried rice. We were so happy not having to face a meal of tripe or, even worse, brains with white sauce and vegetables. My mother forced us to eat these meals, and if she left the dining room for a minute I would run to my bedroom and spit the food out the window. If my mother caught me in the act of doing this, she would go outside, pick the vegetables up from the ground and make me eat them, even if they were covered with gravel or dead insects. Sometimes the dog would get to my spat-out food before my mother and save me from this fate.

For some stupid reason, I would eagerly blurt out what we had been doing with Dad. My sister would call me a tattletale or blabbermouth, and I would call her Miss goody-two-shoes.

Dad survived many drunken nights and would repeat his favourite line, *Nothing in the world worries me – you can all kiss my arse.* My mother would keep nagging, or get his favourite bottles of whisky, and pour them down the kitchen sink. Dad would fall into bed and snore like a Boeing 707 aeroplane. Mum would then always check Dad's trousers and take a few pound notes from his bulging wallet. She'd pretend to fold his clothes, but as my room was behind my father's dressing room I knew what she was up to. Later, when everyone else was in bed, I would creep in to Dad's room and, like Mum, take a few notes and coins to buy cigarettes and special treats at the local store. The next morning Dad would be given a list of jobs that needed doing, which he complied with to the letter. He would spend most of the day in his toolshed, where I knew he had a bottle stashed somewhere, or had poured his favourite whisky into an empty Coca Cola bottle that he hid away from my mother's prying eyes.

Home-life was never boring but I still preferred being around Aunty Rose. We were both born in November, we were Scorpios and I always thought I had inherited her passion and dissatisfaction with leading such a boring life. I was certainly not going to give my life up to Jesus as my mother had. I rebelled every chance I got by running away, or secretly spending time in Girrahween Park, a place I had been banned from entering.

I continued to visit Aunty Rose as often as I could, even when I lived in the mid-north coast of New South Wales from 2000. Then, a few months before Aunty Rose's death, I went to Sydney and drove with my mother to visit her in the Blue Mountains. She was now in her nineties. She had dementia and was living in a nursing home in Leura. I arrived with my mother, and my older cousin Rhonda (Aunt Rose's daughter). My aunt said to me, 'Di. It's good to see you.'

I replied, 'Your hair looks nice, Aunty Rose.' She preened in front of the wall mirror. 'The hairdresser comes around once a week to give us all a set or colour. She talked me into this pinkish number.'

'I like it, Aunt. It makes your eyes look a deeper blue.'

Around the same time, my foray in building a house and permaculture garden on twelve acres with a partner had ended in court proceedings. I faced losing money and having to move on elsewhere. Aunty Rose knew about my plight and said while we were there, 'Di, don't worry about finding somewhere to live. You can always come here and hide under the bed. There's a little dog that visits us during the day, so you won't be lonely.'

'Aunty Rose, that's very kind of you to offer.'

My mother frowned at me and looked at her watch. 'We'd better go before the traffic gets bad on the highway.'

I put my arm around Aunty Rose's shoulder as we walked towards the locked door leading to the gardens outside. 'Hope to see you soon, Aunty Rose.'

It would be the last time I saw her.

One is not born, but rather becomes, a woman.
– Simone de Beauvoir, French author and philosopher

I did not begin menstruating until seventeen years of age. In fact, I felt more like a teenage boy, not a girl becoming a woman. I voraciously read French writers like Balzac and Flaubert. *Cousin Bette* and *Madame Bovary* were two of my favourites books. The writers I read were males but the subject matter was about women like *Anna Karenina* or *Lady Chatterley*. In 1966, a much older boyfriend introduced me to French movies at a cinema in George Street. The first French movie I saw was *A Man and a Woman*. The sensuousness between Jean-Louis Trintignant and Anouk Aimée was a sexual awakening to me, as was the raunchiness of Brigitte Bardot, Charlotte Rampling and finally, Catherine Deneuve in *Belle de Jour*.

Like so many Australians during the sixties, I wanted to travel. My grandmother had been born in the UK, so I was eligible for a work visa. In 1965 when I landed full-time employment as a secretary, I began saving towards my *Grand Tour*. I spent every day dreaming of how to escape from my controlling mother.

On August 6th 1968 I boarded the Sitmar liner the *Fairstar* and escaped to the Mother Country. Because of the Six-Day War in the Middle East, I travelled across the Pacific Ocean via Tahiti, Panama, the West Indies, Lisbon and finally to Southampton.

I was free! My body changed and I became more feminine, I began to wear clothes that hugged my pear-shaped figure. I had time to breathe, to read writers like Aldous Huxley, George Orwell, Henry Miller, D. H. Lawrence and Karl Marx, and talk passionately to my flatmates about the Moonwalk and The Vietnam War. Around 1969 I moved to Archway, a village on the northern road out of London at the bottom of Highgate Hill, which led to Hampstead Heath.

I shared a bedroom with Vivian who worked in a fashion house in the west end of London. My other flatmates were Penny and Jane, both nurses who worked at Guys Hospital, and Rowena and Katherine came from Wagga Wagga in New South Wales. They were sisters and worked as hairdressers. Louis was the only male in our crudely decorated but spacious three-story dwelling that sat atop a disused restaurant. Louis studied at the London School of Economics, had radical political views and a room to himself so he could bed all the females he wanted. We were all in our early twenties and the flat buzzed every evening with literary and political discussions. Most evenings Louis would run up and down the staircase to the toilet completely in the nude, in full view of us all, and it was not unusual for him to walk into our rooms to chat while totally naked. He had an uncanny resemblance to Oliver Reed without the scars on his face, but had hair growing from an area around his tailbone that was half the length of a horsetail. We all had a crush on him, but I also had a crush on one of the hairdressers, the younger sister, Katherine.

Kate was a stunner. Lanky tall with long red hair, unable to sit in the sun for fear of extreme sunburn to her fair, freckled skin. Her behaviour was outrageous. She'd run around the flat in her underwear, perch precariously on the window ledges and flirt with men in the bar of the Green Shamrock pub across the road from us. Her voice was raunchy and she laughed like a hyena, which attracted attention whenever we went out. She looked and sounded like Katherine Hepburn and dressed in pants and jeans most of the time.

It took over a year working in London, before I was able to visit one of my favourite cities, Paris. By late 1969 I was on my way by train through the French Jura Mountains to live and work in St Imier, near Lausanne, Switzerland. I was able to spend ten wonderful days in an apartment on the rue de Narbonne in the 7th *arrondissement*. I was a typical tourist, visiting Montmartre and Sacré Cœur. I walked the stairs of the Eiffel Tower, viewed the *Mona Lisa* by Da Vinci, saw the dancers from the Folies Bergère and tasted frogs' legs. But there was no way I was going to eat snails after being pelted with them during my childhood.

In 1970, after working and living in Switzerland for six months, I returned to London to stay with Katherine and Rowena in Islington. During this brief time back in London, Kate and I began planning our return to Australia overland by bus. It was then I realised I loved Katherine with a passion. We were the same age, but somehow I was in awe of her. I wanted to wear clothes the way she did, but I wasn't quite tall enough. I was 5'6" and Katherine was over 6 foot, with a sense of style and acceptance of herself, warts and all. At this time my self-esteem was low and I had no real idea of who I was.

During our Sundowners bus trip from London to India, my passion for Katherine heightened. Her proximity to me didn't help. We sat next to one another on the bus and the journey lasted two months. The bus had serious mechanical breakdowns where we were stranded in hellholes of towns like Agri in Turkey for nearly a week. Walking down the main street to buy food and supplies at what were called shops became a tortuous affair. We ducked rocks thrown at us by the locals because they thought we were *Poms*. Thank goodness I brought supplies of Sorbent, as what was sold as toilet paper in Turkey was totally abhorrent. Katherine and I passed the time dressing up Steve and Bob, two of our fellow bus travellers, in women's' clothing. Katherine would do their makeup, their eyes with mascara and adorn their lips with the reddest of lipstick, and then we would have impromptu fashion parades to amuse the other bus travellers.

I did not know how to express my feelings of love for Katherine during the time we were travelling together across Europe, Greece, Turkey, Afghanistan, Pakistan, Iran, India and Nepal. We purchased round discs of hashish in Herat, Afghanistan, and would get stoned together while sitting on the floor of the toilet. We'd listen to the flush, which we thought sounded like a waterfall. During the bus trip we continued smoking our hash pipes as we travelled through countries that had the death penalty for those who got caught with drugs. Then from Bangkok we travelled in different directions. Katherine continued her journey to Bali, totally unaware of my love for her.

I flew from Bangkok home to Sydney, desperately homesick and suffering with a severe form of dysentery from the overland trip. I was hardly recognised by my friends and family at the airport, wearing my hand-made silk pants suit. I got my stash of hashish resin through customs in my *Modess* tampon boxes! Thankfully there were no sniffer dogs at Mascot in 1970.

> *Security is when everything is settled, when nothing can happen to you: security is the denial of life.*
> – Germaine Greer, Australian author and feminist

In the late 1980s, a few years after my father died, I was constantly questioning my existence and my purpose in life. I had married in 1972 and my marriage was now failing. I was experiencing extreme stress and panic attacks. My GP suggested I undertake self-assertiveness training at Merrylands Community Centre, close to where I was living with my husband and two sons. On arriving at the centre I met Darlene, a woman slightly older than me. After our initial conversation, I realised she was fiercely passionate and believed every woman should be assertive and not be walked over by any males in their lives.

During the next five to ten years Darlene played a major part in nurturing my passion for women. I completed my self-assertiveness training courses and began movement therapy with Darlene. At her suggestion, I went on to undertake a course of six rebirthing sessions with a group called 'Mandorla' using rebirthing and breathwork techniques developed by Stanislav Grof. The term 'Mandorla' referred to the 'mandala', a Sanskrit word meaning 'a circle'. At the end of a session the participant was encouraged to draw a mandala symbolising their experience. Through this rebirthing process I began to learn about myself and the spiritual connection to my femininity. I came to the realisation that I didn't like myself and found it difficult to communicate with women without feeling sexual.

I attended intensive weekends in Eastwood with other women. These weekends were organised by Darlene and comprised of movement therapy, sand play, meditation and freestyle painting or drawing. Women attending were challenged by Darlene to be totally honest about how they were feeling. Up until then, I had usually answered *fine* to everything asked of me. I also found it very difficult to ask for something just for myself, and I had become very resentful of my family for not allowing me much time for myself. These gatherings became extremely important to me. They gave me the opportunity to find out who I really was.

After the initial course of rebirthing sessions, I felt so connected to my body that I was able to finally have a full body massage. Then in my forties, I'd never had one before, and eventually, in a room lit only by candles, I was able to disrobe and have a massage completely naked. I found myself changing in the movement therapy classes. At the beginning I was unable to move my body at all. I would just lie down on the floor and cry. Gradually, over time I would stand up and allow my body to sway to the music, slowly at first, but as the music changed I would close my eyes and move all over the room, sometimes hitting people with my arms. It was the most freeing experience I had ever been involved in, and it changed my life for the better. Darlene had an enthusiastic and energetic ability to find the right music, putting songs together in such a way that it brought emotions out of people attending the classes. She also made the environment safe, even when men came along to do inner work with the groups of women.

I formed strong and passionate bonds with two other women, Mary and Evelyn. I sat alongside them during rebirthing sessions; these sessions could be very traumatic and confronting. Music was played while each person reclined on a mattress. In a way the music allowed the participants to relax and cross over into their unconscious minds. I remember finishing a rebirthing session and experiencing a profound feeling of being born. I went through a physical process of moving down the birth canal of my mother. I later wrote in my journal that I experienced a feeling of not being wanted by my mother. I went on to write that during my birth my mother was in a lot of pain and not prepared for the trauma of childbirth.

I continued working with Darlene until the early 90s. I kept in touch with Mary and Evelyn as well, finding it much easier to work and communicate with other women by then. In 1992 I felt strong enough through having done the inner work with Darlene to commence Tertiary preparation at Granville TAFE. I had left school at fourteen and gone to business college at the insistence of my mother, and was working in a full-time job as a secretary by the age of fifteen. I had always wanted to go to university and regretted not going further with my studies. Now I had the opportunity in my late forties to complete a university degree.

> ... I am a woman in the prime of life, with certain powers
> and those powers severely limited
> by authorities whose faces I rarely see.
> – Adrienne Rich, from 'I Dream I'm the Death of Orpheus', 1968

When Adrienne Rich wrote the above poem, I was twenty-one and living in London. Now it was 1995, I was forty-eight and felt in the prime of my life. What better time to begin a university degree in English Literature and accept my sexual difference. I was to study a plethora of French female writers such as Simone de Beauvoir and Anaïs Nin during the next five years of my degree.

I had separated from my husband by then and was living with my sons still in the family home near Parramatta. It was time to come out. I was encouraged by Susannah, a friend from college, to find a partner. She dared me to put an ad in LOTL (Lesbians on the Loose). After much deliberation on words to put in my ad, I sent it in with the title 'Coming out late in life'. I described myself as tall, fit with an athletic body, hazel eyes, salt-and-pepper hair, and possessing an eclectic taste in music. I mentioned I was beginning a degree in English Literature at Macquarie University, specialising in Women's Studies and Creative Writing.

I was not prepared for the response from interested lesbians, and after much culling of crappy replies I often drove from my home in Western Sydney to meet with prospective partners in the inner city of Sydney. My first meeting was with Nola at the Stanmore McDonalds restaurant, situated on Parramatta Road, not far from RPA Hospital. Nola told me on the telephone she would be sitting at the first right-hand table from the entrance, reading the *Sydney Morning Herald*. I found her, sat down, and Nola immediately told me she was not attracted to me, but would like to further a friendship. We spent a few hours exchanging our life histories. Nola lived close by in a one-room studio apartment. She had been involved with the Catholic Church and loved singing. She invited me to join her later for choir practice in preparation of a choral performance. I got the impression Nola had a wealthy family but they did not accept her lesbianism. I knew how that felt. There was no way I'd be able to tell my mother anything about my new lifestyle.

Needing a place to meet and mix with other lesbians, I found the Lesbian Space in Newtown. Beatrice, my mother's aunt, had lived close by this area in Australia Street with her grey and pink galah Henry and her alcohol-soaked husband Oliver. My mother had dragged me along practically every week of my childhood to visit my great-aunt Beatrice; she always produced the best cup of Billy Tea with six sugars. The tea always came with small plates laden with my favourite Arnott's Milk Arrowroot biscuits lathered with real Norco butter.

Childhood memories flooded in as I drove from the western suburbs most weekends to the Space at Newtown. A woman I gravitated to on most visits was Virginia, a tall, fierce, redheaded, strangely dressed individual. Virginia eagerly wanted me to join the African drumming group preparing for Mardi Gras the following March. She asked, 'Have you ever drummed Di?'

'I was never allowed to make a noise when I was growing up. Even when I played really good classical music on the stereo, my mother would demand I turn the sound down. I do remember wanting a drum kit!'

'Well, here's your chance. These pottery drums are fabulous and don't cost an arm and a leg. Give them a try before the other girls arrive for their lesson.'

Within a few weeks of visiting the Space I joined the drumming group, I was hooked and found myself signing up to drum at Mardi

Gras (the annual gay pride parade). Something happened when I held the small pottery drum between my legs. The rhythms, the sound vibrating within the room contributed to a feeling of connection with the other women. It was infectious and I lost myself in the moment. Half the group played one rhythm while the other half played another, joining to make wonderful sounds. I was fortunate to have a musical background and a good ear, knowing if rhythms weren't in time. I drummed louder and louder until Virginia begged me to calm down.

My passion for drumming was turning me into a crazy and very loud woman, but I had no hope of calming down. My life before personal inner work had been subdued and controlled by others. The movement therapy with Darlene had opened up the connection between my brain and body. I could move freely and passionately without feeling judged by others. Drumming made things better for me. It gave me an instrument to express the passion inside my body. Virginia saw this, encouraging me to begin the rhythm with a special call to let the other women know the piece was beginning. 'Go Di, let it all out, and tell everyone we are about to make a lot of noise. Go wild Diana!'

Mardi Gras came around so fast. Before I had a chance to say no, I was standing in Elizabeth Street beside Hyde Park with a huge white conga drum strapped around my waist, trying to hide my face from any cameras flashing from the crowd. I had never done anything like this before. The group I was drumming in had a strange name beginning with the word *Lemon*, an image of which was emblazoned on our T-shirts. I had no idea what the word meant in a lesbian context, maybe sour, bittersweet, juicy or tart. All I could think of was, what if my mother sees me on television? As if my mother watched Mardi Gras!

Virginia appeared on the night dressed entirely in black with sturdy Doc Martin boots, colourful socks and long shorts that came just below her knees. She had already participated with the Dykes on Bikes at the beginning of the parade. Her top had the sleeves cut off; they looked like they had been cut with a serrated knife. Her red hair was freshly coloured with henna and Celtic tattoos adorned her arms in circular patterns. Virginia yelled at me, 'If you don't stop that jumping Di, I'll be calling you Tigger.'

'Who's a tigger, Virginia?'

'You are, Di. Like Tigger in *Winnie the Pooh*! Jumping all around with that smile on your face. How long did it take you to come out? Forty-eight years! You'll be called a baby dyke, Di. That's what we call the new girls, or in your case the new older girl.'

The next day I looked at my hands. They were double their normal size. I had drummed so vigorously and hit my hands so hard on the edge of the conga drum, it was lucky I had not done more damage to them. I rang Virginia, hoping to get some sympathy. She answered, 'You'll get used to it. Have you got any Tiger Balm? That works for me. You're not letting the sound lift up from the drum. You're pushing the sound down into the earth. You could also do with a proper drum. There's a great place on Parramatta Road near Camperdown, Drum City. Check it out next weekend. You'll find something there. Look for a Djembe, an African drum.'

Sixteen years later, after many Mardi Gras, International Women's Day marches and lesbian dances in the Blue Mountains, I received a late-night phone call. 'Di, it's Sue … Virginia is dead, she's dead, hit and run over by an idiot on Parramatta Road.'

'No, Sue, it can't be true.'

'She was on the way to a Dykes on Bikes meeting for Mardi Gras, turned into Annandale Road in the bus lane on her scooter.'

'It's not fair. I'm sure she was younger than me, early sixties. That's too young. She had so much passion. She had so much more to give.'

> *… I miss you. I want you. Take me deep within your cavern.*
> *Come and lay beside me on my bed.*
> – Diana Wilde 1995

Carla was the second woman I contacted from replies to my ad in LOTL magazine in 1995. I immediately felt a connection with her.

We completed the obligatory greetings, chat and dinner in Newtown, then coffee at her flat in Dulwich Hill. We listened to George Benson singing 'Masquerade', which was Carla's favourite song. It was late and I still had to drive back to the western suburbs, so I thanked Carla for a great evening, stood up and she hugged me.

At that moment I fell in love with her, losing all sense of reason. I became besotted. She was about the same height, had a petite figure and loads of nervous energy. I remember that night, her skipping along the road as we made our way towards the Thai restaurant on King Street in Newtown. Carla's eyes were chocolate brown with soft centres. They constantly stared into my soul. As we said goodbye on that first night, her hug was so comforting, so electric; I felt a surge of heat through my body like never before. No one had given me this feeling before, not even a man. I was totally hooked.

The next morning I rang her to ask if we could meet again. She agreed to meet me at the Japanese Gardens in Auburn. I had butterflies in my stomach all the previous night and that morning, right up to meeting her in the gardens. She was wearing a cerise top with three-quarter sleeves and black jeans. The top accentuated the delicate line of hair fluffing towards the nape of her gamin-like neck, and her petite but fully rounded breasts. I walked towards her and extended my arms. She accepted them and I hugged her close to my body, feeling the same rush of fierce heat that had overcome me the night before.

We had only walked a short way when I blurted out, 'Come home to my place. It's not far from here.' Carla didn't reply straight away so I added, 'We could pick up some lunch on the way. There's a great Chinese Restaurant at Merrylands, near the station. Do you know Merrylands?'

Carla kept walking ahead of me. All of a sudden she turned around and faced me, but kept walking backwards. 'OK, but I can't stay long. I have to get back to Sydney. I have a mountain of paperwork to finish before work on Monday.' Carla followed me in her car, and later told me she was a State Government Advocate who inspected NSW

Nursing Homes. It was a full-time position plus she was completing a social science degree part-time at UTS in Broadway.

Together we arrived at my blonde-brick suburban house. It had been a couple of years since my husband Vince had agreed to leave. My two sons were still living with me and my college friend Susannah was renting a bedroom. My nineteen-year-old eldest son Luke lived in the garage. He and my other son Jonathan had said very little when I told them I had put an ad in a lesbian magazine. Now I was bringing a woman home and going straight into my bedroom.

I had spent much of my life dreaming about a moment like this, but had never done anything about it until now. What followed for the next four days and three nights felt natural for me, an intense and passionate experience I had been waiting for my entire life.

Perhaps it is better to wake up after all, even to suffer, rather than to remain a dupe to illusions all one's life.
– Kate Chopin, *The Awakening*

Nine months had passed since my older cousin Rhonda had disclosed to me on that humid and hot day in January 2012 that I had been adopted from birth. She had held on to this family secret for almost sixty years. My birth mother, then known as Carol Ann Parsons, was aged nineteen when I had been born and had agreed that I be adopted by Rita and Oscar Larkin. My original birth certificate showed I had been named Sharon Lea by my mother.

Since I had become aware I was adopted, I had begun the process through the Salvation Army to try and find my birth mother. They discovered my birth records were amongst thousands that had been destroyed during the 1940s, and suggested I contact the Benevolent Society in Hurstville.

I became frustrated and began trying to uncover the details myself. After several weeks of research, I discovered my mother's name in family history records on the internet. I passed this information on to my contact at the Benevolent Society. Due to their persistence, my birth mother was found through the electoral roll. She was now eighty-four, went by the name of Colleen Dawson and resided in a nursing home built beside a retirement village in Cootamundra. I was advised she had a power of attorney, a niece called Sandra. Upon contact, this person refused to believe I was Colleen's birth child and threatened to physically harm me if I tried to visit my mother. She told me Colleen had Alzheimer's and was very unwell, too unwell to be asked any questions concerning me.

Even so, I decided to attempt to visit my birth mother.

I was now on my way to Cootamundra with my cousin Rhonda and her husband Bob, to visit and finally meet the woman who had given birth to me. I felt time was running out. Bob, who had known me for over fifty years, had become like a brother to me since I had been told of my adoption. Even though he encouraged me to meet my mother and assured me it would be OK to visit, a feeling of tiredness and fear swept over my body. My *joie de vivre* was severely dampened by the long 500 kilometre drive. Thoughts of what may happen when we arrived rolled around in my brain.

On our arrival, I dragged myself out of the car and walked the short distance to the sliding doors of the nursing home. Inside was a cubicle where an elderly, officious-looking man sat answering enquiries. I waited patiently until he asked me how he could help. I asked, 'Is there a Colleen Dawson here?'

'Well, you're in luck. She was transferred from the main hospital only yesterday. Just go in and ask the girls on the desk. They'll show you to her room.'

For a moment I nearly said her maiden name that was on my birth certificate, Carol Ann Parsons, realising seconds later that she was known by her married name and now also used Colleen, a different Christian name. I felt like I was walking through a time warp, not knowing why or what I was doing in this rather plush, motel-looking building. Rhonda and Bob smiled at me as we walked through the doors into the reception area.

I felt disorientated. 'Rhonda, what if they ask me who I am?'

'It's going to be OK, Di, just say you're a friend from when she lived in Sydney.'

'But what if they ask me my name?'

'Use mine if you like.'

I waited until a young woman came over to the counter. 'How can I help you?'

'I was hoping to see Colleen Dawson. We're from Sydney. I knew her a long time ago.'

'Of course, she's just up the hallway on the left. I'll get a nurse to take you to her room.'

Within seconds we were being escorted to my birth mother's room. Rhonda put her arm around me and Bob just grinned uncontrollably. At no time did they ask who I was or how I knew Colleen. We walked the 50 metres or so up the hallway. 'Here she is. Colleen, you have some visitors from Sydney.'

On a plain hospital bed sat a bright, vivacious and cheerful woman, with grey-white flowing hair, backlit by the sun streaming through a small window behind her. The light gave her skin a translucency, accentuating the blue veins in her neck and arms, leading down to large hands and ending with long, tapered fingers. She gesticulated with her hands, inviting me inside the sun-filled room. Her body language had an eagerness to communicate with us, and she did not take her eyes off me. 'Come in, please come in, come over close to the bed where I can see you.' Her soft and passionate plea snapped me back to reality. For a moment I couldn't move. All I could think of was that this was the woman who gave birth to me, and I was only seeing her now for the first time, nearly sixty-five years later. Rhonda and Bob urged me to go forward. I walked right over to her and she grabbed my hand. I noticed how blue her eyes were. Colleen had a long body, draped in a powder-blue nightgown. She kept moving from side to side. 'I've got a sore on my bottom. The nurses have to get me out of bed soon, and sit me on my lovely chair.'

I remarked, 'That's no good. I can go to the nurses' station if you wish.' I noticed the large poster behind her bed with *COLLEEN* written in texta pen. I began to feel overcome with emotion, so much so that I felt I had to get out of the room or I would burst into tears. But I stayed.

Bob then asked Colleen about the photos on her bedside table. 'Is that you, Colleen?

'Yes, and that's George, the love of my life. He died only a couple of years ago.' She pointed at the other photos. 'That's me when I was about seventy-five. My hair was shorter and a reddish colour.' She looked vibrant and active. I was struggling to hold back the tears still. It had only been a few minutes, but felt like hours.

'We might go now, Colleen, and visit tomorrow on our way back to Sydney.'

She pulled my hand again. 'Don't go yet.'

'We'll be back tomorrow. You need to get that sore on your bottom looked at. I'll let the nurse know on our way out.' I turned quickly, waved to my mother and strode up the hallway. One of the staff at the desk asked me if they could tell Sandra, my mother's power of attorney, who had visited. I loudly proclaimed, 'I don't know Sandra. I knew Colleen a long time ago, when she lived in Sydney. We'll visit tomorrow morning on our way back to the Mountains.'

The woman at the desk didn't ask me anything else. She nodded and I turned and found the exit. My head was spinning. I again felt disorientated. I had no sense of direction. My tired brain was filled with so many thoughts. I just wanted to get to my room, lie on the bed and sob my heart out. Rhonda and Bob walked either side of me, helping me get to the car. I said softly, 'I cannot believe what has just happened. That was my mother who gave birth to me. Why didn't anyone tell me before this, before she became ill? I would have liked to have known her when she was younger.' I cried and cried and cried, sobbing so violently that my sobs became louder and louder. It wasn't far to the motel we had planned to stay at, so I didn't put on my seatbelt I just lay across the backseat, howling.

Early the next day, after another cup of terrible coffee at a local café in the main street of Cootamundra, we went back to the nursing home. No one stopped us as we walked up the hallway to Colleen's room. I smiled and waved to an elderly woman who poked her head out of the doorway before my mother's room. Colleen's hair was pulled back in a ponytail; she looked drawn and tired in the face. Like the day before, she did not take her eyes off me. 'Give me a cuddle.'

I was taken aback. Oh OK, I can do that, I thought. Colleen extended her long arms towards me as I cautiously came over to her bed. She enveloped me with long gangly arms and kissed me on both cheeks. I hugged her fondly and smelled the comforting smell of Johnson's baby powder, the same powder my adopted mother Rita sprinkled on me when I was little. I wanted so much to blurt out who I was. Nothing came out of my mouth. Still holding her hands, I gazed into those eyes again, feeling them pierce my heart right through to my soul. Her eyes were pale blue to grey. She had looked better and brighter yesterday, welcoming us and wanting us to come in.

Colleen said, 'Your hands are cold.'

'It's cold outside; there's a cold wind. Did you have pets, Colleen?'

'Oh yes, I've always had dogs and cats. There are some kittens outside. Would you take them home for me? Better move your car before the kids come in.'

'Do you remember me from yesterday?'

Colleen replied, 'Yes. I have a sore on my bottom.'

Holding back tears again, I put the flowers I had specially chosen at the florist shop, next to her bed. She smiled. 'The flowers will be better tomorrow when the buds come out.' I watched her hands. Mine were the same size and so were my fingers. This is whom I inherited my octave-plus two hands from.

My cousin Rhonda quietly remarked to me, 'Your mother has beautiful translucent skin, Di. Be happy. This is what you'll look like when you reach her age. You have the same mouth and facial structure.' Colleen then asked Rhonda and Bob for a cuddle.

I asked, 'Can I take a photo, Colleen?'

'Yes, of course.' I grabbed my phone and quickly asked Bob to take a photo of me beside my mother. My mother didn't smile and became quite serious.

I whispered, 'Rhonda I think we should go. I don't think she is feeling too well.'

'OK, Di. Let's try and come back again before Christmas, after you get back from Paris.'

Life shrinks or expands according to one's courage.
– Anaïs Nin

One month later by mid-October I was in Paris working on my memoir. I was sharing an apartment with Louise in rue Descartes on the Left Bank within walking distance of rue de Montparnasse, Le Procope and Café de Flore, places that Simone de Beauvoir, Anaïs Nin, Colette, Adjuna Barnes and Gertrude Stein frequented.

During the early part of my life I had been terrified of women, mainly from growing up with my fiercely controlling adoptive mother Rita. Deep within my being, even at a young age, it had seemed impossible that she was my real mother. Many times at night I would climb out my bedroom window at the back of the house and sit in the backyard with my fox terrier Tracy and ask the moon and stars to tell me why I lived in that house with this family.

During most of my life I was encouraged by my accepting Aunt Rose to be myself. And then in my forties, after my divorce and much self-analysis, I had begun to embrace my innate sexual difference and passion for women.

I was now meandering through the Paris streets like a child slushing through mud puddles. I began daydreaming about the journey that would unfold when I returned to Sydney on November 4th 2012, the day of my sixty-fifth birthday.

Passion

for

Family

Roslyn Phillips

They Met in Paris

ROSLYN PHILLIPS

Roslyn is a singer/songwriter, and started writing poetry and song lyrics at a very early age. Some of her childhood short stories about 'Shalala the Cat' and 'America and the Goat' still remain in the family archives. So it wasn't such a stretch for her to travel to Paris to participate in a writing course. It was an exciting way for her to explore Paris and it turned out to be a very fulfilling and rewarding experience. The camaraderie and friendship of the women on the course was so supportive and the collaboration was a wonderful bonding experience. She hopes you enjoy her offering in this 'Passion' anthology.

As I stood with my youngest daughter waiting at the check-in gate to board our flight to Paris, I couldn't help but think of the family I was leaving behind. My wonderful, large, loving family that has expanded over time with husbands, children, grandchildren, lovers, great friends and a few family pets. As I stood there, I found myself also thinking about that hot Australian summer day when my first child came into the world and my own little family came into being. I did not know then that my own family would swell to four children, and at the time of writing this I have nine amazing, wonderful grandchildren. I am also anticipating a great-grandchild to arrive before the end of this year.

What a lucky wonderful life I am living.

The sun dribbled down over the road like warm honey dripping from your fingers to your elbows from a hot crumpet – sweet, hot and sticky. I waddled slowly from the local phone box, moving sluggishly to the relative cool of the house. It was a struggle. My big tummy didn't seem to want to move in the same direction as the rest of me. When I got to the house I unlocked the door and made it as far as the lounge room. There I inched myself backwards onto the lounge and tried to catch my breath. Time warped, bent and buckled, and after some time it cooled. I lay back down on the lounge as the first indications of a miracle about to happen ripped through me.

My husband arrived home from work and I told him it was time. Time for life. We drove carefully to the hospital in the early evening, labour pains pulsating and rippling through my body, and after an impossibly short time, my son was born. And just like that, a family had happened. My son arrived, calmly keeping his watchful eye on everything around him. He was curious, and independent and as he grew older he seemed to make friends easily.

Family comes to us in many different ways. Most often it starts with a mum and dad – a young couple – and a desire to reproduce themselves. Babies immediately attach themselves to your heartstrings and start playing you like a beautiful and ancient song. They wear you out and when they have totally exhausted and drained you, that's when they know they have you. Maybe it's their total dependence on you, their fragility that welds your heart to theirs. However it happens, it is a powerful bond.

Not long after my son was born, along came my first daughter. She was bright and bubbly and sprinkled with beautiful freckles, such a cutie. Over the years those freckles caused much heartache and many questions, and she begged me to tell her when my freckles had faded. Somehow I had lots of ginger freckles as a child, but they faded when I was about sixteen or seventeen. She assures me that hers didn't.

Another daughter, beautiful and olive skinned, was born with a shock of black hair that rapidly disappeared, leaving a beautiful soft golden blonde halo. It amazed me that her hair could change so quickly and be such a totally different colour. She was a different temperament too – she was calm and quiet, contemplative.

And finally a third daughter, my fourth child, was born. She was an actress from birth, busily dressing up and playing pantomime. She was interested in everything, chattered away about anything and demanded a lot cuddles and attention. She constantly entertained our little family. And so my family was complete.

I haven't written much about my children. Their stories are their own to tell. But I have been very proud of their achievements over the years. They have shown me what multi-faceted diamonds they all are.

My father was an oysterman. He was born in Port Macquarie in the 1920s into a family of ten children, which made him a very social and independent man. Oystering is a warm-weather occupation when the oysters are harvested, bagged and sent down to Sydney for sale at the fish markets. At this time of year my father and his brothers had to move quickly as there was limited time to get the oysters out of their beds and off to market, making sure that they remained fresh. During the winter months when the oysters were slowly growing and required minimal handling in the beautiful tides of Limeburners Creek, Dad, his father and brothers went logging in the tall growth forests of the mid-north coast of New South Wales. They had an affinity for the bush and for nature, and were very comfortable in the earthiness of the forests. They lived rough in those cold and rugged conditions, sleeping around a small fire in a lean-to built of corrugated iron and saplings. They would be up at dawn to start the very heavy work of felling trees by hand, talking and laughing and singing as they went.

As they worked, a close bond was formed between father and sons and brothers, and at the end of each day after they had cooked and eaten their very basic meals around the campfire, my grandfather 'Griddy' would pull out the harmonica and play a few tunes. Such was the building of family life in Australia in the 1930s. In those times, people did not have much in the way of material things, but they knew they were loved and they knew they were part of a family unit, unbreakable.

As children, my many siblings and I went to Port Macquarie every year for our Christmas holidays. It was important for Dad to visit family and to check on his ageing parents. My uncle, one of Dad's brothers often came as well and he slept on a camp stretcher in the garage at our rented holiday house. He was always on hand to teach us to fish, go yabbying for bait, swim and surf in the beautiful beaches around Port. Our communal toilet was a large kerosene tin far up in the backyard with a seat attached, and many a time Dad and Uncle Lenny would have to go 'kangaroo hopping' as they called it, to empty the loo tin. There was no sewerage back in those days in our holiday home. Our shower was a bucket with holes in the bottom.

The trick was to get under the bucket quickly enough to get wet enough to wash yourself.

Our holiday was always spent in the same cottage every year, and we learned to live with trapdoor spiders in the backyard, horrible things that we had to navigate around and that seemed to come crawling out of their burrows when the sun went down. We older children slept on the back veranda of the tiny cottage, and often when we awoke in the morning, it seemed that most of the local wildlife had kept us company during the night. Bats and frogs, spiders and geckos would be either stuck in the mosquito netting over our beds or on the floor scurrying to get away from us.

Back in those early years prawning at Lake Cathie took on memorable proportions, and I can remember a year when all of Dad's brothers came down to Cathie to go prawning in the lake. Dad had lots of brothers and sisters, and that year when the prawns ran they all came down to Cathie to help us catch, cook and eat prawns as well as taking away enough prawns to last their families for days. Since we didn't have enough saucepans to cook the quantity of prawns we had caught, we used kerosene tins and cooked them on stove tops and over fires on the back lawn, the entire extended family working together to cook up a great feed of prawns. Bench tops, the dining table and every other available flat surface in the kitchen and lounge room combined were hidden under mounds of prawns cooling on trays. We ate them for weeks, fresh cooked, curried, with vegetables – any way we could find.

One of my most precious memories is sitting on the grass in our backyard at home with my dad one starry night. I'm not sure why it was just him and me on this night, because I have so many siblings and it was extremely unusual to have him all to myself. But on this night as we talked and looked at the stars, he explained to me that light takes time to travel, so the star that we were looking at might have exploded many years before but the light from it was still travelling towards us. So we still see the star as it was before the light set off on its journey to us, not necessarily as it is now. I remember the 'Eureka' moment when I actually understood the concept that he was trying to teach me. Dad worked hard to give each of his children those special 'one on one' moments, whether it was taking us to the footy, helping us with music or even allowing the brothers to use the 'good' oil for their cars.

Friends – sometimes it is a chance meeting with a stranger, someone who embroiders their story on your heart, which creates that unbreakable bond. These friendships fill up the corners of your life, making you feel comfortable and wonderful. Friends comfort you, scold you, advise you, but most of all they are just with you. And it feels good. Schoolyard friendships often last a lifetime and I am lucky to have made a few such long-time friends, whom I met in primary school. These friendships are as cyclic as the seasons and sometimes you are in touch often, chatting and gossiping, catching up on each other's lives and yet at other times life gets in the way and you talk rarely, not having time to return that phone call or email. But when you do manage to reconnect, it's as though you have never had a pause in the conversation.

One such friendship began for me in primary school. Children find it easy to make friends because there is no subterfuge, no filtering of personalities. My friend and I became best friends, staying over at each other's house for sleepovers, walking up to school together. She even taught me to cook a 'fry up' which consisted of putting chops, sausages, onions and tomatoes into a frying pan and cooking it all up together. When everything was just about done, she would throw in a couple of eggs to cook in the fat from the chops and sausages giving them a tasty flavour.

One day we asked my parents if we could go to the Royal Easter Show at the Sydney Showground, the original one at Moore Park. I remember it vividly because it was the first event my parents ever allowed me to go to. Dad was very strict with his daughters. My friend and I had spent quite a bit of time working out what we were going to wear. My outfit was a white t-shirt with long culotte-style trousers that I had made myself. I bought the fabric – green crepe with a large rose pattern – and cut the trousers out myself. Then I used Mum's big, heavy industrial sewing machine to put it all together and they turned out reasonably well. My friend had also made her trousers. They were very stylish corduroy black and white print, and were hipsters. How great was that? We felt really fashionable and trendy and of course, very grown-up.

Another primary school friend and I spent a lot of time singing – she was an excellent singer. She had a natural ability to sing and a very tuneful voice, while I struggled. My voice was naturally low and husky. My dad called me 'gravel voice' as I found it difficult to hit high notes. We learnt lots of modern songs with plenty of harmonies, and while she sang the higher lilting melodies I growled out the bass lines and lower parts. We had so much fun that we formed a vocal group with a few other girls from our primary school and travelled around to all the nursing homes in our suburb where we sang for the elderly residents. One wonderful memory was when an elderly lady in a retirement home asked us to sing 'When I Grow Too Old to Dream'. This wasn't a song in our repertoire, but we learnt it for next time that we went. I think our audience was appreciative, but maybe they were just being polite.

New friends or friends that you have had for a long time are all part of your family as they weave themselves into the tapestry of your life.

Dogs have a funny way of sneaking up on you becoming part of your family and part of your life. Without really trying, their story intertwines with yours and you realise that without them, the family would not be the same zany, crazy place that it is. Being so totally dependant on you for everything, they soon start to repay you with lots of love and sloppy kisses.

One lovely summer morning I was talking on the phone in my

lounge room. I was vaguely aware of a little tiny yelping sound in the distance but took no notice of it. As I finished the conversation I realised that a tiny little ball of snow-white fluff was trying to climb up the step and into my lounge room; it was this ball of fluff that was making the tiny sound. My yard was totally fenced off, so I had no idea where she had come from, and it seemed unlikely that she had crawled in from the street. I played with her for a little while before calling the number she wore on a disk around her neck, only to find that she belonged to a young girl in the block of units where I lived. Her name was GiGi, which stood for gorgeous girl, and she certainly was. My neighbour lived in a smaller unit and had no access to a yard. She said it would be difficult for her to keep GiGi who had been given to her as a gift a week ago. And so it came about that I fell hopelessly in love with this tiny white fluffy gem, my first ever dog.

GiGi was frisky and had a really lively personality that you often find in a Maltese Shih Tzu cross. She would sit on my lap and cuddle up, and loved running around the yard and bouncing into the house. She slept on my bed with me and in winter we cuddled down under the covers. Who would have thought I would allow a dog to do that? In my growing-up years my family had corgis but animals were only to be kept outdoors. But not GiGi. She felt as though she was another child taking the place of my children who had all left home. After some years it became harder to keep GiGi contained as she worked out more and more innovative ways to escape. Opening the garage door to put the car away after work each night became a lesson in strategy, trying to work out where she was and whether I was fast enough to catch her before she came flying out into the driveway and disappeared up the street like a tiny white fluffy Houdini.

I worked full-time and sometimes had to travel for up to a week at a time for my work. On these occasions I put GiGi into the Luxury Dog Resort that she seemed to love. A little holiday for her to play with her friends. GiGi used to bark when I was at work, as these small dogs often do. I started to receive anonymous letters from a neighbour typed in cold ugly font, advising me that I was a lousy thoughtless owner and that GiGi was distressed. As weeks turned into months the letters became more frequent and nastier. I was at a loss to know what to do. I purchased a system that emitted a high-pitched whistle whenever she barked which was supposed to stop her, but that didn't work. Then another system which sprayed citronella in her face whenever she barked. That worked while the citronella was kept up, but it seemed such a cruel thing that whenever she made a noise she would get a nose full of spray and even when a loud or sudden noise was made near her she would get sprayed. It made her become skittish and frightened of noises. I became more and more convinced that I was doing the wrong thing by her and that she would be better off with a family who loved her.

Eventually, after a particularly nasty letter and many sleepless nights, I made the decision to give her away. She deserved better, she would be happier with another family, she needed more attention than I could give, and she needed companionship. This was possibly one of the worst decisions I have ever made as even now – two years later – I still miss her every day, my poor little GiGi. She was a very much loved part of my family and it surprises me that such a tiny little dog could have had such a big personality and take up such a large space in my heart which is hard to fill now she is gone.

The rain tasted warm and tangy as it fell quietly and steadily, cleaning the Australian bush. Eucalypts and bracken alike were surrendering up their fresh scent. I had taken my children and a few of their cousins on a bushwalking adventure in the rain, and we followed the creek wandering down through the new suburb, exploring the bush and the half-built houses around our new estate. I had checked the children's clothes. They should have been wearing boots or sneakers, preferably something that won't puncture easily with twigs and sticks to protect their feet. They needed long-sleeved shirts to stop scratching from overhanging branches, and to make sure any spiders were easy to brush off before a bite. I have always felt comfortable walking in the bush.

This must have been because of the many bush walks with my father and siblings in my childhood where Dad taught us what to look out for, where the dangers were, how to love and enjoy the Aussie bush.

We were all ready and headed single file down into the bush and onto the creek bed. The bigger boys were at the front of the line and I brought up the rear. The creek was small and beautiful. It was mostly about six inches deep with a lovely clean sandy bottom so we could see patterns and swirls on the bed. As we rounded a bend in the creek, a small snake was awoken out of his slumber by our stomping footsteps. He was curled on the sandy bottom of the creek but his head was above the waterline. The children banked up as we came to a sudden stop. Obviously we needed to either get past him or turn back. Since we had come a fair distance and the road was not far up ahead, we decided to try to move past him. So I asked the children for something to throw at him. The idea was if I could throw a big rock slightly to the left of his head, he would dash back into the bush to the right, and we could all run past him and make our getaway. The kids looked around and found a small plastic and very lightweight cigarette lighter. Not really what I had in mind and certainly not large enough to make a big splash!

Finally, we found a large enough rock. I explained the procedure to them all and made sure everyone was ready. The larger boys were still at the front of the line, so that when they moved past, they could be the leaders and take us up to the road beyond. Holding my breath, I threw the rock slightly to the left of the snake. When the splash faded, he was nowhere to be seen. The kids ran on while I stood guard, making sure no one fell over. We made it to the road, and then ran home to safety. We had survived a new and never to be repeated adventure, a bush walk in our new estate, but it was not an adventure that I wanted to repeat often with my little family.

And I'm sure it was as a result of this exciting and terrifying experience that some time later my son asked if he could have a diamond python as a pet. He had lots of weird pets in his childhood. At one time he had an axolotl or Mexican walking fish. One night this poor little creature became sick and my son sat for hours, rubbing his tiny tummy to make him feel better. Incredibly it seemed to save his little life, since he recovered back to good health.

Food and eating is always on the list of family things to do and many cultures do this exceptionally well. Unfortunately for my mother, preparing and cooking food for so many people was a chore to be worked through as quickly as possible. She had many methods of cooking that I have never seen anybody else use. For example, whenever Dad brought home oysters fresh from the lake, she used to heat up a pan of water and vinegar and drop the oysters into it. They came out shrivelled and tangy but somehow creamy, and surprisingly after all these years I still find myself hungering for Mum's oysters, although I doubt anyone else would consider them a culinary delight. She also used to beat eggs for dinner and put leftover bread into the mix to make them go further, and then she would scramble them. She could stretch a meal of six eggs to feed ten people and they were yummy. We never had scrambled eggs for breakfast though, it was always a quick evening meal, maybe for a Sunday night when she wanted to get the evening meal over and done with, so she could sit and relax. Breakfast was always porridge or cereal, and she would put the oats into a saucepan of water to soak overnight. Then the following morning she would quickly boil them into porridge and serve it up, six steaming bowls on the kitchen table to be gobbled up before school.

The Italians I know are great at having large family gatherings and the wonderful thing about their recipes is that they all seem to feed a large family who do lots of laughing, talking, arguing and sharing all around the table. A lot of Italians in Australia still continue the age-old tradition of 'passata day', usually in January when the tomatoes are big and flavoursome and the family gets together to cook passata. The tomatoes are either boiled or steamed in huge pots and once they are cooked, they are peeled and puréed. Everybody had their own job.

Often the children washed basil leaves and one leaf is put into each jar to wait for the puréed passata to be poured over the top. Basil, garlic and oregano are sometimes added to give flavour and body to the passata. After all the hard work of the day and once all the purée had been bottled, it is time to test it, and so the family would then get together around the table for a big Italian meal. Homemade wine and pasta were the order of the day, and lots of laughter and love abounded.

Many Asian cultures also have traditions of gathering together at mealtimes to eat. Women often sit near the rice pot to serve rice to the rest of the family in individual bowls. The rest of the food is prepared in large dishes so that they can help themselves. This gave the family time to bond, for parents to find out what the children had been up to for the day, and for children to learn about how to conduct themselves in company. Young children play with their food, experimenting with taste and texture and possibly even the projectile properties of it, and older children can start to see the many different and delicious ways that food is prepared in their Asian cuisines.

Grandparents hold a special place within a family and it is such an honour to be involved. We are at a stage in life where we are not rushing through each day, doing the washing, cooking and feeding, and in a lot of cases grandparents are not working full-time outside the family home. We have a little more time to slow down and look around. And often that means we can babysit, or spend time with the grandchildren and teach them about their heritage and their history. In many cases grandparents are the custodians of the children's stories, their backgrounds and where they came from. Grandparents add to the knowledge of history, who they are and who their ancestors were.

Amazingly, in this wonderful voyage of life, I now have nine grandchildren. I have to admit this is a tad overwhelming at times but I love it. I love the chaos of having them all around playing, laughing, crying, being noisy and just being beautiful. I also suspect that this is not the end of my collection of grandchildren.

Looking at them through the tunnel of time and having the opportunity of comparing them with their parents, I am able to find the similarities and differences to how my own children were at that age. Their innocence and humour and bravery are just wonderful to experience, and since I know that my own children turned out OK, I have confidence in the future watching these young ones grow. I love to see them all interacting and connecting with each other and with the world around them as they learn about life.

When the first of the grandchildren came along I was trying to record all their sayings and their achievements. I started to keep little books on each grandchild, and when something memorable happened to them, I wrote it down. That lasted about two weeks, because I was forever writing up their exploits and as more and more grandchildren came along the job became more onerous. There is always some wonderful and memorable thing to write about for each of them; now I just leave it all to their parents. It is so much easier in these days of instant photographs and emails than having a paper trail to follow.

I remember my own mother kept a 'red book' and in it she wrote every important event that happened to each of us. This was quite amazing as she wasn't a literary type, never aspired to be a writer, but she wrote in the diary every significant event in her children's lives – new babies, new homes, new cars, new jobs, all got a mention. This was a fabulous and much appreciated record for us all.

One incident that remains in my mind and heart was a time when I had several of the grandchildren over for the weekend. We had a wonderful time playing at the beach, cooking muffins and pancakes and doing all the fun things that I would never do on my own. After they left I decided I needed a haircut so I went up to the local hairdresser, one that I hadn't been to before. I decided on a cut, shampoo and blow dry and discussed with the hairdresser what I needed. As I was explaining to her, she looked through my hair when suddenly – and at the top of her voice – she yelled 'You've got nits!' I was so embarrassed that I almost crawled out of the shop. But now my attitude is different. If your grandchildren have nits and you don't, you are just not close enough!

Children these days have so much more magic in their lives than we did growing up, and that is a good thing. Fireworks are so much more spectacular, computers are magical, books and television are interactive, but relationships are just as confusing as they always have been. People are not as predictable as computers and I often think that's where grandparents come in. To listen, to talk, to comfort and help children know that people all basically feel the same, and that at times we all are happy, sad, angry or nervous. Bringing life back to basics and making sure that our grandchildren know they are loved and there is always someone there to listen – that is our strength, I think. To help our grandchildren feel grounded and safe. And what an honour that is.

Some grandparents volunteer at school and are active in their community or church. As I still work full-time I don't volunteer and I feel that this is something missing in my life. I would love to be a canteen grandma helping out at school and watching the grandchildren go through the ranks. This cements your role as grandparent in their lives, and you find out who the grandchild's friends are, whom they are hanging out with, and it can be a very valuable thing to see who the grandchildren identify with.

Brothers are very useful organisms and I am doubly blessed to have a pair of them – twins. When they were born, they were identical so everyone struggled to tell them apart and things didn't improve over the years as they grew. We called them 'The Brothers', the singular being 'brother' or 'broth' which meant that even the laziest of us didn't have to work out who we were talking to. The generic term covered them both, and our family would not have been complete without them. Born into a family of girls, they were spoilt from the beginning by their sisters who thought they were cute, but mostly by our dad who thought he had won the lottery. As youngsters they received the pushbikes, scooters and every sort of fun toy that never materialised for us girls. And in later years, even cars were subsidised for the brothers. Luckily they were good-looking and loved their sisters. We were even occasionally allowed to ride the scooters but only if enough bribe money was offered!

I remember a time when my very useful and clever brothers, grown to men by this time, had replaced the smoke alarm at my mother's house. They were always making themselves useful and doing little essential chores for Mum and she doted on them. She saved up all the little chores that needed doing for the Brothers. On this occasion they replaced the alarm with a new improved model that was located in the kitchen. One rainy day when I was cooking dinner for Mum the alarm went off. Now you would anticipate that the alarm would go off only when it detected smoke in the kitchen – and given my culinary skills that would not be a rare event – but on this occasion it was steam that started it screaming. Mum and I jammed our fingers in our ears trying to stop the noise. I threw open the back door and grabbed a tea towel, furiously waving it under the alarm to try and stop it. But no luck. The alarm still blared. I grabbed a broom and gave the alarm a vigorous whack to try to dislodge it. It still screamed.

By now there was no smoke or even steam near the alarm but still it klaxonned on, filling up the house and even the whole neighbourhood with noise. I climbed on a chair to see what I could do, and finally managed to prise it from its cradle, still blaring. I threw it outside the sliding-glass back door onto the back balcony yet incredibly the sound was still as loud and violent as ever. I thought there must be a separate sound system. It was only when I climbed precariously back up on the chair with the incredible noise still screaming in my ears, that I finally found the old smoke alarm that my brothers had left on the very top of the kitchen cupboards. Instead of throwing it out, they had left it, hidden and charged, just waiting for some unsuspecting sister to come along and set it off.

Relationships with my sisters are some of the most cherished in my life although we don't see each other all quite as often any more. Life gets in the way and they all have their own grandchildren now. You can tell your sisters anything. They never judge you, and being around the same age, they can give you advice and opinions on all sorts of things. Unfortunately I ended up going to a different school to the rest of my sisters, so I always felt that I missed out on a lot of the fun. They were all so close, while I was 'the outsider'. I remember one fun event though, when I borrowed my sister's school uniform. I went to the railway station in my regular uniform, but then I changed into my sister's uniform and went to her school swimming carnival. I had a fabulous day watching all the events, barracking for my sisters and laughing at the joke.

I have three sisters and they all have very different personalities. One is funny, cute and talkative. She always has an interesting observation to make us all laugh. One is very competitive and works hard in her own business. The other works with autistic children and has a very generous and steady nature. They are diverse and it seemed that we played very different roles in our family. How wonderful that they are all my sisters, and that I can learn so much from all of them.

From my youngest sister I have learnt not to take myself so seriously; life is not so dire and worrying. You can have a laugh and lighten up without losing sight of the gravity of a situation.

From my middle sister I have learned to stick with things, not to give up, to try harder and work more consistently. I have learned to have a plan and work towards it, to make it happen.

From my older sister I have learnt to listen more carefully, not to judge people, and to be more compassionate. She is very courageous and works with autistic children. She has been in situations where she has been pushed in front of traffic, and even physically hurt while working with these children, yet still she is non-judgmental and continues to care for them.

One of my most vivid memories around the end of primary school was the day when one of my sisters almost blew up the house.

We had an above-ground swimming pool that was always green and slimy with algae, and she was mixing up the chlorine to chlorinate and clean the pool. Usually she put the chlorine into a bucket and turned on the cold water to mix it but Dad always put a tad of warm water to dissolve the chlorine faster and my sister decided it would be a good idea to mix a tad of warm water in too. Unbeknownst to her, someone had been using the hot water tap so when the water came out of the tap it was scalding hot instead of slightly warm. When she turned the hot tap on boiling water hit the chlorine which blew up in her face. The explosion was massive, the noise incredible. The stench of chlorine permeated all through the house, making my eyes water. I couldn't breathe. Mum was screaming at me to get out of the house, so with my heart pounding in my ears I grabbed my brother's hand and made a run for the front door and the safety of the street out the front. Neighbours all came running out into the street to see what had caused the explosion. Chaos ensued, Mum and Dad trying to make sure that my sister hadn't blinded herself or injured herself in any way. Some how – incredibly – she was fine, but the memory of that event is still powerfully imprinted on all our minds, even after all these years.

Lovers – I don't think I'm particularly good at being a lover. It seems that I break my heart over and over. Mum and Dad met and married fairly early in their lives and we children came along quite quickly and with monotonous regularity, so although they were happily married and probably considered themselves to be lovers, they gave us no experience of the excitement and devastation of true love. I guess I thought love was meant to be two people just plodding along with a common goal, trusting and liking each other, which in turn was a version of love. I followed in my parents' footsteps. I met a really lovely guy when I was just fourteen and embarked upon a journey to build a family, create a home and live happily ever after.

We married and started to build that dream; after a mere five years of both of us working hard at two jobs, we had built our first dream home. It was in the beautiful Blue Mountains in New South Wales and we loved it there, although the commute to Sydney for work was hard. After a period of time along came our four beautiful children, and things went from being merely busy to absolute chaos.

My husband was a musician so on top of working at a regular day job, he spent most Friday and Saturday nights playing in his band. His band often played extra nights some weeks so it seemed to me now that we didn't spend much time together. New Year's Eve was the most lucrative night of the year but I've always thought that it was overrated and I usually spent most of them babysitting or on my own. I remember sitting in my family room one New Year's Eve after the kids were in bed and opening a bottle of champagne. It was simultaneously the best and loneliest New Year's Eve I have ever experienced. I poured five glasses of champagne for my absent friends and then proceeded to drink them. When I had finished, I washed up the glasses and went to bed. It was 10 pm.

So I was totally unprepared when someone came along who found me attractive, and then worked exceptionally hard for over eighteen months to make me pay attention. It didn't seem possible that anyone could fall in love with a woman with four children, and I guess that was the challenge for my new man. I met him at a very convenient part-time job that I had, and which I was enjoying very much. I felt that I was contributing not only to my family finances but also to the company that I was working for. I was feeling worthwhile. Now that I am older and wiser, I realise that to save my family and the life I had chosen, I should have left that job and found a new position, one that wouldn't have had such catastrophic results on my family and my life. But hindsight is twenty-twenty vision, as they say.

Because this love appeared to be so thrilling and exciting, I actually considered it. I felt as though for the first time in my life someone was actually listening to me, someone valued my opinion, someone wanted to know me – the real me. When I arrived at work each morning there was a little something on my desk – just a small flower picked from its accidental sanctuary on the side of the road, or a new pen, or a tiny drawing of a bug! Yes, even bugs seemed romantic.

Then came the insistence of the first date. This was a tricky one, because as a mother and wife and part-time worker, I didn't have a lot of spare time. It also caused me to delve very deeply into my feelings and to work out what I wanted out of my life. I was aware that this was a turning point, that this step once taken would not be able to be undone. While I loved being a wife and mum, who doesn't feel that they are ignored or overworked on occasions? I loved reading to my kids and making up stories, but making beds and cooking meals which were almost always unappreciated and/or thrown out finally took its toll, and I relished this new concept that someone appreciated me, someone thought that I was funny and clever and beautiful.

So back to that first date. Eventually a way was worked out, excuses given, courage found and I was taken out to dinner. Imagine that! Going out to dinner. Having a reason to get dressed up. You might think that is an odd thing to say because people go out for dinner all the time. But not us. As I said, my husband was a musician so every weekend meant that if I didn't want to go to listen to the band and sit by myself for five hours a night, my only other option was to stay home. And when the children came along there wasn't really even a choice. I was home alone with the children. This was my life, and although surrounded by my very beautiful children, I was very lonely.

That first date was dinner at a lovely little restaurant in Liverpool in Sydney. I was vegetarian at the time and my new man had arranged for the restaurant to provide me with a vegetarian-only menu with no prices, so that I wouldn't be distressed by carnivore meals or feel that I had to consider the expense. When we were seated at our table, the maître d' came over and presented me with a single beautiful red rose. I thought that was very nice of him until I realised that I was the only woman in the restaurant who had received one. And then I was given a dozen red roses when we left. I felt so spoilt, so loved, so taken care of. And I could not believe this was happening to me.

Fast track two years and my husband and I had divorced and I was now living with the new guy. And this little time warp goes nowhere near to describing the heartache and devastation that was caused to my husband and children – and myself, interestingly enough. Because even though I cast myself in the role of the one who decided to end it all, it was still hard to live with. Heartbreak and joy seemed to live simultaneously in my heart as I struggled through the next few years of my life. When my divorce finally came through, separating me from the father of my children, my own father told me that I had 'made my bed' so now I felt I had to live this life that I had created but which was fast turning into a nightmare.

Of course, now that he had won me and achieved the conquest, this new guy was no longer interested. He had moved on to the next conquest but he still managed to keep me on a string with promises of forever and the increasingly fleeting glimpse of a grand passion and a great love. This was, of course, in between his lies, his secret phone calls, meetings and infidelity.

And then there was the violence. They say a woman usually has a pattern, a 'type' of relationship and goes for the same type of man, but this was not the case for me. My father was a thoughtful, but often harried man. My ex-husband was a kind and lovely man and although often absent, he was a stable father to the children. I always felt though that our relationship was more like brother and sister than husband and wife.

But this new guy was violent, no doubt about it. It seemed that when he was in danger of being found out in his latest lie, his standard response was to lash out, to attack and make sure I was kept in my place. Many times the police were called, and amazingly they were always courteous and kind, never hinting that they must have been at a loss to understand why a woman would choose to put up with this type of situation. I must confess I was at a loss to understand it as well.

The night was hot and still, and cicadas were throbbing in the distance. I was face down on the bed with one arm twisted savagely up behind me. I tried to scream, but nothing came out. My face was jammed into the pillow and I was struggling for breath. I was torn between hoping that someone could hear and feeling terrified that somebody would. But even if someone did hear they would not come to my assistance. People don't like to get involved. With one last punch to the back of my head he finally climbed off me and left. Thank God, thank God. I lay there hardly breathing in case he came back, listening, listening. The front screen door slammed and I sucked in a shuddering breath. Now what? I waited several minutes more, just to make sure he was gone. I pulled myself up off the bed and slowly felt all over. No, only bruises this time. I walked into the kitchen and put the kettle on to boil. I made a cup of tea while I thought about what I should do. Somewhere down the street a dog was barking. Yes, I didn't understand why I stayed either.

On one occasion I was sitting in an empty house, my house, with the phone lines ripped out of the wall and a policewoman attempting to ask me questions. I couldn't think how to respond. My mind was blank – like a green school-board with no chalk. I felt as if I was standing above myself, watching this scene play out as though eavesdropping on myself. The officer's comment to me was, 'It's so quiet', and indeed it was.

Early on in the relationship this guy wanted to set up his own company. Of course he had no money, so I came to the rescue and financed him, and ultimately started working with him, mostly to ensure that I still had some say in how my money was being spent. It turned out that he was quite a good salesman (now who would have thought!) but he had few business skills and needed someone to do the paperwork, invoicing and accounting, so we worked well as a team for a while. After several years he asked me to marry him, and even though I knew by then what sort of man he was, I agreed.

I learnt quite a bit about life during this time. I learned how to duck and weave, never telling people the exact story, never indicating that things were less than perfect. I also learned some fabulous new skills such as how to scuba dive, how to ride a motorcycle, how to have fun, and even how to relate to people better. These were all skills that I didn't have before.

Things became trickier each year as I became more and more deeply entrenched financially in the business and it took a long time before I eventually managed to extricate myself from that – well what would you call it? Affair? Relationship? Marriage? Or just a devastating life experience?

An opportunity presented itself to sell the business and after ten years of working so hard at it, we jumped at it. It took some negotiation and after the dust had settled and the final figures were in, my husband had somehow managed to filter most of the profit off into an offshore account in his own name.

A second devastating life experience occurred at this same time as well. My wonderful father who had been suffering for over twelve months from a condition known as Guillain–Barré syndrome finally succumbed to complications of his condition and he died quietly in hospital surrounded by his extensive family. In those last few weeks, while I was trying to visit my seriously ill father and keep the business running smoothly in anticipation of the sale, my husband was spending his time entertaining the head negotiator who had been sent out from London to purchase our business. They went to all the nightclubs and brothels around the city and he would come home so drunk every night that I took to putting a towel and a bucket beside the bed. In the morning I would clean up his mess before heading off to work.

In the end, after the sale of the company I lost my home, my job, my company, my husband, the people who I thought were my friends. Even my car was repossessed. I had to borrow money from my sister to pay a month's rent on a villa for the children and me to move into, to try to rebuild our lives. I had no job and felt so emotionally shattered that I could not formulate a plan of action to even get myself up off the lounge. But at least by this time I knew I wanted a divorce as quickly as possible to extricate myself from this situation.

Ultimately that second husband had a nervous breakdown and ended up in hospital for several weeks. Although some time had passed since we had separated I felt torn at this stage and tried to do 'the right thing' which I thought was to stay with him and help him through this dreadful time, the voice of my father ringing in my ears 'you've made your bed' even after all these years. Of course this was just another manipulation by the second husband, and in the end he hadn't changed his ways. He had met a new woman at the rehabilitation program and commenced an affair with her while simultaneously trying to keep our tenuous relationship alive.

At that very low point, I was lucky enough to meet a musical man. I had joined a local band since I had once been a singer and this was an outlet for me, a way to move forward. At rehearsal one day there was a knock at the door and our new bass guitarist walked in. He was big and tall. He wore tight black jeans and a black tank top, and carried a bass amp which I knew would be heavy, but he moved it around so effortlessly, his muscles bulging with the weight. I stretched a bit taller, tightened my tummy muscles – I couldn't seem to breathe. The leader introduced everyone but it seemed that he knew all the guys in the band and they laughed and joked as they set up the gear. I could feel the heat of him across the room. I kept my eyes on the floor and tried to be cool.

After a while, he arranged to drive me to rehearsals since I didn't have a car; he even cooked dinner for me on one memorable occasion. And after that dinner he gathered me up in his arms and carried me out to the balcony, sat me on a chair. And there he told me many things about his childhood that were buried deep and dark in his past, things that he wanted to share with me, and I thought I understood the hesitancy and trust that he put in me to share those confidences.

After many months of music and singing, I started to feel good again. My guitarist's gentleness and our music had an ability to heal my wounds and to help take the pain and confusion away. Lying in the warmth of his embrace, I'd squeeze in my tummy muscles and immediately I was transported back to the first time I met him. How was it that we had ended here, in this wonderful, safe, loving place? I can still feel the warmth of him cuddled into my back, his strong arms surrounding me, his left hand cupping my breast as he slowly and deliberately moved his hand down over my belly and up onto my hip. His hands were soft and warm and gentle, and he made me feel so smooth and beautiful. He whispered gently that he loved this feeling, this afterglow, and he cuddled me tighter. I knew I never wanted to move from that place.

We worked on chords and timing, new songs and old, and his loving was soothing and healing. Occasionally we dined out at our local restaurant. At the end of one magic night, after all the other diners had left, he held out his hand and invited me to dance. Strains of Glenn Miller filled the room, the proprietors turned down the lights, turned up the music, and I danced close and tender in his arms.

I thought he had the ability to listen and not judge, to talk and make me understand. We discussed everything from international politics to music to animals, and he was knowledgeable on every subject. He encouraged me to see situations from other viewpoints, to look at things from the other side. He had had a very different childhood to me, had grown up in a different country and his experiences were much more brutal and savage than my coddled existence. But I thought he had a beautiful and gentle soul, and he invited me in to learn about him and be part of his world. I so loved him for that. It is amazing that you really never know who a person is, what secrets and hurts they hide. You can never really be sure what their deepest thoughts are – you can only rely on what they tell you.

Lovers dance in, filling up ones heart with love and space and time, and they bring with them a vibrancy and joy to help you through the years. And when they leave, a little piece of family is broken off like a pause in the music that stretches on too long. For a woman, when you invite a lover into your life, he enters your whole being. You invite him into your love, your home and your life. In my case, my guitarist chanced along when I was feeling very fragile. He brought music and a sense of wonder that while everything in the world had come crashing down around me, there was still something wonderful and worthwhile waiting for me. He treated me gently and tenderly for a while, and he slowly helped me rebuild my life. We made some wonderful music together and I thought I had finally learnt what true love was. We played our music, laughed, loved and learned about each other.

In music, when two notes of a different pitch are played simultaneously, they create a harmonic. Of course this is just my simple explanation of a musical phenomenon but I have been told that that same phenomenon happens in electronics and physics as well. I believe this is what true love is, the human equivalent of a musical harmonic. Two hearts, each playing a pure note, creating a vibration connecting you with that person, building a bond of love. It creates a beautiful tone, a true and wonderful connection to that other person. Not every couple finds that harmonic of true love; it has to be a reciprocal, strong, two-part thing. It seems that only rarely do people develop the love and music to make their hearts vibrate at corresponding frequencies. Many people struggle through their lives with their song still buried deep inside of them.

Family: according to the dictionary, one definition of family is 'a group consisting of two parents and their children living together as a unit'. To me that definition is broad enough to encompass all styles of families, and the modern family is certainly diverse. Many couples want to love and be loved as part of a family, whatever their political, religious or sexual persuasion. Families incorporate every aspect of the human condition.

I don't think it matters what the blend of a family is, as long as each adult is a decent and loving person and the children feel safe, protected and loved. And it does take a village to raise a child.

Passion

to

Protect

Susan Mansfield

Susan Mansfield

Susan was born in Orbost, Victoria in 1961. By the age of ten she discovered her love of reading and spent hours writing short stories as a teenager. She left school and underwent a library traineeship, married and moved to Darwin, Northern Territory where she now calls home.

Following the birth of her children she decided a career change was in order and, at the age of forty, she completed a degree in Social Work and has held various positions in child protection, hospitals and allied health. She is currently working in the drug and alcohol sector.

In 2011 Susan blew the whistle on the NT government's failing child protection system, igniting a major inquiry which resulted in greater funding and resources to the Department. With a keen interest in reading memoir, she decided to write about her experience and later attended a writing course in Paris, where she met with ten other like-minded women – and *They Met in Paris* was born.

The evening air was stifling, after the flooding monsoonal turbulence of the previous two weeks. Darwin's wet season feels like being shrouded in a woolly blanket soaked in the heavy scent of frangipani and thick, damp undergrowth. I was sitting on the back verandah watching the grey-black thundering clouds circle overhead and rumble out to sea, while two bush turkeys scurried about our gently sloping backyard looking for shelter, or an escape to freedom. Tracy walked through the front door with her nurse's attitude on, gently placed her hand on my swollen belly and looked into my eyes, telling me it was time for some real action to begin. 'Right, that's it! That baby's been in there long enough and I'm sick of waiting. You're ready,' she stated bluntly. 'I'll be back in fifteen minutes with a remedy to get this show on the road.' She finished off with an air of confidence as she marched out through the door she'd just entered. I totally trusted her.

Tracy was not only a very dear friend and neighbour, but also a natural, nurturing no-nonsense nurse. She was the sort of friend you could always rely on, with a great sense of humour and a good listener; she handed out practical, yet thoughtful and empathic advice and was always there for you when you needed a hand, or an ear. I followed her out the front door and watched her tiny frame stride across the road, get into her car and drive off, weaving through the neighbourhood children playing cricket at the end of our secluded and peaceful cul-de-sac.

My belly was huge, sitting high up under my expanding rib cage, with sunbaked skin stretched to the point of dry itchiness and breasts the size of heavy grapefruits resting softly on top. I stroked my baby-belly gently as I waddled back inside to prepare something for dinner. With swollen ankles, bloated face, fingers and toes, I managed to throw together a filling creamy pasta dish, hoping the heavy carbohydrates would help to satisfy Andrew's hungry appetite when he arrived home from work. This baby was not in a hurry to arrive and I was overdue by one week.

I loved him being in there – not that I knew I was having a boy. The longer he remained in my womb, the longer I daydreamed about what our lives and our future would be like. He was safe in there, pure and untainted by the world. I imagined, as soon as our treasured children were old enough to carry a backpack, we would travel the world together and give them an education far beyond anything they could possibly learn in a classroom. I dreamed of one day heading off to Europe, spending long enough in Paris, or a small French village somewhere, where the children could learn the language, soak up the history and architecture, and become enriched by the cultural experience. We held many a conversation, Jack and I – long before we met face to face. I fancied that we knew each other well, but alas, my life was in for a rude awakening the day I met my gorgeous dark-haired, fair-skinned son.

We were living in a half-finished newly built house. We'd run out of money that year and, true to a typical builders' form when it comes to building their own home, the walls were neatly gyprocked, yet unpainted; no finely polished finishes on the parquet timber flooring, no finished skirting or architraves, no doors closing off the entrance to each bedroom, wardrobes, pantry or bathroom. Basically, there was no privacy at all in our little house. No landscaped gardens. No pool. So much more work yet to be done on the house overall – so much more to be spent on bringing it to completion. I desperately wanted it all finished before I brought this baby home. He did have a room of his own, with no door, no pastel painted finishes or nursery newborn murals on the walls. No intercom. No fancy crib with overhead netting, no 'Welcome Home Jack' banner to let him know 'this is your home' – we just couldn't afford it. At nine months pregnant, I was depleted of all energy and our bank account depleted of all funds to spend on the abundant amount of work still to be done, not to mention all the pretty baby trimmings I desperately wanted to buy. But it was our home, nonetheless, and we had worked hard to get it to a point where we could move in and finish it off over time, using our own money, rather than borrowing more from the bank.

The frangipani scent filtered in through the dusty louvred windows that night with no stormy relief to cool the night air, just a mere gusty flirtation. A storm in a teacup, the wind settled five minutes after it began to stir the heavy moist air. The croaking of frogs and the buzzing of Christmas beetles dominated the music of the dark humid night.

Tracy came back, good as her word, with the show starter. She instructed me to take two tablespoons of castor oil in a glass of orange juice, and she'd be back in an hour to 'monitor' me. I totally trusted her and did strictly as she advised, swallowing the ghastly liquid down as quickly as I could. Within an hour things had started moving, literally. I kept running back and forth to the toilet, my bowels and body working overtime to make room for this baby to manoeuver his way through the birth canal. When Tracy returned to check on me, I was reassured that I would have this baby by the morning. Everything was going according to Tracy's plan and I was definitely in labour. Things were moving quickly, for sure. We got a bit excited at that point and then I had to ask her to leave, as our bathroom had no door and I had to go back in there again!

My labour progressed through the night, with me in the shower, the bath, the toilet, and trying to rest on the lounge or the back verandah for a few minutes at a time. I just couldn't sit still. It was very silent in our neighbourhood that night, as if we were the only ones awake, moving about in our house, music softly playing, making soothing cups of raspberry leaf tea, washing, ironing and cleaning. Andrew hovered about caringly, keeping me company, chatting, giving my back a rub every now and again, checking on Poss (our blissfully ignorant, slumbering three-year-old daughter) while I washed towels, changed the bassinet sheets, rearranged Jack's room, fluffed up the pillows on the rocking chair, folded and refolded nappies and rearranged drawers, finally climbing into bed about midnight. I still couldn't settle. I tossed and turned and wriggled about in the bed trying to get comfortable, until my waters broke and the reality of our baby's impending arrival dawned on both Andrew and me.

We were pretty excited and very relieved, breathing, breathing, breathing, timing contractions that seemed hell-bent on being one minute apart from the very heated outset, once they began. We hastily packed a small bag for hospital and talked about our future, having two children – what would that look like, being a family of four? We called my sister, Ann, and told her we were on our way to drop Poss off. For some stupid reason, we had decided to 'protect' her from the potential painful reality of the birthing experience – a decision I have held with much regret since the day of Jack's birth. She has been a shining light in our lives and, in hindsight, we now know she would have revelled in being present at the birth of her most treasured only brother.

Driving into Ann's in the heart of the holiday van park, just five minutes from our own front door, I felt every speed hump, leaning from one delicate side to the other, cringing at every curvy turn and bump in the road. We quickly handed our sleepy, quietly compliant daughter over, with promises of a progress phone call in the morning, and sped off into the night. I held my breath at every bloody glaring red light at the intersections between Ann's house and the hospital. That was one of the longest drives of my life and yet I noted the frangipani-scented air still managed to waft in through all four windows of the car, catching my attention and imprinting itself into the dark etches of my memory surrounding Jack's birth. Clammy droplets of perspiration trickled down my torso, soaking the flimsy cotton dress I had thrown on before leaving home. No bra. No knickers. The towel I sat on soaked up anything else my body cared to expel that night. I was on a mission.

As we arrived at the front door of the hospital I was convinced I was going to give birth on the doorstep, once I realised the doors were locked. It was about 2 am as I pressed the buzzer-bell at the emergency door. Breathing heavily into the intercom, I announced my labouring arrival, 'It's Susan Mansfield, I'm in labour.' My finger lingered on the button longer than it should have as I buckled under my latest contraction and glanced around me, waiting breathlessly for Andrew to park the car nearby, and willing him to join me at breakneck speed. From the covered driveway of the hospital entrance, I barely noticed the cloud-covered full moon lighting the grey-blue sky above and shining down on the gritty sand-covered mat underfoot – breathing, panting. I wanted to squat down and push – breathing one, two, and three, I held my breath. Andrew quickly appeared at my side, bag in hand and a reassuring arm around my back. The door miraculously opened and we hurried inside to the haven of the hospital lobby.

A midwife met us at the entrance and we were ushered upstairs to the delivery suite, processed in the usual manner, weighed, measured and assessed, contractions timed, reassured the doctor had been called and was on his way. Then, within the hour, I found myself ready to push this baby into the world and finally get to hold him in my arms. What a blissful and blessed moment that was. Time stands still at that instant when you meet your baby for the first time.

Jack was placed gently on my chest, wrapped loosely in a warm brushed cotton duck-egg blue bunny rug. His creamy skin, so silky-smooth and soft, a shot of longish dark hair and large deep-burgundy lips, immediately captivated me. I gently kissed the tip of his nose. He was so deafeningly quiet and serene. His large eyes were so deep in colour that they appeared to be almost black, taking in everything around him, yet focusing on nothing in particular. That first meeting was so vastly different to Poss's arrival into the world. When she was born and placed onto my chest, she immediately looked up into my eyes and we studied each other intently. Passionately. It was love at first sight for my firstborn and me, and the bond immensely binding from that first moment of meeting. Jack seemed to look past me, over my shoulder, somewhere off into the distance. It took another six weeks for him to finally look at me and hold my gaze. I didn't realise just how crucial that feedback is for a parent, until I didn't have it.

The midwives helped put Jack on the breast, for his first suckle. He took to it like a fish to water, the entire time looking anywhere other than at me. We were left alone for about an hour in the delivery suite, Andrew, Jack and I, to get to know one another before being transferred to one of the rooms on the maternity ward. We were too excited to sleep and spent hours holding our new son, touching him, rocking him, just watching him sleep and admiring him – saying his name out aloud and trying it on, like a new glove. 'Jack Mansfield. You've got such a great name, so strong and manly,' we told him.

Jack and I spent a week in hospital following his birth. He had jaundice and required some additional treatment before being discharged home. By day three I was complaining to the nursing staff, 'There's something not right with my baby.' I couldn't put my finger on what it was I felt was 'not right'. He was just different. Feeding seemed to be going well, what went in came out the other end, as required, and he looked normal. I just had a gut feeling something was wrong and it may well have been based purely on the fact that he had never looked at me. I was convinced this was crucial to development.

One night I was wandering the corridor of the hospital, trying to get Jack off to sleep, when I ran into the pediatrician who had been Poss's doctor when she was a baby, Dr Ross greeted me with surprise and congratulations on the new addition to the family. I burst into tears and told him of my concern. He walked me back to my room, took a quick look at Jack and reassured me that nothing stood out at first glance. He would return again for a more thorough examination the next morning. We finally settled for the night and got a few hours sleep.

The next day my feelings of concern were still simmering. Dr Ross came and examined Jack from head to foot, the entire time reassuring me that Jack appeared to be a perfectly normal, healthy baby. He scheduled an appointment for a six-week check-up and reminded me to relax and enjoy the rest of my stay in hospital – not having to cook, clean or do the washing. We had plenty of visitors that day, which helped to distract my thoughts, and I began to think he was probably right; things would improve when we got home and I'd feel better there. Maybe it was just the difference between having a girl and now a boy?

We were finally discharged and went home the next day. My mood improved immensely just leaving the hospital and walking in through the front door of our little house, in my own familiar environment; it felt better just being at home with Andrew and Poss. We quickly settled into a routine as much as we could, becoming immersed in the daily activities of family life, attending playgroups, coffee mornings and play dates, family get-togethers with those who lived nearby and the usual upkeep of day-to-day household chores.

The day before Jack's six-week check-up with Dr Ross, he finally looked me in the eyes. I cried with relief. We studied each other intently whilst he suckled at the breast, one plump and dimpled little fist firmly holding on to my finger, as we gently rocked back and forth in our comfy old rocking chair. Jack had unusually large, gentle sapphire blue eyes, framed by long dark curly eyelashes. I could drown gazing into those eyes of his at times. This single event gave me immediate reassurance that all would be OK; I pushed all other concerning thoughts from my mind that day. We attended the appointment with Dr Ross the next day and received a clean bill of health.

By the time Jack was three months of age my niggling concerns had resurfaced. He was reaching some milestones, eye contact and following a person or object briefly, smiling and an endearing half-hearted laugh (we all worked overtime to achieve that one), gurgling and kicking; however, he seemed slightly weak, struggling to hold his head up at times and he hated lying on his tummy unless his head was flat on the mat and turned to the right. His most comfortable position was to be held with his head resting on my right shoulder, or Andrew would hold him in the crook of his arm, with his head well supported.

We both carried Jack for several hours every day. While he was feeding well and gaining weight during the first few months, there were times I'd go to put him on the breast and he'd struggle to attach; he would become irritated and arch his back, like he really wanted to feed but couldn't latch on to the nipple, as if he was in pain. I had to constantly guide him, or squirt the milk into his mouth until he could settle enough to attach. He only wanted to feed from the left breast and seemed too uncomfortable feeding from the right. I was confused and couldn't work out what the problem was. I'd also noticed Jack often appeared to have a red face which was one-sided. The area around his right eye was often flushed, extending in a diagonal line from the top right hand corner of his forehead down to the bottom left jaw. The other side of his face seemed consistently normal.

I began to wonder if he had a problem with his neck and took him back to the pediatrician. Unfortunately Dr Ross was out of town and we ended up seeing one of the other doctors in the practice. He listened quietly to my concerns, then gently assessed Jack, noting the flushed area of his face and suggested he might benefit from some physiotherapy sessions. 'Nothing too troublesome stands out,' he told me. I left with the referral and hoped he was right.

The physiotherapist came to the house to assess the environment and carry out the first session. She was warm and caring and I could tell she was good with babies, talking to Jack the entire time, trying to soothe him, but unfortunately he cried throughout the session. She encouraged me to persist with the exercise therapy daily and she would return every two weeks for review. It broke our hearts to put Jack through the therapy sessions. We played music and sang gently to him, massaged him with soothing oils. We encouraged Poss to dance around the room and entertain him; she would laugh and squeal with delight, but all to no avail, Jack cried and cried. He hated physiotherapy sessions and so did we. We stopped doing them and I would lie to the therapist when she turned up each fortnight, telling her that we had followed her instructions to the letter. We couldn't put our precious baby through the pain. We'd all end up in tears over it.

When I took Jack back to the pediatrician's clinic for follow-up we ended up seeing yet another doctor, who seemed irritated by my concerns and looked at me quizzically before telling me my son was fine. I left the clinic feeling bewildered and confused. I'd started to question myself. What was I looking for? I didn't want anything to be wrong with my baby.

We always thought Jack seemed to be an old soul, as he was far less active a baby than Poss. He appeared content to wait his turn; an observer in all this chaos we call life. I felt he must take after Andrew in nature – placid, a gentle giant, with those beautiful big sapphire blue eyes taking in everything that surrounded him, taking a mental note for later.

By the time Jack was six months old my concerns were not just my own. Andrew had wholeheartedly agreed with me from the get-go, however, now our family and friends appeared to be seeing what we were seeing and worrying along with us. I began to withdraw socially from outings, preferring to stay at home rather than risk causing him more upset and discomfort by going out, getting him in and out of the car or the pram. Even having friends over, there were times when I felt too many people and too much noise would upset him and, in turn, I became anxious and couldn't wait for everyone to leave. Poss, on the other hand was absolutely delighted to have visitors, the more the merrier. She'd drag out her paints and paper, peg it to the fence and spend hours painting, both the paper and everything around her – made easier by living in the tropics when your day as a three-year-old is spent in just a bikini bottom, or nothing at all. She played tea parties, dollies, making things from play dough, dress-ups, cutting and pasting, and under the hose, or in the wading pool. Three-year-olds are so easily pleased.

The health clinic I attended for immunisations and baby health checks advised me Jack was in the lower percentile. His weight had dropped off and they started to question his feeding regime. I'd lost a bit of weight, so they suggested my breast milk might not be good enough for him, he's not getting enough nourishment, he should be on more solids, or perhaps he's a fussy baby. They wanted to see him more regularly. I talked these concerns over with Tracy and Kris, who had been present during many a breastfeed and they reassured me that it couldn't possibly be my milk, or Jack's diet. They told me what I wanted to hear.

It was about this time that I started to document Jack's feeds (liquids and solids), his nappy changes, sleeping pattern, and times of the day he became unsettled and irritable. Basically, I began to document Jack's life. Whilst we had started him on solids, at about four months of age, he really didn't seem fussed on eating food. He usually managed the first mouthful, but then he would just roll the food around in his mouth until it fell out. Me being the anal-retentive Virgo that I am, immediately wiped his chin, the chair, his hands and everything around him clean then gave him a few more mouthful attempts, before I gave up and threw it all away. I thought he didn't want it and I didn't want to play food games, because that's messy. I figured when he's hungry he'll eat. After a short while of documenting this I realised at seven months of age Jack was about 98% breastfed, which was also becoming problematic.

Demand feeding essentially had taken over my life for the past seven months. I was feeding, or attempting to feed, Jack every hour to two hours – day and night. I also realised that he had only ever rolled over once, after a great deal of coaxing, clapping and cheering from an audience of Tracy's family and ours. He was so happy when he finally did it. His 'startle reflex' had gone by about four months of age and then recently returned. If I compared Jack to other babies the same age they seemed to be more advanced, sitting, rocking on all fours, crawling commando-style along the floor to get a toy or to get somewhere. Jack was floppy and far from mobile. The other babies even spoke some words. Jack spoke one word 'mum' and it was only when he was crying or laughing. It was an effort for him to get the word out, and it sounded more like 'marrrrrm'. When I think back to that sound it breaks my heart.

I had taken a job back at the university library, where I had worked prior to having the children. It was just two mornings each week and a bit of extra money, which we could really do with at the time. Poss went to kindy and Jack went to spend the morning with Kris and Mark, our very dear friends who we had befriended when our daughters were born.

I was asked to work back an extra hour one busy Friday, to cover the chaotic lunch hour rush on the front desk, and called Kris to ask if she could have Jack a little longer than usual. When she answered the phone I could hear Jack quietly crying in the background. Jack's cry was a gentle 'err-herr-herr' noise, which sounded as if he was far too tired to put any real effort into it. Andrew and I were never able to leave our children crying for more than a minute or two without picking them up to pacify them, or attend to whatever the need was. Kris said Jack had seemed really unhappy and she hadn't been able to put him down all morning. She wondered if he was coming down with something as she'd noticed he was spiking temperatures off and on over the past four hours. Kris asked if I'd mind if she gave him a breastfeed to see if that comforted him. She was still feeding Scott, her son, who was almost five months older than Jack. I thought this was a brilliant idea, given that we spent so much time together, it was as if she was his second mother anyway.

By the time I got to Kris's an hour or so later Jack had fed and eventually settled, although the minute he saw me he started crying his gentle little cry again. He seemed to be relieved once I picked him up and he snuggled into the crook of my neck, with his head resting on my shoulder – his favourite position. Whilst I stood rocking Jack back and forth to soothe him I discussed my concerns with Kris. She added to my ever-expanding list with the temperature spikes and I realised I'd noticed them as well, but put it down to our humid weather, given they would eventually resolve themselves.

It was time to go back to the doctor. We were worried. It took a couple of weeks to get in to see Dr Ross. I didn't want to waste any more time going from doctor to doctor. Basically, during the first seven months of Jack's life, I had taken him to three pediatricians, two general practioners, several community health nurses, a physiotherapist and received varying degrees of concern, or lack of concern. I'd been told by one or the other that it was my breast milk, he's not getting enough, or enough nourishment, he needs solids, he's lazy and doesn't want to work for his feed, there's nothing wrong with him, he looks fine, he's perfectly healthy, he'll grow out of it, and my favourite one of all: 'You're neurotic and looking for a problem that doesn't exist'. I had to go home and look up the meaning of neurotic. I was offended and held a grudge against that doctor for many years. And to think these comments all came from highly educated, well regarded medical professionals.

I had one friend who told me I was looking for the perfect baby and I didn't have one. 'You've got a fussy one instead, so just get on with life and forget it,' she said. Of course I had started to doubt myself months ago, but when others who saw Jack on a regular basis started to see what we were seeing, we felt justified in pursuing the issue.

Tracy worked with our own GP and I asked her if she would talk to him about our concerns just prior to the appointment with Dr Ross, which she did, however I didn't fully understand his prognosis. Tracy carefully advised me that he had wondered if it was something genetic. What did that mean? I had no idea, and in 1991, it was a good ten years or more before the luxury of computers, internet access and Google were a given in every home.

Dr Ross was welcoming and receptive to my teary concerns. I told him about Jack's weight loss, floppy limbs, irritability, feeding problems, startle reflex, dry nappies and constipation, sleep routine, milestones – the list was endless. He listened intently as I read it out aloud to him, then he examined Jack thoroughly. He advised me, 'When a mother thinks there is a problem, nine times out of ten she is right.' At the conclusion of his examination Dr Ross confirmed he also held some grave concerns and he would like to arrange a neurological examination by a specialist pediatrician in Brisbane.

Within two days Jack and I were on a flight south. Naively I thought there maybe a blockage in the spine around the neck area, causing the redness, the temperatures and his growing irritability. I imagined the specialist would fix it and we'd be back home within the week. Andrew and Poss stayed at home in Darwin, as there was no possible way we could afford for all of us to fly down to Brisbane. We didn't have a credit card back then, either.

We attended the specialist appointment two days later and I was shocked to hear the pediatric neurologist comment whilst examining Jack, 'Yes, there seems to be some spasticity there.' I couldn't believe my ears. Who says spastic these days? I was transported back to my childhood and teens, when my sisters and I would tease each other saying, 'Get out of my room, you spastic', or 'You're a spaz'. Indignantly, I thought, my son is not 'spastic', that doesn't happen to me; this guy must be mistaken.

We were admitted to the Royal Children's Hospital the next day for further testing and assessment. All types of scans, blood test after blood test, lumbar puncture, nerve conduction testing, skin biopsy, MRI, then they seemed to repeat many of the tests over and over again. During the week in hospital we were moved from a six-bed share ward to a private room. I was surprised by this privilege and put it down to our having private health insurance, rather than isolating us.

Groups of trainee doctors came and went. They'd file into the semi-darkened room and gather around Jack's cot (or me if I was holding him); poking and prodding him, study his file notes, make murmurings on how curious his symptoms were, scratch their heads, nod to each other, then leave, giving nothing away. I had no idea what was going on. Nurses appeared to be tiptoeing around us, at times avoiding eye contact, in case I asked too many questions. If I managed to corner one of them they'd return with a few medical textbooks under one arm, hand them over, check on Jack, then leave me alone again to find my own answers. I was medically naive and became mildly frustrated over the lack of answers to the puzzling confusion of my son's condition. At one stage the doctors suggested

Jack might have mild cerebral palsy, but the next day they ruled that out.

A week later we were discharged from hospital and went to stay with Andrew's dad, Allan and his partner, Betty, until the test results came back. I called Dr Ross to let him know there were still no answers and he seemed somewhat surprised that we were still down in Brisbane. He immediately arranged for Andrew and Poss to be flown down to support us. Unfortunately, due to our dire financial situation, Andrew had to get back to work and he returned home after only a few days. Two weeks later the pediatric neurologist finally had some news and arranged a meeting on Friday 13th September. An ominous date, by all accounts, which we now refer to as the Black Friday of our lives.

The diagnosis and prognosis hit me like a cascading avalanche of rocks. I was crushed and drowning in the million thoughts flooding into my mind, as the doctor stammered on with his unforgiving delivery of horrific news. 'Your son has a rare genetic disorder called Krabbe disease, or Globoid Cell Leukodystrophy.' I struggled to get my mouth around the words he was using. He went on to describe the degenerative illness that would wither away at Jack's little body and brain, eventually taking our precious baby's life before the age of two.

The doctor knew of another family who's son had died the week before Jack was diagnosed. He would put us in contact with them, if we liked, to get some support and information. I could barely hold the pen to write his words down. My body was shaking uncontrollably; tears tumbled down my face, plopping in large heavy droplets onto the edge of the desk, my crumpled piece of paper and then onto Jack as I cradled him on my lap. His parting words were, 'Take Jack home and make him as comfortable as possible, because he's unlikely to see his second birthday.' My eyes were stinging, my heart pounding in my heavy chest. I stumbled blindly out of the doctor's office, bereft and disoriented. Poss, worried and confused by my reaction, tried to steer me towards the door that would lead us out onto the busy street and bright sunlight. I sobbed out loud as I manoeuvered the pram, the bulky nappy bag and Poss out through the door. In hindsight, how did that man ever let me leave his office in such a state?

I found the nearest phone box and called Andrew at work. He was working in Oenpelli, a remote Aboriginal community, building houses. This was before mobile phones so someone had to go and get him from the building site and take him back to their house to receive the call. Telling Andrew the news would have been like taking a sledgehammer to his heart. His son was terminally ill. He describes the news as numbing. Neither of us recalls that conversation exactly, as we were both in shock. I called my mother at some point after speaking to Andrew, but she was a couple of thousand kilometres away. What could she do to help me? The distance between us, at such a harrowing time, must have devastated her. I somehow managed to drive back to Allan and Betty's house that day. I seemed to have an endless supply of tears and continued crying with disbelief.

Waves of grief and fear would engulf me out of the blue, my tears would tumble down my cheeks in a rapid torrent, then suddenly dry up just as quickly as they arrived. I could be anywhere and at anytime of the day or night. Grief is exhausting. I'd quickly suck it up; I had to keep strong and vigilant for Jack's sake. I had to protect him and keep him safe. 'We will fix it and prove them wrong. This doesn't happen to us' became my mantra.

We flew back to Darwin two days later. My thirtieth birthday was the next day. I'd imagined my thirtieth birthday to be a day of laughter, fun and celebration. It wasn't. We spent the next couple of weeks watching Jack's every move. Documenting, making lists of questions, going to the library and gathering as much information as we could possibly lay our hands on. Ann became our research expert, collecting articles through inter-library loans and medical journals. We then took it all to Dr Ross for his interpretation. He was wonderfully patient and understanding. He emphasised the rareness of Jack's disease by telling us many doctors wouldn't see a child with this disease in their lifetime and, as far as he knew, there were no others in Australia with this disease at that time.

Krabbe disease affected both males and females; both Andrew and I had to be carriers to pass the defective gene onto our children. A one-in-four chance that one of our children would inherit the disease and a one-in-four chance that one of our children would have carrier status. One of each of our parents must be carriers to pass the carrier gene onto Andrew and me. We immediately questioned whether we were related, but the disease has been traced back to Vikings and has been found in all corners of the world. We were not related.

As we learned more about Jack's condition, we realised his little body had already started to deteriorate. We had been compensating along the way without fully understanding what was going on for him. His muscles had been wasting away for the past couple of months, which explained his weight loss and weakness in the neck, his inability to hold on to things, his inability to sit, roll or hold his head up; he was losing his suck and swallow – I'd been squirting milk into his mouth, he couldn't manage solid foods, he no longer managed to suck a dummy – it just fell out of his mouth; he didn't have the energy or ability to have a hearty laugh or cry, his smiles were becoming fewer and further apart. He no longer said 'marrrrrm'.

Every two weeks, it seemed, Jack would regress further.

We started to notice tiny seizures (usually accompanied by spikes in fever). Several times each day a wave of pain and stiffness appeared to grip his little body, causing great distress. We would hurry to hold him and reassure him that we were there for him. We soothed him any way we possibly could. We massaged and sang, we danced around and rocked him, we took walks around the garden, lazed in cool baths, tickled Jack's face with feathers and deeply scented frangipani petals, we put drops of eucalyptus oil on his pillows, sheepskin rug and toys, we swabbed his mouth with moistened lemon swabs.

I reluctantly gave up breastfeeding Jack at ten months; it became too much effort for him to suck, although he seemed to love the comfort. Dr Ross got us to try thickened feeds, special milk formulas, bottles and teats. Jack also saw a dietician and a speech therapist, to no avail. The milk just sat in his mouth and his little body became weaker and more susceptible to infections. Mouth thrush was the first of many such infections, making him miserable and initiating a strict hand-washing routine for everyone who touched him, or touched anything that went near him.

My heart was breaking as we also commenced an endless round of medications to try and alleviate some of his discomfort; Coloxyl for constipation, Baclofen, Frisium and Diazepam to relax his muscles and help with the seizures; Painstop to reduce pain and fever. None of these medications gave our son true relief. He had always been a light sleeper, however, by the time Jack was ten months of age he and I had no more than two hours sleep in one sitting. It became around the clock nurse parenting. Ann and Kris became our lifelines, Tracy our in-house doctor and medical interpreter. They were always there to lend a helping hand and mop up the tears.

Watching Jack regress at such a rapid rate was like water falling through a sieve. You just can't stop it. Every two weeks we noticed another change in Jack, a new hurdle, and it was always a regression. Poss also started acting out of character. It must have been so confusing for her. She would tuck Ken or Barbie under one of Jack's arms, telling him about the game they were playing together and then she'd change the doll for another one, or place a different toy in his hand, because he hadn't moved. She was so gentle and loving towards him, fussing like a little mother. If she noticed a dribble, she'd wipe it away; if he leaned to one side, she'd prop him up and rearrange his head support. She held books in front of him and told him stories (although she could not read), she helped with feeds and bathing, always giving him lots of loving care and attention. If someone came to visit and she didn't know them she'd throw a tantrum, lie down on the floor and start screaming, 'I don't like you!' She wet the bed a couple of times and started sucking her fingers and clothes. My poor firstborn wanted our old life back; she was starving for attention and totally confused by all that was going on in our little family and the many people that would come and go from our home.

My parents came to visit just as Jack and I were hospitalised to have his feeding problems sorted. He was losing weight rapidly, couldn't get his feeds down and had only three semi-wet nappies over a 48-hour period. He was immediately started on nasogastric tube feeds, and a couple of days later we were discharged home with a supply of tube feeding paraphernalia and a suction pump, to clear the ever accumulating mucous which Jack struggled to expel. We became experts at tube feeds and medication regimes in a very short space of time. In one respect I felt I had given in too early with breast-feeding and the introduction of tube feeds, however, Jack's body needed the nutrients from the special formula and sucking took way too much energy. I wanted a miracle to happen to save him from this intrusive method of feeding, but alas, he was too weak to manage it alone.

I also fantasised that the doctors had made a dreadful mistake; Jack would be the exception and prove them all wrong. He would pick up and roll over, sit up, talk, walk and grow up to be a normal child, teenager and adult, and on his twenty-first birthday we would tell this story – which would all be a dreadfully bad dream – because this sort of thing does not happen to us. Did we have to battle for everything in life?

My parents' thirty-six-year marriage had come to an end and I had not an ounce of attention I could pay them, I was far too consumed by my own dire situation to give them any real empathy or support. My father painted our house and built a stand to hang Jack's feeding bag from, which enabled us to be more mobile with his feeds and made life a bit easier. He also delighted in Poss and was able to give her the extra attention she needed for the couple of weeks they were visiting. My mother helped with the cooking and washing for all of us, but this was not a happy home.

The Seating Clinic custom-built a car seat, a sling and an amazing sponge wedge, specially designed for Jack to lie in for bathing. The Health Centre delivered a special ripple mattress and baby hammock.

The humidity combined with Jack's lack of mobility meant constantly moving him to avoid pressure ulcers or heat rash. The doctors kept us supplied with feeds and medication samples when they could get them. The local playgroup mums got together and developed a roster for meals, which were delivered every Tuesday and Thursday – unfailingly. The community spirit that pulled together to help and support us was humbling and we will be forever grateful and indebted to those wonderful, wonderful people.

We were on one wage, we had no money to spare and Jack's medications were expensive and not covered by our health insurance. We couldn't even afford to get rolls of film developed from our camera. Every cent mattered and we lived from pay to pay. Occasionally Andrew bought himself a can of Coke, as a treat.

My parents returned home to Victoria by the end of November. They parted ways, sold their caravan park and tried to move on with their lives. I'd never seen my parents argue – ever; I'd never seen any indication of relationship breakdown between them in my life. This was alien territory for my sisters and me. My father moved in with a new woman, which seemed to make him happy and Mum returned to live in Ballarat, with my sister, Wendy. Our family and our lives were changing and we seemed to have no control over it.

The physical, emotional and financial stressors took their toll at times, although I could not hand Jack's care over to anyone else. I maintained the vigil twenty-four hours a day. I literally coped on about two hours sleep each day. Of course Andrew was there at nights and on Sundays, but we needed the income and he had to keep working as much as he could to keep a roof over our heads, to pay Jack's medical bills and to keep food on the table. We lived on spaghetti and rice; I became a whiz with budget meals. If Andrew got up to Jack through the night, I could not remain in bed – I had to tend to him as well. We were a team, Andrew and I. We were living life one hour at a time. We could not look further than one day ahead and our passion to protect Jack and our little family from losing him was what kept us going.

A newly religious friend of mine told me one day, 'God sent Jack to you because you were on the wrong path.' All I could think was: if there is a fucking God, He accidently gave this debilitating disease to my baby, but it was supposed to go somewhere else. Not another baby, but rather like rust to a car, or rot to a tree – not a baby! If there were a God, surely He would not make innocent children suffer. I just didn't get it; Jack had done nothing wrong, yet we watched him suffer every day. I did, however, begin to think I was a very bad person. I pushed people away if I thought they were negative or demanding of my attention – away from Jack. If they didn't acknowledge Jack or Poss when they came to visit, I cut them off and made excuses as to why they had to leave immediately. I screened all phone calls; I made excuses as to why people couldn't come over. I kept a very tight schedule of feeds, cuddles and play, medication, quiet time, and jobs that had to be done. If there was a knock at the door, I would open it a crack and quickly assess whether they were worthy of entry or not. I became the mother from hell.

I had a falling out with my sister, Ann, who was wonderful and a lifeline, but the fallout was over money. Andrew had done some building for her and her husband, but when it came to asking for payment, Ann didn't want to pay. We desperately needed the money to cover Jack's medications, put food on the table and to pay our mortgage – all essential items in our lives that we could not do without. I was so stressed at the time and I could not bear to have us at loggerheads. Thankfully, her husband David smoothed the muddy waters and we navigated our way through the dilemma.

I had no time for my parents when they called; I had no sympathy for their relationship breakdown and the awful situation they must have been going through. My sister, Wendy, and brother, Richard, were interstate – supportive, but not there on a daily basis, as were Andrew's family. I screened their calls too.

Some friends suggested miracle solutions: we should travel to China, America or England for the latest and greatest genetic engineering cures of all time – based on nothing concrete other than those countries surely have more to offer than Australia, and living in Darwin had to be the last place we should be. Wendy was up visiting when a doctor from Sydney called to tell me that my son was 'a disaster'. I had contacted him about Jack's eligibility for bone marrow transplant, after reading information sent to me from the American Leukodystrophy Foundation and the trials they were doing in various countries around the world – I held high hopes that this would be the cure. When the doctor finally returned my call on a Sunday afternoon, Wendy and I were beside ourselves with anticipation for the answer we wanted to hear. He told me he had heard of our plight and Jack was not suitable for the bone marrow trial, due to his juvenile form of Krabbe's; he said Jack was too far gone and he probably wouldn't survive the transplant, let alone regain any of the mobility, mental and physical deterioration that has already occurred in his body. I hung up the phone and dropped to the floor crying and deflated. Surely it's worth a try? Can't we just try? I didn't understand.

The neurologist in Brisbane had introduced us to Liz and Paul, the couple whose son, Tyrone, had died at the age of two, just prior to Jack's diagnosis. Liz was a nurse and a fount of knowledge; her clever interpretation of each stage and change in Jack's condition made sense to us – they had lived it all before us. She was never too busy to talk on the phone and we bonded and connected through our son's illness immediately. If we needed advice or information about medical issues, Liz was like the master of 'Krabbe's for Dummies'; if we needed a distant shoulder to lean on, Liz had shoulders the size of Ayers Rock; if we just needed to say hi, Liz said, 'hello' in such an empathic voice I immediately felt heard and totally understood. We are forever indebted to Liz and Paul and the lifeline they threw to guide us through the turbulent current that kept dragging us under.

As time went by Jack became weaker and weaker. His one and only Christmas was the saddest Christmas of my life. We had two hundred dollars to spend on the children's presents. We had no credit cards (what a blessing) and we had saved for months to buy Poss's bike, the ham and trimmings. We bought every noisy attention-seeking toy known to man (under ten dollars), with the hope of catching Jack's interest and try to get a smile out of him. Ann and David literally fed us that Christmas. We spent the day at their house in the spa and grazing on the feast they had prepared, with Jack having catnaps in the air-conditioned bedroom – a total luxury, as we had no air-conditioning in our own home.

Poss and Jack's birthdays followed, born three years and six days apart in early January. We had a huge birthday party in the park at the beach – everyone was invited. A friend from playgroup made an amazing cake and everyone brought a picnic lunch to share. This was a stress-free birthday party. Just prior to leaving home that day, I noticed a blockage in Jack's feeding tube. Clearing the blockage was paramount and I felt as if I had to cancel the party, because I couldn't risk taking him out with everything not being one hundred per cent right. After several flushings the blockage was finally cleared and we arrived on time, although I was a mess for the rest of the day, constantly worried about all the children and whether their hands were clean before touching Jack. I wanted to shoo them all away and keep him in a bubble of protection.

Even in such a compromised state, Jack continued to respond to our voices and touch. He would wrap his little fingers around one of ours when we placed it in the palm of his hand and he made lip-smacking kisses when we put our cheeks against his mouth. We constantly showered him in butterfly kisses, told him wonderful make-believe stories, read brightly coloured picture books and sang lots of songs to him every day. We really didn't know if Jack had lost his sight and hearing by that stage, because sometimes he responded to tests and sometimes he did not.

We tried to keep things as normal for Poss as we could manage, even though our major outings had been reduced to doctor's visits, tube changes and medication management at the pharmacy. She happily came along, sometimes bringing her dolls and toy pram with her. I would go for days without consistent sleep, having thirty-minute power naps here and there to keep me going. Once each month Jack would be hospitalised for at least twenty-four hours, so that I could have a night's sleep. Sometimes I was given a room at the hospital as well so that I was on hand, if things were touch and go. We were given the option, early in Jack's diagnosis, to have him made a 'Ward of the State' – this would essentially have taken all financial responsibility off us and the public health system would have picked up the bill. This would also have meant Jack was no longer legally our son, and therefore we would have no control over his treatment and care. This was not an option for us. We loved our son and wanted to protect him with a passion.

Come March, Poss was at pre-school for half the week and we had an added agenda to our daily routine. Pre-school was just a five-minute walk from our home, so this was often done on foot with Jack in a twin stroller, kind of like the stretch limousine of prams. At school the other children would gather around the funny-looking pram to take a look at Jack; they were all very curious about Poss's special brother and asked lots of questions about him and the tube attached to his cheek. Poss took it all in her stride, as if everyone's little brother was like Jack. She was totally accepting of his condition and his inability to play with her. She was the perfect altruistic sister, whose empathy for others like Jack has continued on throughout her life.

Jack developed breathing difficulties and his high temperatures seemed to become more prevalent. Suctioning didn't appear to clear the congestion and he developed a wheeze and a weak cough. A doctors visit confirmed Jack had an infection. We'd been warned that Krabbe's patients become so physically compromised that they end up dying of secondary complications, such as pneumonia. We felt Jack's life was hanging by a thread; his little body was exhausted, depleted of all energy, yet he kept fighting infections, complications and battle after battle. Dr Ross suggested Jack may be over-sedated and it was time to reduce some of the medications, which would aid his ability to fight off chest infections. That and a hefty round of antibiotics! Andrew and I cradled Jack between us late one night and told him we loved him, we told him that we hated watching him suffer and we would understand if he had to give up the fight and leave us. We comforted ourselves in thinking that there had to be something better than the life Jack was currently living, and perhaps we'd meet again some day.

We watched Jack constantly, awake or asleep. Whilst he sometimes looked peaceful, his little body was super sensitive, he was jumpy and the bouts of choking that Jack endured scared us. There were times when I could not close my eyes, days when I was too afraid to rest, or too afraid to even peg the washing on the line, or do anything that took my attention away from him. Jack could not be left alone. There was so much care to be done, with feeds, medications, bathing, enemas, massages, nappy changes, suctioning and then the routine started all over again. Andrew and I worked our parenting-nurse routine around the clock. When one of us grabbed a quick nap, it was usually snuggled up with Poss, as her room was directly opposite Jack's and she would happily slumber on unaware of the crisis in the next room.

Dr Ross introduced us to the Sunshine Association, a volunteer organisation who had raised some money and wanted to make a wish come true for Jack and our family. They very generously offered to send us on a holiday to Ballarat, where Jack could meet his cousins and our extended family could spend some time together. We initially declined the offer and felt overwhelmed by such charity. Dr Ross and the people from Sunshine were very persuasive, and after much consideration and reassurance we finally agreed to go. At about this time Jack appeared to become slightly more alert, the reduction in Valium gave us a false sense of security and I secretly started to believe Jack might be getting better.

Within a week we were on a flight to Melbourne. The airline stewards paid such wonderful care and attention to us on the lengthy flight south, assisting with Jack's feeds and medication requirements, as well as entertaining Poss. We questioned that perhaps Jack didn't want his usual routine interrupted, as he seemed to be rejecting his feeds throughout the entire time; the tube kept blocking up, as if his stomach was rejecting it. We managed to get some formula into him, but put the problems down to travel and unfamiliar environment.

We arrived in Ballarat just after midnight, welcomed by the entire family who were so excited to meet Jack and to have us all together at such a poignant time. We finally fell into bed, after tending to Jack's last medication at about 2am. Andrew, Poss, Jack and I slept snugly in the one room. I awoke before six the next morning to give Jack his next meds, and glanced outside to see the early morning was still covered in darkness. Windows frosted over from the heavy dew-like condensation of cold temperatures on the outside and warmth from within. The house was very quiet, with everyone still sleeping off our late-night arrival. I imagined it would be another couple of hours before the family began to stir.

I rugged Jack up and told him all about the family he had met last night. He stared at me as he peacefully took in all that I had to tell him. The medications struggled to go down the tube again that morning and it took a bit of flushing to finish off. We had a cuddle on the lounge before I placed Jack gently back into bed and tucked the blankets snugly around him. Just as my head touched the pillow I heard Jack sigh the most amazingly restful sigh I'd ever heard him utter. In blissful ignorance, I shut my eyes in anticipation of more sleep, when the alarm on Jack's pump deafeningly alerted me to an emergency. Andrew and I both flew out of bed and I lifted Jack from the warm soft mattress, knowing full well he had just passed away. That final sigh was one of extreme exhaustion and Jack's decision that the 'time was right' for him to leave us.

At some point someone called an ambulance and the family huddled around us as we cradled Jack in our arms, waiting interminably for help to arrive. Again, time stands still the moment your child passes away. The uncontrollable shaking that overtook my body the day Jack was diagnosed returned to me that morning, overwhelmed by my aching grief and loss. It wasn't until the ambulance officer took Jack from Andrew's arms and placed him on the floor, carefully cutting his clothing from Jack's tiny body, that I could reach out and stop them from attempting to bring my son back to me.

We had talked about this moment and worried what we would do about resuscitation, if we had the choice. Andrew and I both knew Jack was exhausted. He had put up one hell of a fight to stay with us as long as he had. He had suffered enough and we needed to let him go in peace. Our son was gone and his fight was over.

We held a funeral service in Ballarat, for family and friends down there, all the time just wanting to return to Darwin with our son and lay him to rest at home. It took another week before we were able to leave Victoria and as we sat on the tarmac in Darwin, waiting to disembark our return flight, I glanced out of the plane's rear seated window and watched my son's tiny white coffin slowly travel down a conveyer belt from the belly of the 747 aircraft.

That was twenty-two years ago now. Our lives took a turn in the road that neither Andrew nor I anticipated. As parents we expected our children to outlive us, we expected this to be a parenting right of passage and we fought passionately to protect and hold on to Jack as long as we could. Poss has been a blessing; she comforted us in our grief and gave us new hope in dark times.

We've since learned Poss is a carrier of the Krabbe's gene and her soon-to-be husband, Tim is not; so the disease stops for now, no more life will be given to this fatality in our family and her children will be safe from Krabbe's. Her grandchildren, however, may still be at risk.

Jack was buried in a large grassy cemetery on the outskirts of Darwin. We planted a weeping fig tree at the foot of his little grave, tapped into the sprinkler system in the garden bed. When we planted it, we imagined that tree would grow big and strong over the years, sheltering him in storms and shading him from the harsh sunshine, wrapping its lovely big roots around our son to cradle him and keep him company.

Initially, we'd go and visit the gravesite daily, then weekly, monthly and now yearly. On birthdays we took him helium balloons, the number we took depended on the age he would have been turning that year. We'd release them together, sent with a bright red lipstick kiss, or a message attached to the ribbon, all the while imagining that he would be receiving them up in the clouds somewhere.

Over the years the weeping fig has grown into a majestic masterpiece, densely covered in glossy dark green leaves, its graceful drooping branches providing a canopy over Jack's grave like a sprawling Australian verandah. There has been many a balloon captured by that canopy and now I'm sure that beautiful big tree has many a story it could tell us.

Passion for Vintage

Sierra Phillips

SIERRA PHILLIPS

Sierra is an actress, writer and model. She was born in the beautiful Blue Mountains and now lives on the Central Coast of NSW.

Sierra completed her Bachelor of Arts Degree in 2005, with a major in Drama and a minor in Writing. She enjoys travelling, dancing, reading and futile attempts at turning the patch of soil at the back of her unit into a lawn.

Passion for VINTAGE

The French have a wonderful saying. Actually, the French have many wonderful sayings, and one of these is *Plus ça change, plus c'est la même chose*. It means 'The more things change, the more things stay the same'. There must be some truth to this, given that in the past six decades, the world has changed dramatically (we've created political instability, the internet, Billy Joel, climate change …). There have been many profound changes in the world, and yet I can walk down any suburban street of Newtown in Sydney and suddenly it could be 1953. The cars, the clothes, the hair, the make up, the diners … It's almost as if the people here have collectively decided that it's now the 1950s again and hit pause on their iPhone stopwatches.

I remember the first time I ever heard the word 'rockabilly'. I was about fourteen years old. It was a warm day, far too warm for the jeans and sneakers I was wearing. Dad was driving as I talked incessantly, babbling on about everything and nothing. When we arrived at the café in Mount Lawley, Dad pulled the car over and put the handbrake on. I pushed the door open and climbed out of the car onto the footpath then turned around and closed the car door. I looked up as I began to walk around the car to cross the road. That was the moment when I first saw it, a sight that would stay with me for years to come.

I saw women sporting jet-black hair with blunt fringes. I saw hair rolled and manipulated into cylindrical and conical shapes. I saw Cadillacs and Chevrolets parked in the street. I saw a woman in her wedding dress – but it wasn't a traditional wedding gown, it was a knee-length white dress with an impossibly full skirt. I saw the bridesmaids in dark coloured dresses with cinched waists and full skirts boosted by layers and layers of petticoats in contrasting colours. I saw the men, with huge sideburns and slicked-back hair, perfectly styled pompadours. They wore jeans with huge cuffs folded at the bottom and colourful braces crossing over their backs. They were all smiling and laughing and looked as if they were having the time of their lives. Dad smiled, and tried not to stare. I was not so polite. I gawked, and it must have been obvious. This was the coolest thing I had ever seen.

We entered the café and sat down in a booth with Dad's friend. 'We just saw a rockabilly wedding out the front,' Dad told his friend. Rockabilly. I mentally implanted that word into my consciousness. It was an aesthetic I loved. It resonated with me in a way I couldn't quite place. Where did they get those clothes, I wondered. How did they make their hair go like that, and stay like that? I didn't understand why I was wearing jeans and sneakers and a tee shirt when I wanted to look like *that*. But I had no idea where to begin. Nobody I knew dressed like that, styled his or her hair like that, drove a big old shiny car like that. I was immediately drawn to it. But I never dreamt it was something I could be part of, something I could enjoy. It was for other people, the people who dressed like that and drove those cars, the cool kids.

Ten years later, I was working in an office job that was stifling my creativity, to the point where I hardly recognised myself. I was beyond miserable. I didn't even care about being creative anymore; I was just trying to survive through life. Then Amanda, a workmate who went on to become one of my best friends, invited me to a concert – Reel Big Fish were coming to Australia! My boyfriend at the time didn't want to go, saying he didn't like their music. We broke up shortly after this (simply because we weren't having fun together anymore). So I went to the gig with my girlfriend and her husband and immediately fell in love with the support act, a quintet from Queanbeyan near Canberra called Los Capitanes. Their sound was rock, ska, punk, reggae … it switched and smoothed its way between genres not just over the course of the album but within each song.

It suited my ADHD listening personality perfectly. I rushed over to the merchandising stand where groupies and girlfriends giggled and tossed their hair. I bought their second album, Rest for the Wicked, and a couple of days later went to a music store and bought their debut album, No Fun Intended. I liked both so much, it was as if these songs had been written and recorded just for me. If music was to be made just the way I wanted to hear it, it would sound like this.

After a few days of listening to these two albums almost without pause, I was looking at the Los Capitanes' Facebook page when I saw a comment from someone who had the same surname as one of their song titles. I sent a message saying something along the lines of, 'Hi, have to ask – are you the Mr Cooper of *Hangin with Mr Cooper*?' He replied immediately saying, 'Yup, that's me!' So from there we began chatting. It turned out he'd been in a ska band that Bekky, a high school friend of mine, had liked back when we were in high school. She used to drag me to shows where they'd play. I told him I'd seen his band as a teenager and remembered having fun skanking (that's a dance, not nearly as crude as it sounds!) to their music. It wasn't long before we exchanged mobile numbers and email addresses; we talked every day and sent each other links to songs we enjoyed. We ended up dating for two years, and in that time I learnt a lot. Essentially I learnt that there was a whole subculture, an entire world, existing right around me that I hadn't been aware of since the rockabilly wedding I had seen a decade earlier.

There was the music; there were the car shows, the festivals, the burlesque shows, and the pinups ... Girls just like me, creative and quirky, only not like me in that while I was in my stable, steady, corporate nine to five arranging meetings and coordinating travel for middle management, they were at home sewing sequins and Swarovskis crystals onto corsets, dying their hair bright pink and coming up with inspiration for their next burlesque routine. While I was at home, tucked up in bed fast asleep, they were strutting around stages in venues I'd never even heard of. I felt like Alice through the looking glass. This whole new world of glamour, red lipstick and high heels opened up. I felt like I had come home.

Vintage has been defined as 'the time that something of quality was produced', or 'something that is of the highest quality of its kind'. However, generally when people use this term they are referring to an era or period of around fifty or sixty-plus years ago. Over the past decade we have seen a huge resurgence all over the world in the popularity of the styles and fashions of the 1950s. Almost everywhere you look, women like me can be seen wearing full dresses with petticoats, or wiggle skirts, carrying parasols as they totter along in their heels. Restored classic cars carry them and their greaser boyfriends to regular nostalgia festivals where rockabilly bands play.

These styles originate from around 1945. World War II had just ended, America was victorious. An air of celebration had spread throughout the Allied countries. (Sparklers had not been invented yet, so people could not celebrate the cessation of big explosives by playing with smaller explosives as they would today.) The Great Depression was finally over – the average family had gone from living on rations to again having disposable income.

But the 1940s and 50s was not all rosy cheeks and good family values, as adverts from the time may have you believe. There was a terribly dark side to the period that nostalgic types often forget or deliberately omit when reminiscing about 'the good old days'. This was a time when many prejudices were still very much a part of most people's beliefs and attitudes. Intolerance, prejudice and discrimination were part of an accepted cultural norm – so much so, that television and print advertisements which were considered humorous or even completely mundane in their day are these days viewed with a mixture of shock and bemused intrigue.

A print ad of the time which really amazed me, for example, was for a certain brand of coffee. It depicted a man with a grown woman bent over his knee, (can you imagine) his hand raised, a look of shock and fear upon her innocent face. 'Woe be unto you', it warned, 'if your husband ever finds out you're not *store-testing* for fresher coffee.' Indeed, woe be unto any woman who dares be so inattentive to her domestic duties. Such a woman clearly fully deserves (and can therefore assuredly expect) violent punishment. A woman's place was in the home. Her worth was dependent upon her ability to provide her husband with a clean house, a tasty nutritious meal and a pretty smiling face to greet him at the door after a hard day's work. This was the generally accepted view of women in the 1950s.

Racism was also rife in mid-century America. From what I have read there was still a pervading belief that people of African descent were somehow different or 'other' than white Americans. They were seen to be second-class citizens, which led to them often being employed in menial jobs, if employed at all. This belief manifested in many venues having a main entrance, and tucked behind this, a separate flight of stairs with a neon sign reading 'coloured entrance' and an arrow pointing to the entrance designated specifically for the 'coloured' patrons.

Even on television back then, coloured people were not shown dancing together with white people. In fact, 'Star Trek' was the first ever television show to depict white and coloured people occupying the same roles. Before this, coloured people were always depicted as either working for white people, or at least holding a position of lower power and authority.

When watching the movie *Hairspray*, I am always surprised at how shocked and appalled Penny's mother is to learn her daughter is 'a checkerboard chick!' meaning that she embraces integration and is even dating a 'coloured boy'! Even Tracey's mother, who is portrayed as comparatively open-minded and enlightened, admits to being afraid to be in the 'black neighborhood'. Even in the movie's popular fictitious television program 'The Corny Collins Show' they have a dedicated 'Negro Day' once a month, in which 'negroes' are invited to dance on the show, although of course still segregated from the white dancers, separated by a rope partition.

They Met in Paris

This was also a period during which many people were far less accepting of gays and lesbians than today. Homosexuals had to stay in the proverbial closet, and much propaganda was distributed to create fear of anyone different to the societal norm. In fact, the judgement and fear of what some people so misunderstood led to 'educational videos' being shown in schools to warn children (particularly boys) of the dangers of homosexuals. In these videos, the gay person was almost always portrayed as a sleazy pedophile. Today we have laws such as the Anti-Discrimination Act to protect people's rights, and this sort of prejudice is almost incomprehensible to most educated people nowadays.

So with all of these past negative aspects, the seemingly endless judgment and intolerance, why the sudden nostalgic fascination with this period that I and many of my friends have embraced? There are many things about the styles and fashions of the 1950s that have contributed to their resurgence in popularity and made them so interesting to me and those around me.

Post-modern theorists will tell us that nothing is new anymore, we cannot create anything original. All we can do when 'creating' art is to take something that already exists and change it in some way. Now, you're probably thinking 'Explain Tim Burton then, post-modernist know-it-all hipster!' Tim Burton is indeed creative, but he is essentially putting a new spin on what has already been done. Was 'Edward Scissorhands' just a modernised adaptation of the 1931 film Frankenstein? Both depicted a scientist creating a being that becomes a monster. The medium of film as we know it is certainly not new – the first recorded motion picture dates back to 1895.

I would even dare go so far as to say that Lady Gaga's meat dress, which was so controversial at the time that the media went on about it for almost a whole week, has been done before. She was not the first person to create a dress from a material not traditionally associated with dressmaking. In fact, just last week, a friend sent me an image of a woman in the 1930s wearing a gown made entirely from grapefruit skins. So you can see, it could be argued that our capacity for originality has been exhausted and we are now all merely rehashing all that has gone before.

Enter 1950s fashion. It was a time of seeming decadence and glamour, yet household budgets were very modest when compared to ours today. During the war, the phrase 'waste not, want not', and the image of the little housewife with the 'mend and make do' mentality, were commonplace. Women like my grandmothers were thrifty, and spent their time sewing and stitching, making and mending clothes. Their husbands, meanwhile, tinkered away in the shed, repairing appliances rather than throwing them away.

These resourceful habits of those living in the 1940s and 50s, such as our grandparents, form part of another reason we are choosing to buy and wear vintage clothing today. By lowering the demand for production of new clothes, we are helping the environment. It's not only eliminating (or at least significantly reducing) the demand for production of new items, but also reducing the requirement for packaging and transportation of clothing that also has an environmental benefit for all.

In fact, even the plastic hair bun boosters that I wear today were much more environmentally friendly in the 1950s. I've heard that women in the 1940s and 50s would collect their own hair from their shower and their hairbrush to make hair bun boosters. They would place the hair into an old stocking that had been mended until it could no longer be worn. Yes, even stockings were not discarded. They were darned and mended until they could not be worn anymore, and even then they were not tossed out with the trash, but used to create these hair-volumising accessories. Today, I use a plastic and foam device which will not biodegrade and will inevitably become landfill, and the wonderful stockings with seams that I so enjoy wearing are more or less designed for a single-use and considered somewhat disposable.

However, with the Global Financial Crisis during the last decade, many families have been turning away from this disposable way of consuming, and have begun to mend and repair what they already had, just like in the post-war years. It's friendlier on our budgets, much kinder on the environment, and we generally tend to get a sense of personal satisfaction when we are able to repair something that has been broken.

In one of the most exciting period in fashion, the 1950s saw the creation of modern fabrics such as nylon and spandex. This means that while back in the day my Nanna would have had to hand wash her dresses and hang them out to dry, during my mother's teenage years dresses became durable enough to withstand being thrown in the washing machine – and, to their delight, a few years later, the tumble dryer.

From the full circle skirts that I often wear which emphasise a tiny waist, to the figure-hugging wiggle skirts that flaunt a woman's curves, the styles that were worn by women in the 1950s are universally flattering. They celebrated a woman's feminine shape, regardless of whether she was tall, short, thin or solid. These fashion trends that I adore originated from Christian Dior's 'New Look' of 1947, and the cinched waists with dramatically full skirts were perhaps the most iconic silhouette to arise out of these collections, and become iconic of 1950s fashion.

Today, reproduction, or 'repro' garments (newly made clothes in vintage styles) are readily available in such a wide range of fabrics, prints and colours that it's easy for me and other women to find something we will love. This is another reason for the broad appeal and popularity of vintage style.

This, combined with lower production costs and online shopping, means that 50s-style dresses are more affordable and more readily available than ever before, for the many that want to adopt these styles. In fact, they are probably even more affordable than in the 1950s! This accessibility and affordability has contributed to the popularity immensely – I can see a dress on the internet, and with the click of a mouse it's delivered to my door, more or less overnight!

For example, pinup model Bernie Dexter designs and models her own dresses, and the results are simply breathtaking. She captures the fresh-faced, wholesome look of the 1950s pinup girls, with just a hint of a 'naughty girl' edge that made them so intriguing. Her Facebook page has over 185,000 fans, reaching a wide audience all over the world. She posts photos of herself modelling the dresses that she has designed, accompanied by links to her online store, where we can browse all of the beautiful designs and perhaps even make a purchase when the budget allows.

However, this ease of access was not always the case. When the resurgence began, around fifteen years ago now, savvy city-living women would dress as 50s housewives as a tongue-in-cheek statement about women, their previous place in society and how this was reflected in fashion. Prior to the internet, men and women with an interest in 1940s and 50s fashions would go to libraries, and study books on the era, or they would need to watch films from the period and try to reproduce the makeup, clothes and hairstyles of the silver screen. Now that the clothes are so readily available and so popular, the statement made by dressing in this fashion has lost its original meaning and intention, and vintage is now considered by some as 'just another fashion trend'.

You only have to look at a modern television set in comparison to one of the earliest sets ever produced, and you'll begin to understand the impact of mid-century design. All household appliances, from the toaster to the refrigerator, were not only built to last, but in my opinion were designed to look great as well as being functional. Designers used shapes and lines that were pleasing to the eye. Materials used were of the highest quality. Possessions were truly built to last a lifetime. This was true of household appliances, furniture, cars and of course, even houses.

Rose Seidler House in Wahroonga is a magnificent example of mid-century architecture. It plays home to the Fifties Fair each year. I simply love attending this event where I and many other people who enjoy vintage fashion meet to browse the stalls, enjoy the fashion of other patrons (there is even a best dressed competition) and dance to bands playing rockabilly and swing music.

⚜

With feminism came this wonderful new belief that women should have the freedom to wear whatever they wanted, without judgment from men or other women. We were entitled to dress however we chose. This relatively new-found freedom was a wonderful thing – but did it lead to a decline in pride in appearance? It was perhaps this new belief that lead to a rather distinct (and, if I may say so, somewhat disappointing) lack of style throughout the 2000s.

I noticed that many women seemed to no longer care about their appearance or personal grooming. Even in a corporate environment, I saw women wearing inappropriately short and tight miniskirts, chipped nail polish, transparent tops and, God help me, leggings worn as pants. Women that I worked with would come into the office with their hair thrown carelessly into a messy bun and last night's mascara smeared under their eyes. Outside of the office, I saw women wearing jeans with fluoro-coloured g-strings clearly visible over the top. At the supermarket, I saw people doing their weekly grocery shopping in flannelette pyjama bottoms and ugg boots, with twisted bra straps sliding down their shoulder. The tide of majority taste needed to turn.

This 'anything goes' attitude eventually brought about a desire for a return to 'the good old days'. Myself and many others began to find ourselves looking back to a time when women were ladies and men were gentlemen. We began looking at photos of our grandmothers in beautifully pressed dresses, their hair curled, their bright shiny skin that looked great, even in those old sepia photos ...

At the time these photos were taken, the war was creating uncertainty about the future, and people at that time began living as though each day could be their last. Women would set their hair before bed most nights, and in the morning they would get up and tend to their homes with a face full of flawless makeup. I even found this helpful advice published in the manual of a Singer Sewing Machine manufactured in 1949:

When you sew, make yourself as attractive as possible. Put on a clean dress. Keep a little bag full of French chalk near your sewing machine to dust your fingers at intervals. Have your hair in order, powder and lipstick put on. If you are constantly fearful that a visitor will drop in or your husband will come home, and you will not look neatly put together, you will not enjoy your sewing.

Attitudes in society towards women of this era demanded that they always look their very best for their husbands, even when their husbands were not at home, even when a woman was home alone sewing. If a wife failed to present immaculate personal grooming, their husbands thought they had every right to stray.

Hairstyles are, in my opinion, one of the most important aspects of creating a vintage look. One of the main differences between the aesthetic of the 1940s and 50s and today was that then women made an effort to look neat, tidy and polished while today, it seems, absolutely anything goes. With lowered standards of what is considered acceptable, we have women making very little effort and the result is appearing unfinished, unpolished. In the 1950s, it was not the done thing to go to the shops immediately after washing your hair, allowing it to drip down your back and soak your shirt. It simply wasn't done.

There are as many vintage hairstyles as there are women to wear them. One of my personal favourites is Bettie bangs, a short, blunt fringe named after the most iconic woman to sport them, Bettie Page. Another style that I love is the 'suicide roll' that rolls off the forehead to the side. My absolute favourite hairstyle, but the most complicated and difficult to achieve, is victory rolls (so called because they mimic the manoeuver airplanes would do when their pilots were celebrating a victory during the war). These can be terribly frustrating – and while you are learning, your arms will get sore. But with patience, persistence and practice, anyone can learn to style their hair in this way within ten minutes.

Moving to the back of the head, the classic 1940s roll in which the hair is rolled up to the nape of the neck is a very elegant and feminine hairstyle. An alternative to this is the twist, in which a section of hair at the side of the back of the head is twisted, and then more and more sections incorporated and intertwined across the nape of the neck until all hair forms a roll. I enjoy playing with all of these hairstyles and I did during my time in Paris, mixing and matching and creating something new and different every day. They are all beautiful hairstyles that are flattering on most face shapes and they all espouse glamour and elegance.

However, it's often frustrating when I'm running late for work, or a party, or meeting a friend and my hair simply won't do what I want it to do. This does not apply exclusively to vintage hairstyles – some modern hairstyles are also tricky, but given that styles such a victory rolls in a sense defy gravity, it can be difficult to achieve this look. There is also the fact that all these vintage hairstyles must be neat and tidy, unlike the modern tousled beach waves or 'windswept look', for example.

I really admire burlesque star Dita Von Teese, who has been quoted as saying that it is precisely the discipline of looking flawless that she enjoys about her style. The discipline is in always having neat and tidy hair, flawless makeup and wearing high heels – even on those days when she would rather be in jeans and sneakers. For her, the discipline gives her confidence. However, the other side (perhaps, may I say, the 'sad side' of this quote), is that she also said she was not as confident when she was comfortable and relaxed as she was when she was 'made up'. Dita Von Teese has stated that she doesn't like how she looks naturally – which boggles the mind, coming from a person considered by many to be the most beautiful woman alive today. The aesthetic has become a mask for her – she is unhappy with how she looks naturally, and therefore prefers to present a carefully cultivated and constructed image of herself to the world.

⚜

I've found some fabulous skincare and makeup tutorials online that were filmed in the 1930s, 40s and 50s that have been uploaded onto YouTube. They instructed young women of the day how to do their makeup in a way that was becoming and suitable for their age. For me, vintage makeup, particularly pinup makeup, has three distinguishing factors – a flawless base, black liquid eyeliner and ruby red lips.

Max Factor created pancake makeup at the beginning of World War I. Originally created exclusively for Hollywood film starlets, it created a flawless base, smoothed out skin tones and therefore presented the actress in the best possible light on screen. The formula had to be changed with the introduction of Technicolor, as movies in colour obviously had very different makeup requirements than movies filmed in black and white. Max Factor's pancake makeup soon became so popular that it went into mass production and became available to ordinary, everyday women. I use Max Factor Pancake Foundation when I want 'heavy coverage'. It creates a flawless base which becomes my 'blank canvas' to work on.

Like most women, it took me a long time to master the liquid eyeliner. It was terribly messy at first, as it is for nearly everyone. It doesn't matter how confident or experienced with other makeup you are, the first time you experiment with liquid eyeliner, you *will* look like a disappointed panda. Don't fight it, it will happen. With patience and practice, however, you can command the liquid liner and transform the appearance of your eyes in minutes. The winged 'cat's eye' look is more of a 1960s look, and is very popular with lovers of vintage.

The most fabulous and iconic makeup trait of the 1950s was the red lipstick. A fact about lipstick that I find very interesting is that in times of economic uncertainty or decline, sales of lipstick (in particular, red lipstick) rise. The most plausible theory behind this is that when times are tough, women are not able to treat themselves to, say, an overseas holiday or a new fur coat. Instead, we boost our mood with a cheap, quick and easy fix – a new lipstick. A lipstick can cost anywhere between ten and a hundred dollars, so there is something for us all, no matter what our budget. There is also a shade for us all. I have heard many women proclaim that they 'can't wear red lipstick', or that 'it just doesn't look good on me'. There are so many shades of reds, from blue-based through neutral through to orange-based reds, so there is no reason why anyone cannot find a shade that complements their skin tone and complexion. The only reason a woman would claim that she 'cannot possibly' wear red lipstick is because she lacks the confidence to wear it. Perhaps ironically, it is these very women who could benefit most from wearing red lipstick, as it does wonders to boost a woman's mood, confidence and self-esteem.

As Elizabeth Taylor famously said, 'Put on your lipstick, pour yourself a drink and pull yourself together.' This quote exemplifies the extraordinary impact that something as simple as putting on lipstick can have on a woman. It can help her regroup, rebuild her strength and boost her confidence in a matter of seconds.

Dita Von Teese has been quoted as saying that, 'It's amazing how people listen when they have a pair of red lips pointed at them'. Lipstick makes the wearer appear more confident and therefore, more attractive. It gets her noticed. Perhaps it is for this reason that it has been claimed that men like red lipstick on other women – but not on their wives!

Hollywood screen sirens of the 1930s, 40s and 50s epitomised glamour and effortless elegance and style.

Marilyn Monroe, born Norma Jeane Mortenson, has been called the most beautiful woman who ever lived. What to make of the fact that the most praised and desired woman in history was an insanely sensitive, messed up, fragile little girl in a woman's curvy body? Her iconic hourglass figure, blonde hair, red lips and permanently sleepy-looking eyes made Marilyn a star. She was an invention, a product created to sell movies and the merchandise that went along with it all. She had a fragility and warmth about her that made moviegoers – men and women alike – want, at times, to protect and nurture her.

Audrey Hepburn, a perennial favourite of mine and many others, redefined beauty. Here was a woman who literally very nearly starved to death during the war. As a child, she risked her life by carrying and delivering messages hidden in her dance shoes in return for a loaf of bread. Yet towards the end of her life, when she was asked to sum up her life in one word, she smiled and said 'lucky'. This showed an extraordinary spirit and a level of courage and grace that was truly unique to her alone. For me, hers was a whole new level of beauty and grace that goes far beyond red lipstick. She possessed an elegance and inner beauty that transcended traditional notions of glamour and radiated off the screen.

Pinup models during the 1940s had a rather important role to play. They boosted soldiers' morale during the war and provided inspiration for young men to survive by reminding the men what they were fighting for; the pinup posters gave them a reason to look forward to coming home again.

Gil Elvgren remains one of the most popular and well-known pinup artists of all time. His art almost exclusively depicted innocent-looking young women with bright eyes and rosy cheeks, often caught in a compromising position or embarrassing moment. I find it fascinating to see some of the women who posed for him, the actual photographs that inspired his work, next to his finished paintings. The images in the photographs were altered until the finished products we see in his paintings are impossibly cute – the eyes wider, the mouth poutier, the hair curlier and more golden ...

Bettie Page is today known as 'The Queen of the Pinups'. Although she is arguably the most well-known and iconic pinup of all time, she actually only posed for a few years. She then found religion, gave up her modelling and retreated into solitude. It was only decades later when she was 'rediscovered' that she found out just how popular and iconic she had become. She is a favourite of mine and many others, not only because of her intriguing life and story, but also because she had that mixture of playful innocence with a bit of cheeky sassiness mixed in. Her photos conjure images of fun and playfulness with a hint of naughtiness and mischief.

Today there are hundreds of thousands of pinup models, all over the world, each with their own unique style and mannerisms, each carrying on the legacy of the original pinups. Although these types of images are no longer used as inspiration for soldiers as they were originally, pinups still have a purpose nowadays, often providing creative inspiration to other artists.

Miss Pinup Australia is Australia's premier pinup competition. This isn't just because it's bigger and more prestigious than any other competition in the country, but because it's so much more than a beauty pageant. While entrants do technically compete for the ultimate title of Miss Pinup Australia, it is more a journey of self-discovery and self-acceptance. Miss Pinup Australia is open to women of any age, shape, size, race and background. Since the competition began, every year women (and more recently, some brave men) have walked away with a new-found self-confidence and self acceptance because they have taken the plunge and pushed themselves outside of their comfort zone in a loving, supportive environment.

There are seven categories – Miss Perfect Pinup, for all lovers of vintage fashion, Miss Vava Voom, for ladies over a size fourteen, Miss Classic Pinup for ladies over thirty years of age, Miss Prestige for ladies over forty, Miss Illustrated for the tattooed pinups, Miss Neo for those with a modern, edgy twist on the look and finally, Mr Pinup, for the gentlemen who don't want to miss out on all the fun.

Over the course of several months, entrants take part in several events. The first of these events is a series of workshops, including hair and makeup, deportment and posing. These workshops not only teach entrants the skills they will need when they get to strut their stuff on the Miss Pinup Australia stage, they also provide a new level of confidence in everyday life. Deportment skills such as learning how to walk, sit and move gracefully used to be taught in schools. These days, however, there is no such grooming or self-development on the curriculum.

There is a meet and greet held early on in the competition, in which entrants meet each other. While technically these ladies are in direct competition with each other, they're strongly encouraged to form bonds and friendships based on a shared love of vintage glamour. The meet and greet is an opportunity for family, friends and fans to come along and meet or support their favourite pinups.

Things really start to get exciting at the State Finals. Entrants are required to 'bring a vintage photograph to life'. This involves three clothing sections – sleepwear, beachwear/swimwear and daywear. Each entrant has forty-five seconds on stage for each clothing category, and must demonstrate between six and eight classic pinup poses. Entrants must also do their own hair and makeup. There is also a talent section, in which each pinup has sixty seconds to demonstrate a hidden talent or secret skill. In the past, this has ranged from singing and dancing to making a sandwich or mixing a cocktail. If successful at the State Finals, entrants move on through to the National Finals. This follows the same process as the State Finals (sleepwear, beachwear, daywear, talent) with the addition of an eveningwear segment. An opportunity to turn the glam factor up to full – a vintage evening gown!

Vintage prom dresses are a personal favourite of mine. When I buy a vintage dress I know I'm buying a piece of history. Perhaps this was the dress that a young woman wore on a first date with her sweetheart and had her first kiss in. Or perhaps it was her first heartbreak after he stood her up. Either way, I get the feeling that a life has been lived in these vintage dresses. Party dresses for me represent dreams and fantasy, escapism and glamour. Tulle and lace, satin and velvet – these were not the fabrics of clothes worn every day in the 1950s. They were made and worn for special occasions, and some of the excitement seeps into the woven fabric and becomes part of the dress and, in turn, part of all those women lucky enough to bring these dresses back to life today.

I feel there is also mystery and intrigue woven into the fabric of vintage garments and accessories. Every pair of gloves, each handbag, every hat has a story, and when I can find out snippets of a story when buying them, it becomes even more intriguing. Who owned this dress before me? To which occasions did they wear it? Did their parents buy it for them, or was it a gift from their beau? Was it a Christmas or birthday gift?

Teen culture arrived in the 1950s. This was the first decade where pop culture was directly marketed to teenagers. Until then, advertisers sought only to influence men to buy for the family, to purchase appliances for their wives. (Who doesn't now laugh about the Hoover ad that proclaims 'This Christmas, she'll be happier with a Hoover!' showing a woman all but making out with her beloved new vacuum cleaner?) Women were then only encouraged to buy skin creams and hair care products to ensure their husbands didn't stray (because if you get a wrinkle, darling, it's your fault if he cheats!).

Teenagers were finally being recognised as consumers, and advertising and marketing quickly jumped on board. When 'Rock'n' Roll' first hit the scene, it was the first time ever that music was being recorded specifically for teenagers.

Rockabilly music of these times originated from rhythm and blues. According to the lyrics of any rockabilly song, there are only two stages of any romantic relationship: the beginning, in which he loves his gal because all she wants to do is rock'n'roll all night, and the end, in which he is fed up with his gal because all she wants to do is rock'n'roll all night.

The musical movie *Cry Baby* was a great depiction of the attitude towards 'squares'. To be cool, you had to be a rebel. Johnny Depp in *Cry Baby* plays the sensitive and troubled teen full of angst and potentially fatal good looks. Comparisons could be drawn between Depp in *Cry Baby* and James Dean in *Rebel Without a Cause*, who also portrayed a teenage male struggling with his own identity, wondering where and how he fitted in.

Of course, nothing says 1950s like a woman with pointy boobs wearing a poodle skirt, sucking on a milkshake through a straw from a tall frosted glass, her chin resting in her palms as she gazes at the picture of Elvis on the wall of the diner. The American Diner itself has become another iconic part of American mid-century history. This was where teens would go on dates, and while the pointy-boobed girl drank her milkshake, the boy wearing his leather jacket with his father's Brylcreem in his hair would order a hamburger and give his sweetheart a dime for the jukebox, and secretly hope she would put on a Gene Vincent track and not another Sam Cooke ballad. Today, many 1950s themed diners have opened with varying degrees of success.

An interesting thing for us wearing 1940s and 1950s fashion is the number of comments and remarks we receive from complete strangers. It is rarely a reaction of neutrality or indifference. More often than not, these strangers were young women around the 1950s who are reminded of their own youth. They smile and say things like, 'I like your dress – I used to wear things like that when I was your age,' and others say, 'Oh, I used to wear my hair like that!' Sometimes it's as quick an exchange as a passing 'Great look!' accompanied by a smile, but it more often generates conversations and discussions, with people stopping to ask questions or relay their own experiences with the style ('I have a friend who dresses like that, she loves it!').

The flip side of this positive reaction is the surprising and negative reactions people have to women adorning themselves in 1950s attire. Some people jump to the conclusion that women who dress this way must hold the same beliefs and carry the same attitudes as the women of a dishearteningly racist and homophobic era.

Some of my friends have been criticised and condemned, even attacked, and accused of being like a *Stepford* wife, only interested in painting their faces and ensuring feminism rolls backwards until women are no longer burdened with having to earn and manage their own money. They have actually been told they deserve to be beaten by their husbands – presumably because dressing in a style from an era in which domestic violence was terribly common and not often discussed automatically means they are willing to accept such abuse.

Nothing could be further from the truth. I and every woman I know who enjoys vintage fashion and style is an empowered feminist who lives her life on her own terms. Whether this life includes a husband, children, a career, or any combination of these three things, it is our own personal choice.

Many of us lovers of this period really enjoy nostalgia festivals. Nostalgia for me means a longing for the past, a bygone era. I doubt that many of us are truly conscious of just how different the world was then. One of the most fabulous things about the world and culture we live in today is the fact that we all have the ability and the freedom to pick and choose. We can choose to leave the prejudices and preconceived notions in the past, and take the cars, the music, the clothes, the makeup and hair and even the furniture from the past and transpose it into today!

Like any fashion trend or fad, there will be an inevitable decline in the 50s style's popularity. Some, including myself, who have embraced this style, will continue to do so for many years to come. Others who have been drawn to it because of its popularity, accessibility and availability will possibly move onto the next trend or revert to whatever style they'd adopted before vintage became fashionable. One thing is for sure – the 1950s vintage style was an aesthetically beautiful and glamorous era that should never be forgotten.

Epilogue

The group of women who have written these stories you have just read are some of the most interesting and enthusiastic women I have ever met. The range of skills many of them have in addition to writing is amazing.

All the women lead very busy and demanding lives so meeting the strict production deadlines that were set for them for this book was not always easy for some of them, especially as we are scattered geographically.

Five of the women are still in the workforce so I must compliment them for the extra effort they made to keep up with us others who naturally had more time to spend on our stories.

During the story development process we arranged to meet as a group at Avoca on the Central Coast of NSW to review and discuss our first drafts. We stayed for a week in a rambling beach house that our savvy writer Diana found on-line. The group was at the meeting table by 9.30 am each day with detailed agendas and kept at it most days until 1.30 pm. It was almost the same structure that we had during our time together in Paris, but this time we were putting into practice what some of us had only dreamt about doing one day.

Anna Blay of Hybrid Publishers edited the final draft of the stories. Anna was very generous and patient, given she had the task of dealing with the work of ten very different writers who were naturally all very passionate about their stories.

Miriam's story told you about her travels in France and Louise described to you in her delightful way what she saw as she walked the streets of Paris. Judith told you about her love of books even before she could read and about how books have influenced her life. I took you back to how food was in the 50s and relayed my experiences growing up with parents who had witnessed food shortages during the war. Valerie wrote about romance, love and passion and the part it played in her life, and described to you delightfully her first experience of love. Anne wrote about her love of life and described her adventures in Alaska, her passion for the Kimberley and about her time in Paris. Diana told you how she rebelled against a controlling mother and how she finally discovered her passion for women. Roslyn reminded us how important family is and wrote about the wonderful warm family she grew up in. Susan's heartbreaking story demonstrated the love a mother has for her child, while Sierra's story told us how she became fascinated with all things vintage from seeing a rockabilly wedding in her teens.

I hope you have enjoyed these ten diverse stories and have been informed and entertained by them. I expect you would have laughed at times and no doubt even shed a few tears.

Carole Lethbridge
theymetinparis@gmail.com

www.ingramcontent.com/pod-product-compliance
Lightning Source LLC
Chambersburg PA
CBHW051937290426
44110CB00015B/2019